PAPER CURRENCY IN INDIA

PAPER CURRENCY IN INDIA

B. B. DAS GUPTA

WITH A FOREWORD BY

J. C. COYAJEE

GYAN

Published by

GYAN

Gyan Publishing House
5, Ansari Road
Daryaganj, New Delhi-110002
Phone: 011-47034999, 9811692060
E-mail: books@gyanbooks.com

Distribution Network
gyanbooks.com
India, USA, Canada, UK, Australia, France

ISBN : 978-81-212-3873-1 (PB)
First Published, Calcutta, 1927

2nd Impression 2020

Printed at: Gyan Press, Delhi.

Paper Currency in India
Author: B. B. Das Gupta

PAPER CURRENCY IN INDIA

BY

B. B. DAS GUPTA, M.A., Ph.D.,
B.Sc. (Econ.), Lond.

Premchand Roychand Student, Calcutta University, Lecturer in Economics, Lucknow University, formerly Professor, Presidency and Scottish Churches Colleges, Calcutta, and Lecturer, Calcutta University

With a Foreword
BY

Prof. J. C. COYAJEE,

Member of the Royal Commission on Indian Currency and Finance 1925-26, and of the Indian Fiscal Commission 1921-22

Calcutta

PUBLISHED BY THE CALCUTTA UNIVERSITY

1927

To

J. C. KYDD, Esq.,

Teacher and more than a teacher

FOREWORD

It is a pleasure and a privilege to be asked to write a Foreword for such a scholarly treatise as that of Prof. Das Gupta's on Paper Currency in India. The literature of Indian Currency is already rich and has been of late increasing in volume as well as maintaining its quality. The days are gone by when the late Prof. Marshall could say "There are five thousand pages of able reports for the students of Indian Economics but no good text books." The last fifteen years have given us quite a number of good and able works on Indian economic topics; and the work of Prof. Das Gupta will form a notable addition to that list. Where the subject treated is so wide and complex, as in the present work, it is only natural that a few of the opinions expressed in it cannot command my assent; but I admire the general soundness of the exposition.

A monograph on the Paper Currency of such a great and important country as India, was in fact overdue. It is surprising, indeed, why some one out of our many well-trained economists did not single out the subject ere this for special treatment. It would appear that even in our days when so many scholars are on the look-out for suitable theses, we can still find, occasionally, an eligible subject seeking an able author. Prof. Das Gupta has seized the opportunity afforded to him by the want of special works on the Indian Paper Currency System and has made the most of it. Apart from the practical importance of such a subject, the record of six decades of the working of a Paper Currency System under such special circumstances was, if ably handled, sure to throw light on problems of theory, and our author has not failed to treat his subject in the light of the evolution of monetary theory and practice.

He has also shown in his handling of his thesis originality of thought and treatment, and his work is based on careful and painstaking research. He has spared no labour in collecting his facts and has founded his conclusions on a course of wide reading which included some sources of information of a *prima facie* unpromising and remote character.

A word might also be said about the general arrangement of the material. The problems in hand must have taken a lot of careful thinking out before they could be developed into the lucid and well-thought-out scheme of the book—the more so as the problems of Paper Currency are mixed up almost inextricably with other monetary matters. Our author has adopted the most logical course under the circumstances. The tangled mechanism of Paper Currency has been taken into its component parts, and each part is examined in isolation, so far as isolation is possible. This is a more convenient method than that which is usually followed in books of the sort. A complicated and difficult subject is thus made attractive to the reader. The author has a clear and attractive style, which has greatly facilitated the difficult work of monetary exposition.

I have read with special interest, attention and instruction the last chapter of Prof. Das Gupta's work—the one dealing with the recommendations contained in the Report of the Royal Commission on Indian Currency and Finance. I only wish that many more critics of that Report possessed the scholarly erudition and the well-balanced judgment of our author. Even where he is inclined to differ from the recommendations of that Report, he is fully aware of the special circumstances and difficulties which justify those recommendations. Criticism leads the way, but justification follows hard on its heels. Thus, on the one hand, he notes that "the transference of the note issue to a bank, whatever pompous name we call it by, is fraught with certain risks" (p. 272); but, on the other hand, he has emphasised how the transference of note issue to such a Reserve Bank—by whatever name it is called—would prevent non-monetary considerations from influencing the administration of the paper currency (pp. 268-70). On the one hand he regrets the necessity of the partial "scrapping" of the permanent provisions for our paper currency laid down in 1920 (p. 263); on the other hand he clearly perceives that "a project of paper currency reform to suit and supplement a Rupee standard, silver monometallism or bimetallism. would of necessity be different in nature, from a project fitting into a gold standard" (p. 266). As a theorist he is impatient of the restraints—such as they are—imposed on the discretion of the management of the Reserve Bank (pp. 280-81); and yet he is aware that the transfer of the note issue from the Government is not without its risks, and consequently should not be without its safe-guards. In fact, the chapter is a very good commentary on the Hilton-Young Report.

But there are many other topics of the monetary economics of India discussed very well indeed in the book; and on controversial matters the author is particularly interesting. I would instance his handling of such problems as the amalgamation of the Paper Currency and gold standard reserves, and the methods and proper meaning and measure of 'elasticity.' On the importance of price-stability as a basic principle of monetary policy the author has justly laid great stress.

In conclusion, I would emphasise the fact that the publication of the book is very timely. The whole monetary organisation of India is at present being discussed and examined by the public as it never was before; and it is to be hoped that this book which deals exhaustively with our Paper Currency but incidentally also with many other phases of our monetary system, will be carefully read by many of the public and will enlighten and guide their judgment.

PRESIDENCY COLLEGE, CALCUTTA,
3rd March, 1927.

J. C. COYAJEE.

PREFACE

The following work attempts to give an account of the past and the present of the Paper Currency System in India. It was prepared substantially in its present form and approved by the University of Calcutta as a thesis for the degree of Doctor of Philosophy. I have now revised the work, making additions and alterations in nearly every chapter. Chapter ten, dealing with the Future of the Issue, has been practically rewritten. I have endeavoured to be up-to-date, having noticed the latest landmark in the currency history of India, namely the Report of the Hilton-Young Commission. There is however no fixity or finality of things during a transition period. New happenings may soon make new currency history and events move too quickly to be caught by the camera of a passing publication. Although this uncertainty of outlook is a handicap, it leads at the same time additional weight to the necessity of a clear understanding of the past and of the present. To this end perhaps the book may be regarded as a timely contribution.

My purpose has been to deal exclusively with the paper currency, isolating it, as far as it bears such isolation, from the rest of the monetary system. This has been no easy task and I have had constantly to resist the temptation of embroiling myself in discussions of the monetary system generally or of parts of that system comparatively foreign to my purpose. I realise however the essential unity of the entire monetary structure of which paper currency forms an organic part.

Perhaps I need say a word about the arrangement of the work. I have divided the subject matter into two parts, dealing respectively with the period of bank issue and the issue as in the hands of the State. Within these two broad divisions, it has appeared to me as the most convenient method to break up the different aspects of the issue into separate discussions and trace out their history and developments separately. The usual practice whereby all the departments of Paper Currency organisation are studied, rather mixed up, in a system of chronological presentation of Paper Currency Acts, seems hardly conducive to a quick and clear understanding of the various and many-sided developments of our Paper Currency. I have taken the machine into pieces and tried to examine each aspect as far as possible separately from the others. But the Paper Currency System, in all its aspects, forms of course one whole.

A history of Indian Paper Currency needs hardly any apology for it. The subject is important; and with the growing part that paper is destined to play in the circulating media of the country, it will continue to grow in importance. Indeed, in the new currency order outlined by the Hilton-Young Comission, paper will form the outstanding part of the circulation, if not the sole circulation. A study of Paper Currency again is full of interest, both from the theoretical standpoint as also from the point of view of practical experiments in currency administration. Nowhere else in the world has the State attempted to run a Paper Currency, the only one of its kind in the country, on such a scale and for such a long time. Lastly, the subject may also be said to be necessary. Much of our Paper Currency System is a tangle, and much of it, although beginning considerably after Tutankhamen, seems as much buried in the past as his remains. Sir Basil Blackett has said that one of the first things that he did on becoming the Finance Member was to ask for the existing Paper Currency Laws and after a hard day's labour 'he had to give the subject up.' An historical background, if I have not succeeded in making it still more complicated than the picture itself, may perhaps help to clear up the matter. At any rate seeing that Japan and a few other countries possess excellent monographs about the story of their Paper Currencies, there is no reason why we should not have ours.

I am deeply indebted to Prof. Coyajee for the Foreword which he has kindly written for the book. It is no small privilege to be introduced to the reading public by one who is regarded as one of the most distinguished Indian economists living and whose experiences as a member of the Royal Commission on Indian Currency entitle him to speak with unique authority on Indian Currency questions. I am also grateful to Prof. Cannan for looking over a good part of the work and making a few corrections and suggestions. Through the courtesy of Mr. Denning, Controller of the Currency, I have had the advantage of consulting an officer of his Department and verifying my account of the technique of paper currency administration. I take this opportunity of thanking Mr. Denning and the officer.

THE UNIVERSITY,
LUCKNOW
16th March. 1927.

B. B. DAS GUPTA.

CONTENTS

Part I.

Paper Currency before 1861.

CHAPTER I.

Some General Features . . . . . 2—9

Sec. 1. Influence of English example, p. 2.—Sec. 2. The beginnings and the growth of Bank circulation, p. 3.—Sec. 3. General character of the issue, p. 6.

CHAPTER II.

Details of Bank Issues . . . . . . 10—32

Sec. 1. The circulation of the first banks and agency houses, p. 10.—Sec. 2. The Presidency Banks and their issues, p. 14.—Sec. 3. The circulation of the non-Presidency Banks, p. 22.—Sec. 4. The conditions of Bank issues, p. 24.—Sec. 5. References to Part I, p. 29.

Part II.

Government Paper Currency.

CHAPTER III.

An Act to provide for a Government Paper Currency . . . . 34—54

Sec. 1. The first suggestions for a government issue, p. 34.—Sec. 2. Reasons for transference to the State, p. 36.—Sec. 3. The Act in the making, p. 39.—Sec. 4. The principal makers of the Act, their ideas and their share in moulding the Act, p. 41.—Sec. 5. The main provisions of the Act, p. 49.—Sec. 6. Contemporary estimate of the measure, p. 51.—Sec. 7. Plan of studying later history, p. 53.

CHAPTER IV.

The Agency of Issue . . . . . 55—76

Sec. 1. Presidency Banks made agents for the management of the issue, p. 55.—Sec. 2. The Wood-Laing controversy. Laing's case for enlisting the co-operation of the Banks and Wood's objections, p. 58.—Sec. 3. Wood's victory and the final dissociation of the Banks from the issue, p. 65.—Sec. 4. Fresh attempts to connect banking with the issue early in the 19th century, p. 67.—Sec. 5. The Imperial Bank and the question of the transference of the issue to it, p. 70.—Sec. 6. The proposal of the Hilton-Young Commission for a Central Bank Issue, p. 74.

CHAPTER V.

The Mechanism of the Issue . . . . . 77—111

Sec. 1. The building up, in stages, of an independent Paper Currency Department under a Controller of the Currency, p. 77.—Sec. 2. A glance at the office work and the officers in a Currency Office, p. 82.—Sec. 3. The designing and the printing of Currency notes, p. 85.—Sec. 4. The denominations, p. 87.—Sec. 5. The Circles and the Sub-Circles of Issue, p. 89.—Sec. 6. Other subsidiary establishments—Currency Agencies, Currency Chests, Mint Chests, p. 94.—Sec. 7. The process of universalisation, p. 97.—Sec. 8.

The question of legal tender and of facilities, legal and extra-legal for convertibility. The War-time crisis and the steps taken to meet it, p. 103.

CHAPTER VI.

The Cover of the Issue. *The Paper Currency Reserve, its functions, its location and its relation to other Government Reserves* 112—141

Sec. 1. The functions of the Currency reserve exceed mere convertibility and are rather undefined, p. 112.—Sec. 2. The influence of the two main schools of elasticity and convertibility on the history of the reserve, p. 114.—Sec. 3. Various non-currency uses of the Currency reserve. Some early instances of such unorthodox use, p. 118.—Sec. 4. The inseparable connection between the Currency reserve and the gold standard reserve, p. 124.—Sec. 5. The case for amalgamation of the Currency and the gold standard reserves, p. 132.—Sec. 6. The location of the reserve. Beginnings of the system of holding parts of the reserve outside India, p. 133.—Sec. 7. Further widening of the area of holding of the reserve during the War and after, p. 138.

CHAPTER VII.

The Cover of the Issue (*continued*). *The Composition of the Reserve* . . . 142—191

Sec. 1. The history of the composition of the reserve represents progress from rigidity towards elasticity, p. 142.—Sec. 2. The gold portion of the reserve as it grew up under successive Currency Acts, p. 143.—Sec. 3. Criticism of the policy of holding gold in the reserve, p. 147.—Sec. 4. The silver portion of the reserve, p. 154.—Sec. 5. The history of the security portion of the reserve. The process of expansion through successive stages,

p. 158.—Sec. 6. A detailed examination of the War and post-War inflation of the Paper Currency, p. 166.—Sec. 7. The sale of reverse councils and the security reserve, p. 171.—Sec. 8. The unsatisfactory fiduciary issue, as it stood in 1920, p. 176.—Sec. 9. Provisions of Act 45 of 1920, p. 178.—Sec. 10. The futility of the permanent provisions, p. 181.—Sec. 11. Limit of fiduciary issue further raised in 1925, p. 189.

CHAPTER VIII.

The Cover of the Issue (*concluded*). The Question of Elasticity . . . . 192—216

Sec. 1. Elasticity of issue, its different interpretations and its connection, in theory, with the market rate of interest, p. 192.—Sec. 2. Conscious and unconscious developments in connection with the growth of elasticity. Various suggested methods of promoting elasticity, p. 196.—Sec. 3. The reason why the Currency reserve has been suggested in preference to other sources, p. 202.—Sec. 4. The recommendations of the Chamberlain Commission and of the Smith Committee with a view to increase the elasticity of the issue, p. 204.—Sec. 5. The suggestions of the Smith Committee, somewhat modified, incorporated into the Paper Currency system in 1920. The first regulations in this connection, p. 206.—Sec. 6. Changes in the procedure of the issue of emergency Currency made in 1923, p. 208.—Sec. 7. The existing double opening for elasticity in the Currency system summarised, p. 210.—Sec. 8. Further changes in the procedure of the issue in 1924, p. 212.—Sec. 9. The question of valuation, depreciation and sundry other points relating to the security reserve, p. 213.

A note on the Federal Reserve Note-issue system of U. S. A. in comparison with the Indian system 217

A note on the rates of interest charged for the issue of seasonal emergency currency . . 222

CHAPTER IX.

The Growth of the Issue . . . . . 227—259

Sec. 1. Summary statistics of the growth of the circulation, p. 227.—Sec. 2. Explanation of the growing popularity of the notes despite several unfavourable factors, p. 229.—Sec. 3. The division into gross and active circulation, with figures of such circulation, p. 232.—Sec. 4. Comparison of circulation and the price-level. A typical currency return, p. 235.—Sec. 5. Seasonal demand for Currency and its bearing on the gross and active circulation, p. 237.—Sec. 6. The distribution of the issue by circles and denominations, p. 239.—Sec. 7. Sources of information, p. 242.—Sec. 8. Currency profits and Currency forgeries, p. 243.—Sec. 9. A chronological survey of Currency legislation, p. 244.—Sec. 10. A biographical notice of Lushington, p. 250.—Sec. 11. Of James Wilson, p. 251.—Sec. 12. Of Sir Charles Wood, p. 253.—Sec. 13. Of Samuel Laing, p. 254.—Sec. 14. Of Sir Malcolm Hailey and Sir Basil Blackett, p. 255.

CHAPTER X.

The Future of the Issue . . . . . 260—287

Sec. 1. Programmes of reform, long called for, have now taken definite shape and direction in connection with coming vital changes in the monetary framework, p. 260.—Sec. 2. Two basic principles to be recognised, p. 263.—Sec. 3. First, regarding the relation of Paper Currency to the entire monetary system, which is a relationship of the part to the whole, p. 264.—Sec. 4. Secondly, regarding the aim of sound monetary policy, which is price-stability, p. 267.—Sec. 5. Of false considerations, the consideration of profit leads to a baneful subordination of Paper Currency to general finances, p. 268.—Sec. 6. In the altered monetary outlook, transference of the issue to a central bank, logical and inevitable, p. 271. Sec. 7. Facilities of convertibility, legal and extra-legal, p. 273.—Sec. 9. A combined reserve for rupees and notes, p. 277.—Sec. 10. The composition of the reserve, p. 279.—Sec. 11. The location of the reserve, p. 281.—Sec. 12. The Paper Currency and the gold standard reserves amalgamated, p. 283.—Sec. 13. Provision for elasticity, p. 284.—Sec. 14. Sundry suggestions regarding the technique of the issue, p. 285.

BIBLIOGRAPHY for Part II 288

APPENDIX A. Act 19 of 1861 292

APPENDIX B. The existing Paper Currency Law, Act 10 of 1923, amended by later Acts 300

APPENDIX C. Proposed new Currency legislation 315

INDEX 327

PAPER CURRENCY IN INDIA

PART I

Paper Currency before 1861

" It was the country of Shuh, now the province of Sze-chhuen, into which a true paper money was first introduced............A certain Chang-yung brought them into circulation, in order to supply (supplant?) the iron money which was too ponderous and inconvenient. These assignats were called chetse or cuts. Under the sign of Chiu-tsung of the Sung (from 997 till 1022) this example was followed and assignats were made under the name of Keaon-tsze or bills of exchange..............Every Keaon-tsze represented one ounce of pure silver."

Klaproth, Origin of Paper Money (1823)

CHAPTER I

SOME GENERAL FEATURES.

§ 1. Influence of English example, p. 2.—§ 2. The beginnings and the growth of Bank circulation, p. 3.—§ 3. General character of the issue, p. 6.

§ 1. Before 1861 the business of issuing notes in India was left entirely in the hands of banks. It was left to banks in exactly the same way as any other kind of banking business was so left. Note-issuing was not then looked upon as in any way separate from general banking work. No one thought of it except in terms of banking generally. The ideal was the English banking system with its tradition of bank issues. India followed this ideal at a respectable distance, and consequently there was at first no question of disconnecting note-issuing from banking. Banks issued notes more as a matter of course than as being deliberately chosen to be the best possible agency of issue. It was simply taken for granted that they should issue and they issued. It was unusual to think of any other rival method of issue. Here, as in most other imported institutions in India, English experience showed the way and equally limited the field of choice. Upon the whole history of Indian Paper Currency, the lessons of English experience are clearly traceable. There is a marked parallelism in ideas and in practice between the two countries. In the last half of the 18th century, as English banking came into India, it brought with it its characteristic function of note issue. These early issues were, so far as is known, free from all restrictions. By and by, as English opinion veered round, after much painful experience, in favour of regulating the issues of banks, India took up the tale, and then we meet with a period in which the Charters of new banks contained controlling clauses regarding the note issue. Finally, the conservatism of the English Bank Charter Act of 1844 was matched in India by a very drastic procedure. Government itself took over the issue of notes in its own hands,—relieving the banks altogether. The English doctrine of safety first was also faithfully echoed and the new issue was hedged around with all manner of restrictions. The result was as rigid an issue in India as in England.

§ 2. The earliest note issues in India are lost behind the mists of a century and a half. Not much light can be thrown upon them now. It is impossible to say, in the first place, how many banks there were in India before 1800. The 18th century was a period of unsettlement in India. The East India Company was turning gradually from a trading to a governing company. The boundaries of British territories were being extended on all sides. It might be described as an era of acquisition of new territories,—rather than of consolidating the existing ones. There was no uniformity in the monetary system between different parts of the Company's possessions. Communications were extremely undeveloped. It was not therefore a time suitable for the growth of banking. Of the few names that come down to us as banking houses existing before 1800 only two seem to have been banks in the strict sense of the term. They were the Bank of Hindustan and the Bengal Bank. There were a number of other institutions, the so-called agency houses which passed for Banks, but which rather mixed up trading business with pure banking work. It must be remembered however, that combining trading with banking was not an unusual thing to do in those times. Anyway, it is better to put the Agency Houses out of the category of banks. Their number, further, could not have been large. The East India Company exercised a jealous monopoly in those days in its trade with India, and it was not easy for any new banks to be started in the country in the face of its opposition. There is no doubt but that the migration of banking capital to India was seriously hampered by this exclusive monopoly. Whatever the causes may have been, the situation towards the end of the 18th century was far from satisfactory. The few banks that issued notes were all very weak. The impression one receives by going through some contemporary correspondence is that, neither the trading community nor the Government thought much of the note issue. The famous letter from C. S. Tucker, Accountant General to Lord Wellesley, which Dr. Dhume reproduces in full in his Banking in India, may be cited as giving expression to a feeling held universally.* 'There is not in Bengal,' regrets Mr. Tucker, 'as in the commercial countries of Europe, an artificial capital arising from the circulation of a paper currency.' He therefore proposed the establishment of a bank that

* C. S. Tucker, Letter to Lord Wellesley, 1801.

among other work, was to take up the issue of notes. He however did not consider it yet safe to attempt to circulate notes beyond the limits of the Presidency, under the existing system.

In the early part of the 19th century the number of banks in India was gradually increasing. Not all of them however issued notes. The note issues of some banks are said to have been very satisfactory. The people of the country were slowly taking up the note habit and Government, which was apathetic at first towards these issues, thought it worth while to give some sort of official recognition to them. The Bank of Bengal, under its Charter granted in 1809, was given permission to issue notes, under certain conditions. These conditions did not and were not meant to put any kind of direct control on the note issue. They did not treat the Bank's liability for its issue in any special way different from its other liabilities. By 1839—when two more Charters had been given to the bank—the reference to the note-issue grew more conscious. The Charter of 1839 definitely put down a limit beyond which the issue could not rise. Although thus it was being realised that in the conscious. The Charter of 1839 definitely put down the State had a part to play,—still much remained to be done. The notes were not yet legal tender, nor were they freely received in the Government's Treasuries. By 1843, two more Presidency banks had been started, but no important change was noticeable in the Government policy towards the note-issue. The Charters of these new banks contained almost exactly the same provisions regarding the note issue as did that of the Bank of Bengal. In the meantime the other non-Presidency banks, those that had a free note-issue, were considerably eclipsed by the new Presidency banks, and declined in importance. Some disappeared altogether, as commercial bad weather set in, while others escaped, shorn of their issues. What with their own internal weakness, and what with the formidable rivalry of the new Presidency banks, basking in official recognition,—their note issues swiftly declined in amount, until by the time the Act of 1861 was passed, the three Presidency banks between them practically monopolised all the note issue of the country. No figures are available as to the amount of notes issued by the non-Presidency banks in 1861, but that it had dwindled almost to nothing is apparent from the fact that in transferring the issue to Government hands, no compensation was at all proposed to be given to them.

§ 3. Between the years 1770 when the Bank of Hindustan 'probably the first banking institution in India on European lines' was started, and 1861, when the note issue was made a Government undertaking, it is possible to count as many as 35 banks that at one time or another, with good or bad fortune, operated in India. Of these only some ten, including the three Presidency banks, seem ever to have issued notes. There was besides, the so-called Government Bank of Madras which Lord William Bentinck, the Governor of Madras, established there about the beginning of the 19th century (Brunyate). It is said to have possessed a limited circulation. But its notes were more like Treasury Bills than notes proper, and the bank cannot be regarded, correctly, as an issuing bank. The note-issue between 1770 and 1861, was therefore wholly a private bank issue. Although issued by different banks, under varying conditions, certain features are noticeable about the issue. It is possible to summarise these characteristics as follows :—

(1) It was a period of issue by private banks. These banks were scattered all throughout the country, and did not seem to have much relation with each other. Onward from 1839 the issue more and more concentrated in the hands of the three Presidency banks. But the older banks still continued to issue.

(2) Very little of Government assistance was extended to these bank issues. They were not legal tender money and quite frequently the Government refused to accept them.

(3) It was a period which, beginning with absolute non-interference with note-issues, tended more and more towards regulation. No conscious policy however was yet evolved. Government was feeling its way, as it were. The necessity of doing something to improve the note issue was keenly felt. But it was left for James Wilson in 1861 to strike out the line of advance.

(4) The circulation of the notes was unsatisfactory. It was mainly confined to cities, and its amount was very small, compared to the size and population of the country. Dr. Arnold quite rightly questions Conant's assertion that before 1861 India

already had a prosperous system of note issue. The issue was at most a moribund and small one.

(5) There was no uniformity in the system of issue. A uniformity in the issue of notes, when there was no uniformity even in the coins that circulated in different parts of the country, was more than could be expected. It was only in 1835 that much of this currency confusion was finally cleared. In that year the Company's rupee of 180 grains was made the only standard money for all India. Formerly the rupee most in use was the Sicca rupee, of 173 grains. The denomination of the notes issued, also varied from one bank to another. Even the definition of a bank note was not universally agreed upon. It comprised, besides what are now regarded as currency notes, an elastic range of negotiable instruments. In the statistics of those times bank post-bills are nearly always included in estimates of note-circulation, while as Macdonald * records, promissory and treasury notes of the Government were also usually considered as and passed for notes. ' The former of these corresponded to bank certificates, being in fact obligations on the treasury for the payment of the interest on the public debt, the second partook of the nature of exchequer bills bearing a certain rate of interest per diem, which from time to time varied considerably. The practice of regarding Government promissory notes and treasury bills as belonging to the same category as bank notes is rather confusing and leaves much

* A. J. Macdonald, Banking in India, Journal of the Institute of Bankers, May, 1890.

uncertainty about the statistics of paper currency of that time. Both Arnold and Brunyate bear testimony to it, but they might have just borrowed the idea from Macdonald.

The uncertainty about the definition of a 'note' remained for a long time. It was only after 1861 that the paper note took its specific form in which we see it to-day.

CHAPTER II.

Details of Bank Issues.

§ 1. The circulation of the first banks and agency houses, p. 10.—§ 2. The Presidency Banks and their issues, p. 14.—§ 3. The circulation of the non-Presidency Banks, p. 22.—§ 4. The conditions of Bank issues, p. 24.—§ 5. References to Part I, p. 29.

§ 1. Very few particulars of the note issues up to 1861 have come down to us. The available details, which we owe mainly to Brunyate and Cooke, may be conveniently arranged in two parts :—1st, the circulation, dealing with such facts as the amount, the vicissitudes and the territorial range of the issue, and 2ndly, the conditions of issue, dealing with the restrictions, if any, imposed upon it. Since there was not one, but really a number of issues, in both these parts, the many issuing banks will be treated separately. First, then, about circulation.

1. *Circulation.*

As far as is known, the earliest bank to issue notes, was the Bank of Hindustan, established in 1770. This is taking no account of course of the so-called Agency Houses. Historically, these Agency Houses were however the first dealers in credit (although, among other things) in the country on anything like Western lines, and they grew up along with the growth of British power and British trade. The Agency Houses were ' agents for the planters and merchants settled in the Upper Provinces. They were bankers receiving deposits...........and bankers issuing paper-money. They had a note circulation which was extremely beneficial to them in carrying on their diversified operations as shipowners, house-owners, farmers, manufacturers and money-lenders' (Cooke). We also read (Institute of Bankers Journal, Oct., 1898) that ' the Commercial Crisis at the beginning of the third decade involved the failure of many of the merchant princes, such as the firms Alexander & Co., Ferguson & Co., and Macintosh & Co., names familiar with the history of our banking from the strain that their failures created here and to take their place joint stock associations were rapidly formed, for instance the Agra and United Service Bank Ltd., established 1833.'

To return however to the Hindustan Bank. The circulation of its notes was confined entirely to Calcutta and the immediate neighbourhood. The Government refused to confer on the notes the standing of legal tender money and did not accept them in any of its Imperial Treasuries. The circulation varied considerably in amount from time to time, occasionally reaching 40 or 50 lakhs, but on an average remaining at about 20 lakhs. Its notes are said to have been received freely at all the public offices in Calcutta, ' scarcely excepting the Treasury itself.' That the bank's position was quite strong is apparent from the fact that it met promptly and successfully two severe runs upon it,—one in 1819 and another in 1829. The causes leading to the first are instructive of the atmosphere of distrust in which the banks in India lived in those times. Some forgeries had lately been brought to light. The bank thought it wise to issue a notice to the public pointing out how to distinguish the genuine from the forged notes. This was all that the bank had done. Some 'evil-disposed persons' at once gave to the notice a false character and spread the report among the natives that unless the bank-notes were brought in by a certain day they would not be cashed. The consequence was an immediate run which brought in nearly all the notes outstanding—about 18 lakhs. The reasons for the 1829 run lay in the failure of an important trading concern, Messrs. Palmer & Co., and on this occasion notes to the value of about 20 lakhs of rupees were cashed. It is to the credit of the Bank of Hindustan that it met both these runs with the utmost promptness,—which is the only sure way of staying a panic. It closed down in 1831, not being able to stand the 'most awful crisis that ever visited India' (Cooke). Very few of its notes however were in circulation at the time of its failure.

The Bengal Bank,—not to be confused with the Presidency Bank of Bengal started later in 1806,—is mentioned as a going concern in 1790. When exactly it was founded it is impossible to say. It had also a note circulation, but possibly a very limited one. Cooke gives a specimen of a note of this bank—which is reproduced below:

বেঙ্গাল ব্যাঙ্ক	No. 2 / 2749	BENGAL BANK
CALCUTTA একশত টাকা সিক্কা		*15th Nov., 1791.*

I promise to pay, Ramcaunt Dutt or Bearer on demand One Hundred Sicca Rupees

One Hundred — **For the Bengal Bank**

Exd. — **Benjamin Mee**

The Sicca rupee contained 173 grains of silver. The specification that the payment is to be in Sicca rupees indicates that there were other kinds of rupees also current.

In the beginning of the 19th century was founded the Government Bank at Madras. But, as said before, it was in reality more a treasury than a bank. 'The Treasury Bills by which the government raised funds at that time were also a species of paper currency. But they were expressed in amounts which were too large for the bills to be a popular form of currency' (Brunyate). They bore interest and were inconvertible and consequently circulated at a discount. Although in consonance with the loose monetary nomenclature of those times they were also styled as notes and often passed for such, it is better to leave them out altogether, as differing in many important respects from genuine paper currency. They were simple loan-certificates, only fit by courtesy to be called money. They seem to have been a feature of the Government finance of that time. Brunyate says that it was partly with the object of assisting in the gradual withdrawal of bills of this kind from the market that the Bank of Bengal was created and its notes were originally issued only in exchange for Treasury Bills and for a short time were payable in the same currency. In a few months however it was decided to pay all notes in specie on demand. The Madras Government Bank continued to issue such 'notes' for some years, until it was displaced by the Presidency Bank of Madras in 1843.

§ 2. By far the most important issuing agencies were however the Presidency Banks. Although the same lack of information as in the case of the other non-Presidency Banks makes it impossible to draw up a complete picture of their issues, yet enough is known of them to say that their circulation, both in amount and popularity, far outshone that of all other banks. The Bank of Bengal, of the three of the kind, was the first to be started (1806). Its notes were not made legal tender or accepted by the Government unconditionally. That would have been too much unlike a self-less Government, anxious above all for security. The condition therefore was the deposit of 20 lakhs of Company's paper in the Public Treasury as a security for the credit given by the Government to the Bank in receiving its notes. Perhaps it was a small price for the privilege. In 1835 this condition was removed. At first the Government did not receive its notes outside of Calcutta but afterwards 'directed their acceptance at all Government Treasuries in the Lower Province' of Bengal. This order limiting the recognition of the Bank's notes to a certain area only, seems to have been still in force in 1836, for in that year we find the Bank asking the Government to accept its notes at the Treasuries of the North Western Provinces (modern United Provinces). The Bank was then trying to open a branch at Allahabad. The Government however refused to extend its patronage to the notes, explaining that it could not do so 'unless the Bank made its own arrangements for cashing its notes on the spot.' * This indicates that the bank's notes were payable only at the Head Office at Calcutta. It is curious that in spite of this very limited opportunity for encashment the Bank's notes should have commanded any wide circulation, yet Cooke says that the 'Bank of Bengal notes had a circulation which extended to Benares 560 miles above Calcutta.' He remarks, however, that the notes were subject to a discount of about 4 per cent. That they should have at all circulated so far away from the office of payment, speaks if anything of the strong confidence that the people had in the Bank. There was not even a breath of suspicion attaching to its notes. The Government, if it liked, could have assisted the Bank in many ways. But apart from consenting to receive its notes under certain conditions, it did not do anything else. It never cashed them in the Lower Provinces even, nor re-issued them, except when demanded by people willing to receive them. The Court of Directors seemed uneasy at this small amount of official connection even,—for they had given orders to see that more than Rs. 50 Lakhs worth of notes by no means accumulated in their treasuries. Any excess was to be presented to the Bank for immediate payment. This order seems to have been repeated in 1848 and regarded by the Secretary of State at any rate as holding good up to 1861. It was more than could be practically observed however in times of emergency. Once in 1839 the holdings amounted to Rs. 72 lakhs.

* Bank of Bengal Charters—(G.L.).

Pp. 53-54 deals with the Government's objection to receive notes at 'Bunares.'

The Bank of Bengal, by virtue of its expanding volume of business and scrupulous soundness of administration, enjoyed a unique position, not only among other private banks, but also among the Presidency Banks. Its circulation far surpassed that of any other bank, Presidency or non-Presidency. It had an average circulation of Rs. 120 lakhs yearly, about the year 1829. But although by 1861 it still continued to function as the one great Bank of Issue in India, its circulation did not, strangely enough, show any appreciable increase. The highest average for the 6 years preceding the withdrawal of the right of issue in 1862 was only 176 lakhs, while in two of the six years the circulation was actually under 150 lakhs. One would have naturally expected a far greater increase than that, in 30 years' time. This stagnancy in circulation may be explained by three sets of causes :—

(1) In the first place, although the note habit was growing among the Indians, it was still confined more or less to cities. The Indian in the country was still unfamiliar with this form of currency. The methods of his business were mainly on a coin basis. He had also difficulty in storing this new paper money.

(2) Absence of facilities for encashment, outside of Calcutta, seriously limited the circulation. The costs of carrying specie from one place to another in those pre-railway days were very heavy. Gang robberies were the order of the day. Consequently increase of centres of encashment, which was a necessary condition for extension of circulation, did

not appear as a paying proposition to the Bank. Brunyate says that it naturally preferred the profits of an internal exchange to those of an extended note issue.

This question of facilities for encashment came prominently before the Bank when it was thinking of opening out branches. Making notes issued at Calcutta payable at the branches meant undertaking considerable transfer of specie. The appeal to the Government was bound to be coldly received. Government could not be expected to bear the cost of remittance when it had no share in the profits of the note circulation. Still, without multiplying facilities for encashment it was idle to expect any increase in the circulation. The bank's plan to meet this difficulty was an anticipation of the later Circle system. It proposed to separate the branch note-issue from the Calcutta issue, with two distinct reserves at the two places. The notes of the branch bank might be cashed by favour at the head office if funds permitted, but there was to be no obligation. This circle or compartment plan was bound to suggest itself to any one as the only possible way to reconcile a desire to extend the circulation and avoid the costs of remittance. It came to G. Udny, Secretary to the Bank of Bengal. "The safest way," he writes in a minute on the point,* "I conceive to be the erection there (at the place where the branch was proposed to be opened) with a certain amount of capital, of an independent

*Bank of Bengal Charters (G. L.), p. 97.

Branch, by which I mean a Branch with a circulation of notes entirely distinct from that of Calcutta and which though payable if convenient at Calcutta, shall be cashed alone as a matter of right at the branch only (Allahabad.)'' Such a proposal was actually made by the Bank to the Government on the 27th January, 1837—but Government thought that some modification in the Charter of the Bank was necessary before the proposal could be carried out. Hence no further progress was made with the idea. As however no branches were opened until a few months before the withdrawal of the right of issue the question never assumed a pressing nature. The Circle solution, as later experience proved, extended the note-circulation, but did not extend the same issue. More notes circulated in the country, but the notes were of different kinds and were not interchangeable as of right—a fact that considerably minimised the importance of the increase of circulation. The extension was, if one may say so, quantitative but not qualitative.

A notable event in the history of the Bank of Bengal issue, was the necessity in 1860, of increasing the circulation beyond the maximum limit granted by law. It was only once in the whole life of the Bank that such a necessity had ever arisen of overstepping its Charter. Normally, the Bank's circulation stood far below the maximum of Rs. 2 crores allowed by the law of 1839. But in 1860, in respect of the subscriptions to the Government $5\frac{1}{2}$ per cent. loan, a heavy demand for accommodation rapidly pushed the issue up to the legal limit, and still much of the demand was left unsatisfied. On an application to the Government it permitted the Bank to issue notes up to the amount of 275 lakhs, *i.e.*, 75 lakhs more than the usual amount, and "in consideration of the fact that excess notes were all held in the public Treasury and really represented an advance from the Government to the Bank, the Bank was charged interest on the excess issue at the rate of 5 per cent. per annum."* This seems to be the earliest evidence, in India, of the principle, so well recognised in our times, of keeping an outlet for seasonable increase of currency, modified by a safety brake of charging a price for it. It is curious, this precedent was entirely overlooked in the framing of the Government paper currency system of 1861. Perhaps it was regarded as an abnormal instance involving a breach of law—more to be ashamed of than emulated. That it was in any way a contribution towards introducing an element of elasticity in the note-issue was not yet realised.

It has already been remarked how, owing principally to lack of facilities for encashment, the note issue of the Bank of Bengal did not grow as fast as was to be expected. The circulation outside Bengal was in fact quite insignificant. Major Hyde, Head Commissioner of Paper Currency, in his evidence before the 1867 Commission said, "I do not remember ever having seen a note of the Bank

* Brunyate, Account of the Presidency Banks (not published). Also Macdonald.

of Bengal, in upper India "* Some idea of the growth of the circulation of the Bank during the earlier part of its existence can be had from the following figures :—

Years	1809	1812	1815	1818	1821	1824	1827	1830	1833	1836
Circulation (Lakhs of Rs.)	29	35	39	47	54	91	84	91	104	106

These figures are taken from the "Papers relating to Bank of Bengal." In 1851, we find in "Die Banken," the note circulation stood at 7,600,000 Thlr. (Pr. Cr.)—which would be perhaps approximately equal to 1 crore and 14 lakhs. Macdonald says that the note issue of the Bank of Bengal seldom exceeded 1 crore and 60 lakhs.

For statistics of the Bank's circulation from 1857 to 1862, reference is to be made to the Report of the 1867 Commission. The average circulation in 1862—the last year of issue—was about 176 lakhs. The denominations of the notes were Rs. 10, 15, 16, 20, 25, 50, 100, 250, 500, 1,000, 10,000.†

The account of the other two Presidency Banks will take far less space. The Bank of Bombay was founded in 1840. In the development of a paper circulation the Western Presidency of India was very

*Minutes of Evidence, Commission of 1867.

† It is curious Hübner writes—' Ihre Noten von bis 10,000 Rupien werden bei allen Aemten in Unterbengalen an Zahlung genommen.' But the 1839 Charter of the Bank of Bengal grants a note issue only provided that " no such note shall be for a smaller amount than 10 Rupees."

much behind the Eastern. It is said that previous to the foundation of the Bank of Bombay—"note circulation was almost unknown in the Presidency." * Hardly anything is known about the circulation of the Bank. It was a very well-timed issue, for we are told that the "advantage of bank notes as a medium of exchange was at once and fully appreciated by all classes." It is, however, difficult "at once and fully" to believe the statement. It is easier to appreciate it as a compliment to India's go-ahead Presidency. The maximum limit of circulation as in the case of the Bank of Bengal, was Rs. 2 crores,—the highest point actually reached was Rs. 1,28,12,000 (including again a small amount of post bills). In December, 1843, the circulation stood at Rs. 63,50,000, the highest figure for any year up to 1852—the average being Rs. 35,00,000 (Huebner).

Our knowledge of the paper circulation of the Bank of Madras (founded in 1843) is equally scanty. It replaced the so-called Government Bank of Madras, the note-issue of which was discontinued. Its notes were convertible into cash in all public treasuries.† If that is so, it enjoyed a privilege which was certainly the envy of the other two Presidency Banks. About its circulation it is known that the average was "about 15 or 16 lakhs. At one time it reached 30 lakhs and in the negotiations

* The late Government Bank of Bombay, 1868, G. L. Almost the only source of information about the Bank.

† Münz—Mass—und Gewichtsbuch (A Directory of money, measures and weights). Leipzig, 1858, G. L.

of the Bank with the Government it struggled hard for an extension. With the exception of the year 1860 the circulation was always under 20 lakhs, but in that year it rose to 24½ lakhs, the surplus being generally held by the Treasury and the Banks in Madras " (Macdonald). The circulation in 1852 was approximately Rs. 12,71,950 (Huebner).

§ 3. If so few particulars are known about the Presidency Banks, little or almost nothing is known about their other contemporaries. The Union Bank, which arose out of the ruins of a number of trading or agency firms in 1829, had a respectable circulation for some years. Starting with Rs. 3,63,020 in 1830 it reached its maximum issue in 1837 when the circulation stood at Rs. 7,05,175. Then it declined. Brunyate says that the Union Bank's notes were for a time freely accepted by the Bank of Bengal. But in 1834 it decided to refuse them and its monopoly of Government recognition enabled it to persist in that decision in spite of much protest on the part of the well-wishers of the Union Bank, "who attributed this action of the Bank of Bengal to the desire to strangle the infant Hercules." The notes had no wide circulation and the bank itself disappeared in 1848. Another bank, the Commercial Bank, whose dates are given as 1819-33, also had a circulation of a fluctuating nature. The average amount of notes in circulation was about 16 lakhs. The circulation in 1828 had considerably contracted. Its notes were not accepted by the Government at all. The Calcutta Bank was another institution to claim an issue between 1824-29. Its notes outstanding averaged Rs. 20 lakhs. The Bank of Mirzapore is also said to have obtained for its notes a limited circulation. No figures are available. The Bank of India, projected in 1828 by Raj Kissen Dutt, a name long remembered for the forgeries associated with it, "had a note circulation which was received by the natives." These banks are all mentioned by Cooke in his Banking in India (1863). Another bank not mentioned in his book, the Bank of Western India (Die Bank des westlichen Ostindien), founded in 1842, also seems to have a note issue.* But no details of its circulation are available. Perhaps this was the same bank as the Nordwest Bank von Indien which Huebner mentions but gives no details of its issues. Huebner also mentions two other banks, *viz.*, the Oriental Bank Corporation and the Agra and United Service Bank of Agra as having a note circulation. The amount of circulation of the former was approximately Rs. 5,18,910 in 1851, of the latter approximately Rs. 10,00,000 in 1852.

So much about circulation. How quickly all particulars of the note issues by the banks became in India a thing of the past, will appear from the testimony of the Head Commissioner of Paper Currency. Only five years after the transference of the issue to the Government he says, in answer to a question before the 1867 Commission :—"What was the actual average circulation of the Presidency Banks? I do not know. I have no information on

* Münz—Mass und Gewichtsbuch, 1858, G. L.

the subject, nor have the means of obtaining the data that would enable me to answer the qustion."

2. *The Conditions of Issue.*

§ 4. We now come to the second part of our subject—the conditions of issue. These conditions might be described as very easy and simple. Apart from the three Presidency Banks there were no restrictions imposed upon any other banks in the matter of note-issue. This was the general position, although, as Huebner notices, the constitution of the Oriental Bank Corporation contained provisions for a one-third cash reserve against note-issues, in the case of all its branches. Whether this was at all operative is difficult to say.*

Even in the case of the Presidency Banks the restrictions, as experience amply showed, were meant not so much to hamper the growth of a paper circulation as to insure the general stability of the banks. The Government's attitude—so far as it knew itself—was perhaps *laissez faire*, neither an attitude of active support, nor of active repression. Cautiousness—perhaps born of indefinite ideas and policies,—was the motto. In the first Charter of the Bank of Bengal no attempt is made at any direct control of the note-issue, although there are clauses prescribing certain relations between the liabilities,

* Die Banken. I think Brunyate also mentions this but passes the fact by as of no importance on the ground that before any note issue was contemplated under these provisions, the Paper currency passed into the hands of the Government.

assets, and the capital of the bank. The later Bank Charters, however, marked a slight deviation from this policy and contained direct regulations about the note-issue. But even then the restrictions were small in amount. The limit imposed still left much room for the circulation to grow freely. Only once, as an exceptional occasion, as has already been noted, did the limit actually prove to be a barrier for the expansion of the circulation. Taking the whole period at a glance, from 1770 to 1861, it would be true to say that the growth of the circulation was never really hampered by these restrictions. The period of the bank issue is thus, on the whole, a period of minimum State regulation.

Historically, as has been remarked, in the beginning, the control grew, as Government, in the light of developments, slowly felt its way on. At first there were no restrictions whatsoever. Then the restrictions were indirect and insignificant. Only as late as 1839, they hardened into any definite shape. No evidence is forthcoming that they really obstructed the note-issues in any material way. That normally the actual circulation of the banks stood far below the maximum amounts permitted under the law—leaving a considerable margin of expansion—is proof enough of the harmlessness of the legal interference. The banks themselves, or any public associations, are never known to have made any protests against the restrictions imposed—which indicates how mild they were. The same conclusion has to be drawn from a letter by the Secretary of State of India to C. L. Cumming Bruce, M.P.—(November,

1852) wherein he notes that although the three Presidency Banks were allowed together to issue notes up to Rs. 5 crores, according to the latest returns they had only issued a little more than Rs. 2 crores. He found also that the cash reserve of these banks were "extraordinarily large in proportion to their liabilities." He therefore argued against the necessity of starting any more banks in India.* A publication in 1837† says, "the Bank of Bengal issues its notes as long as there are any takers." Whatever the reason, there were not enough "takers" to push up the circulation of notes to the point of seriously conflicting with the restrictions imposed. No intending takers were perhaps ever disappointed. In view of all this evidence, it would be idle to suggest that paper currency in India could not grow on account of the chains of legislation. The chains were remarkably light.

It may seem rather strange that only the Presidency Banks were subjected to regulations regarding the note-issue. Others escaped free. This partiality, however, need cause no wonder. The Presidency Banks were far and away the most important of the issuing banks, and gradually swallowed up the issues of their weaker rivals. By the side of the Presidency Banks the other Banks became very puny institutions, with trifling issues. It was expected that most of these private circulations, lacking

* Letter from Secretary of State to Cumming, Parliamentary Accounts and Papers, 1860, XLIX, B. M. L.

† Bank of Bengal Charters, pp. 53 and 54, G. L.

Government support and recognition would eventually dwindle and die off,—an expectation that proved true, in time. In the meantime the policy of the authorities seemed distinctly to have been *not* to favour the growth of any new banks of issue. In 1853, for instance, the Court of Directors were of opinion that it would not be expedient to grant such powers of issue either to the Oriental Bank, the Bank of Asia, or the Bank of India, Australia and China * (the last two having been proposed).

Coming to details, the first Charter of the Bank of Bengal (1809) empowered the directors to issue promissory notes payable on demand for amounts of not less than Rs. 10 and not more than Rs. 10,000. No special condition was laid down as to the reserve for the notes, neither was there any maximum limitation of the issue. Indirectly, the note circulation was touched by (*a*) the provision that the total liabilities of the Bank were not to exceed the Bank's capital of 50 lakhs of rupees and (*b*) secondly the actual cash in hand was never to fall below one-third of *all* the outstanding claims payable on demand. Notes being only a part of this demand liability, the total cash reserve normally thus stood at much higher than one-third of the total note-issue. For fourteen years the Charter remained in operation and during this period notes were not distinguishable from the other liabilities of the Bank payable on demand. There was only one reserve for all.

* Letter from Secretary of State to Cumming, Parliamentary Parliamentary Papers, 1860, XLIX, B. M. L.

The Charter of 1823 kept up the two-fold restriction on the issue, although relaxing the screw to some extent. Regarding capital restriction, the directors were empowered to extend the note-issue as they might think expedient for the public accommodation up to a maximum of four times the Bank's capital, which then stood at half a crore. Regarding the cash reserve restriction, from the previously compulsory one-third minimum the Bank was allowed to have a minimum of one-fourth of the outstanding claims.

In the Charter of 1839, the system of pegging the maximum issue to a multiple of the capital of the Bank was abandoned. Instead was laid down a definite amount beyond which the issue was not to rise. Article 31 of the Act, No. VI of 1839, granting a new Charter to the Bank of Bengal stipulated that the Bank might "issue promissory notes payable on demand or at a date not exceeding thirty days after sight...............provided always the total amount of such notes in circulation at any time shall not exceed 2 crores of rupees and provided also that no such note shall be for a smaller amount than Rs. 10." The capital restriction was thus given up in favour of a maximum limitation. But this limitation, as we have seen, had little practical effect, as the normal circulation never reached, except on one occasion in 1861, Rs. 2 crores. The maximum reserve part of the restriction was kept unchanged as before, in this Charter. Article 26 said that the amount of cash was to be at least one-fourth of all the claims against the Bank payable on demand. The provisions of

1839 held good up to the time when the right of issue was taken away from the Bank.

The story of the other two Presidency Banks, is practically the same story as that of the Bank of Bengal. Their constitutions were more or less modelled on that of the Bank of Bengal. Consequently the same restrictions as imposed on the Bank of Bengal by the law of 1839 were imposed on them. Act III of 1840 (for the incorporation of a Bank at Bombay) reproduced under articles 25, 26 and 31, very nearly the same clauses as regulated the note-issue of the Bank of Bengal. The circulation was limited to a maximum of Rs. 2 crores and the cash reserve to one-fourth of all the demand liabilities. Three years later the same principles of control were embodied in the constitution of the Bank of Madras. Act IX of 1843 (for the incorporation of a Bank at Madras) provided that the total amount of notes issued by the Bank must not exceed Rs. 1 crore in all (article 33) and at least a one-fourth cash reserve must be maintained against all liabilities payable on demand (article 28).

References.

§ 5. The principal materials that have been consulted in the preparation of this Part, are the following :—

1. Sir James Brunyate—An Account of the Presidency Banks. This book was written for official information. It has not been allowed to be

published, although it is impossible to say why. It is at present out of print, Sir James personal copy being perhaps the only one available. My thanks are due to Sir James for having kindly lent me his book for some time. Full of valuable historical materials, it is a source book which writers having anything to do. with the financial past of India, have largely, and in some cases, even without acknowledgment, drawn upon. Chapter 5 of the book, where the note-issues of the Presidency Banks are dealt with, has been the most useful to me.

2. Charles N. Cooke—Banking in India, published 1862. Goldsmith's Library of Economic Literature (referred to before as G.L.). This is another important work. Besides giving some account of the Presidency Banks it attempts a running survey of all the banks that ever operated in India up to 1862.

3. Bank of Bengal Charters, published 1837. Full of correspondence and minutes by various directors of the Bank, a difficult book to extract any desirable information from. G. L.

4. The late Government Bank of Bombay. Published 1868. Some glimpses into the early history of the Presidency Bank of Bombay. G. L.

5. Otto Hübner—Die Banken—published 1854. Contains particulars about some of the then existing banks of India including a few statistics of note-issue.

6. Two papers in the journal of the Institute of Bankers. One in May, 1890 and the other in

October, 1898. Short references to the pre-Government note-issue.

7. Anton Arnold (A Reichsbank official)—Das indische Geldwesen unter besonderer Berücksichtigung seiner Reformen seit 1893. Some few particulars about the issue before 1861.

8. Münz—Mass—und Geweichtsbuch, Leipzig, 1858. Very scanty references to note issues of the banks in India. G. L.

9. Sketch of the Commercial Resources and monetary and mercantile system of British India. By John Crawford, 1837. Contains two or three paragraphs on the note-issue of the Bank of Bengal. G. L.

10. J. M. Keynes—Indian Currency and Finance, 1913, Chapter on Paper Currency.

11. F. Shirras—Indian Finance and Banking, 1920. Containing more particulars than any other recent books.

12. Dhume—Banking in India (University of London, Ph.D. thesis) not published.

These works supply as much light as is practically available on the note-issue before 1861, yet the information is very scanty. I have added here and there any new stray information that has come my way in my labours among old official papers in the British Museum Library (referred to as B. M. L.) and in the India Office.

Of these, mention might be made of—

1. Copies of Acts for Incorporation and Regulation of the Bank of Bengal, Bombay and Madras (Parliamentary Accounts and Papers), B. M. L., 1860, 49).

2. Copies of Acts' Notifications, etc., concerning Coinage Currency and Legal tender of Territories in India from 1st May, 1834 (B. M. L. Parliamentary Papers, 1857-58, 43).

3. Acts and Ordinances regulating Currency and Legal Tender, 1855-1860 (B. M. L. Parliamentary Papers, 1860, 49).

PART II

Government Paper Currency

There were Three Little Men
And they made a Little Pen
And they said 'Little Pen, you must flow, flow, flow

And write our names away,
Under promises to pay
Which how we are to keep we do not know.'

Then the Little Men so gay
Wrote their promises to pay
And lived for many moons royally, ly, ly.

Till there came a stormy day
And they vanished all away....................

They who sought the Little Men
Only found the Little Pen....................

—*Paper Money Lyrics by*
Peacock (1837).

CHAPTER III.

AN ACT TO PROVIDE FOR A GOVERNMENT PAPER CURRENCY.

§ 1. The first suggestions for a Government issue, p. 34.—§ 2. Reasons for transference to the State, p. 36.—§ 3. The Act in the making, p. 39.—§ 4. The principal makers of the Act, their ideas and their share in moulding the Act, p. 41.—§ 5. The main provisions of the Act, p. 49.—§ 6. Contemporary estimate of the measure, p. 51.—§ 7. Plan of studying later history, p. 53.

§ 1. The business of issuing notes passed in 1861 from the banks to the Government of the country. It was a bold step to take. It meant going on a wholly untried path. It therefore marks an important event in India's currency history. Just for how long the Government had been contemplating the change it is difficult to say ; but that the unsatisfactory state of the paper currency must have suggested some such course long before the first official proposal was actually made in 1859, admits of no doubt. Ideas often gather in volume silently in people's minds, until the time comes when they find expression through a chosen medium. The experiment of bank issues had practically proved a failure. The necessity of doing something to vitalise the issue had long been felt. It was indispensable that some new methods should be tried. The idea of Government's taking over the issue was not an altogether new or foreign idea. That it existed, as an under-current, even as early as 1837, is apparent from the fact that in a publication of that year (Bank of Bengal Charters, pp. 65) we find one John Fullarton attacking it with all the force at his command. 'As to the idea,' says Mr. Fullarton, 'of Government taking over the issue of paper money entirely on itself and making it a State monopoly'—it is one with which he finds it impossible to reconcile himself. Whether Mr. Fullarton was attacking a definite suggestion made by some one—or only disposing of an imaginary proposition which was the creature of his own mind, —it is true to say that in his time there were only a few people perhaps who could reconcile themselves to such an idea. Still fewer of them could have the courage to speak out their revolutionary opinions. But by 1859, the lack of any appreciable improvement in the note issue was too obvious for the authorities to sit idle.

It is immaterial to quarrel over the question to whom belongs the credit of first suggesting a Government paper currency for India. James Wilson, whose name is most commonly associated with the transfer of the issue to the Government may have independently thought of it or may have borrowed it from the Secretary of State for India, Sir Charles Wood, with whom he is known to have had conversations on the subject before leaving for India (Secretary of State's reply 26th March, 1860). But in point of time, the Government of India's first Despatch, accompanied by a Minute by C. H. Lushington seems to have anticipated them both. This despatch is dated 27th April, 1859. But the idea, as distinguished from the first concrete plan, is perhaps older than that. It may have been in the air for some time before 1859. The despatch of 1859 for the first time gave utterance to a sentiment that may have been current for a long time. It was by no means the beginning of everything. The true beginning, as in all history, is beyond anyone to trace out. What matters most is the end, the result. The result in this case was a very definite one —the law of 1861, transferring the issue from the banks to the State. The events that led to the passing of that law—the provisions of the law—together with an account of the part played by the individuals who had a hand in making that law, will form the subject matter of this chapter.

§ 2. Broadly two motives seem to have actuated the desire to transfer the issue to State hands. In the first place, there was a very laudable motive of extending the note issue, which had grown stagnant in the hands of the banks. Nothing but a State issue, it was believed, could infuse life into it. The banks were quite good theoretically. But in the peculiar circumstances of India, they could not be safely entrusted with the function. Both Lushington and Wilson had strong faith in banks. Both believed or pretended to believe, that the banks were the ideal agencies of issue, the Bank of England being the nearest approach to the ideal. But Lushington reasoned that to try to extend the note-issue by means of new branches in the country, would call for very self-sacrificing banks, willing to forego all prospects of earning a dividend. None was likely to be started. Wilson argued that the creation of a bank in India of the magnitude of the Bank of England was then out of the question, and hence the State was the only proper agency competent to run the issue. Sir Charles Wood's belief in Government was more direct and straightforward. He was against the Banks having any connection with the issue, simply because they were banks. Samuel Laing was as much anti-Government as the others were anti-bank, but coming rather late into the field, he could not entirely change the policy to his liking. He had to put up with the idea of Government directing the issue, but he tried to introduce the banks by the back door as 'agents for the issue.' Even in this he was ultimately unsuccessful.

The second motive for transferring the issue—was an argument of powerful economic—though of doubtful moral validity. It was, to put it simply, the idea of making a profit out of the note circulation. The notes that were to be issued against coins would of course yield no revenue to the State, but the uncovered part of the issue would serve to withdraw some of the Government's securities from the market and thereby reduce the burden of national debt. Lushington said it would in effect amount to a public loan, bearing no interest. He might have gone further. The securities in the fiduciary reserve might be replaced by creating other securities of equal value when they fell due,—and thereby the revenue of the State might be increased, not only by the amount of the interest of the debt, but virtually by the principal also. It would provide a new source of revenue as if by magic. But this magical increase of income would have another side of it also, which would be more than Government would like to contemplate. It is important to note this profit idea even at the inception of the proposals for State paper currency—for this idea still seems to haunt a good many people anxious to reform that currency. Nothing could be a more false and dangerous base to found an issue of paper money upon. It is true that Wilson, in his first minute, dated Camp, Meerut, 25th December, 1859, disavows this intention of making a profit out of the circulation. But later on in another letter (Govt. of India—No. 102 of 1860) he makes no secret of the existence of this motive. 'Our belief is that,' says the letter, 'whatever amount of Government securities we may gradually absorb as representing a portion of the circulation, may be regarded as being permanently withdrawn from the public and the debt of India will be practically reduced to that extent.'

Yet after all is said it remains true that the Government was prompted less by its own interests than by the general interests of the country in taking over the issue. It acted on a genuine desire to improve the state of the paper currency. In this respect, the origin of the state paper currency of India is a far more honourable origin than that of most state paper currencies. M. Subercaseaux in his interesting book on paper money * shows how

* G. Subercaseaux, Le Papier-Monnae, Paris, 1920.

wherever the paper currency passed from the hands of the banks to those of the Government, for instance in Chile and in Brazil, there, behind the transference lay either some difficulty forcing the hands of the Government, or some doubtful financial motives. The fact that M. Subercaseaux overlooks totally the case of India—her paper currency history finding no place in his work—leads him almost to generalise that the origins of Government paper currencies are forced or dishonourable. This, as India's case proves, is not quite true.

§ 3. The first proposal for a State paper currency, as mentioned above, was made in April, 1859. It went through a career full of vicissitudes, until it was finally passed into law in 1861. During this period it was hammered on the anvil and forged in the fire by a number of blacksmiths who had altogether different ideas about its proper shape. It crossed and re-crossed to England many times to accept benediction or chastisement at the hands of the Secretary of State. It would be too long to try to follow its progress, step by step, in all its details, through the mass of Minutes and Memoranda, Despatches and Counter-Despatches in which it was being discussed. All that can be attempted is a bare historical outline. In April, 1859, we come across the Despatch by the Government of India to Lord Stanley, the Secretary of State, embodying the first proposal ever made of transfer of the issue to the Government. It was 'prepared by our Financial Secretary' Mr. C. H. Lushington—not to be confused with another officer of the same name who served later. A note by Lushington was appended to the Despatch. To this Despatch His Majesty's Government, after being, as usual, 'fully sensible of the advantages of a well-regulated paper currency' replied that they regretted they were not disposed to direct its introduction at present. Towards the end of the year James Wilson arrived in India as Finance Member of the Governor-General's Council. He re-opened the question with a Minute (Dec., 1859) which was sent to the Secretary of State (now Sir Charles Wood). Discussion with Whitehall followed. Meanwhile, on the 20th November, 1860, Wilson introduced his Paper Currency Bill in the Legislative Council. The Bill was read a second time in the Council on the 22nd September, 1860. After that it was referred to a Select Committee. Wilson having died on August 11th, 1860, Samuel Laing had to enter the Select Committee in charge of the Bill. Thanks to his entirely opposite views to those of Wilson, the Bill underwent some severe handling in the Committee. When it came out it had changed almost beyond recognition. All along, the Secretary of State, Sir Charles Wood, had kept up a constant fire of enquiry, suggestion and criticism about the Bill. And when finally the Bill passed into law in July, 1861, it was difficult to say how far it was influenced by Wilson, how far by Laing and how far again by Sir Charles Wood. It was the product of a number of brains, working together in a kind of Joint Committee—not of one single brain. Each of the members of the Committee held different views from the others and it was a wonder how anything could come out at all from their deliberations. Although the Bill was passed in an Indian Legislature, it was perhaps from outside India, from one who was behind the scene, but who pulled the strings, *viz.*, the Secretary of State for India, that the greatest influence came. It is however difficult to apportion the credit, or the blame—whatever it might be—for the Act between the different individuals who had lent a hand in producing it. Samuel Laing, Wilson and Sir Charles Wood—these were the outstanding figures, as Lushington disappeared entirely from the scene with the rejection of his proposal. They equally fought for their own and tempered each other's views. If a verdict has to be pronounced at all, one would say that Sir Charles came out the winner ultimately. He had one great advantage, and that was that while Wilson died and Laing resigned, he continued in office and continued there long enough to purge the Bill of what he considered to be the last objectionable feature about it.

§ 4. Before passing to summarise the provisions of the Act of 1861, it would be interesting to compare the views held by the Big Four—who were jointly responsible for its fatherhood, namely, Lushington, Wilson, Laing and Wood. Lushington's scheme, which was just an outline, the details of which he had not yet developed, hinged on two important features. The first was that the necessary legislation should be made by the British Parliament, rather than by the Government in India. The reason was that, if the power of doing so was left in the hands of the latter ' in future the temptation to take dangerous advantage of this power ' would be great and there would be really no check to over-issue. The importance of the suggestion was bound to be lost upon the people of a time who only defined over-issue in terms of the convertibility of notes, rather than in terms of the general price-level in the country. That Governments also require to be controlled as much as banks in the matter of currency inflation, nations had not yet realised by sad experience. The second important point about the scheme was that the notes were not to be legal tender. But it is doubtful whether according to his proposal, any extension in the note-circulation would have at all resulted. Without an extension of the issue the experiment would not have been worth while to make, and the main purpose of the transfer to Government would have remained unfulfilled. Other features of the scheme included the division of the country into Circles ' 300 or 400 miles in diameter.' Since the demand for conversion, judging from the experience of the Bank of Bengal, would ' never be likely to be in excess of one-fourth of the total issue,' a cash reserve to that amount might be maintained in each of the Circles—against their issues. Lushington advocated denominations of Rs. 10 and upwards. On the whole his scheme retained many of the characteristics of the bank issues and would not have meant as sharp a departure from the existing practices as the proposal of Wilson and others did.

James Wilson had a more detailed scheme. The principle that guided him was well known in England at that time. It was that the paper circulation should be only allowed to fluctuate in quantity in exactly the same way as if it were purely metallic. If there were more metal in the country the note circulation should correspondingly increase. If less, the note circulation should automatically shrink. The way to ensure such an elastic response was to base the issue on a metallic reserve preportionate to the size of the circulation. Wilson suggested a coin reserve which might fluctuate, but which was never to fall below one-third of the value of the notes outstanding. By this means the convertibility of the notes would be fairly safe-guarded and according to Wilson's ideas as long as the notes were convertible, there could not be any over-issue of them. There was much in Wilson's scheme which was founded on sound monetary principles, but much of it, on the other hand, would be thrown out by modern economic science. Wilson had experience enough with currency questions at Home to know that limitation of quantity was the one absolutely indispensable condition to give to the notes any value at all. His plan aimed at securing this limitation by ensuring the convertibility of the notes—a recognised, though by no means the best method of limiting the quantity. How far in India with a silver currency which rapidly went towards bi-metallism, this convertibility method would have proved a success, is more than can be said now. Convertibility into which of the precious metals ? Gold or Silver or both ? Convertibility into silver rupees, themselves merely notes printed on silver and convertible at the option of the Government at uncertain rates, still further reduced the effectiveness of this limitation after 1893. But Wilson could never foresee these changes. He was for all that is known about him, against a double standard. How his plan would have worked it is therefore idle to speculate upon. It contained at least two very valuable features about it—which were unfortunately dropped by the later pilots of the Bill. One was the idea of introducing some element of elasticity into the note-issue. Wilson's plan of proportionate and fluctuating reserve would have given much scope for such expansion and contraction of the circulation. In the final Act, any trace of elasticity is conspicuous by absence. The second feature was placing the department of the issue in charge of a Commission, independent of the Government of India, and hence aloof from all unhealthy influences. Wilson contemplated a Department solely to be directed to this end, and 'to undertake no other business of any kind' (Minute, 25th December, 1859). 'The officers might be suspended for incapacity, negligence or misconduct by the Governor-General in Council, but should be removable only by the Secretary of State for India' (Wilson's Bill). These were important provisions, the significance of which was entirely over-looked in the final constitution of the Bill. Unlike Lushington, Wilson insisted on a legal tender note currency. He thought quite rightly that the main purpose of the paper currency would be defeated if the notes were only optional tender. No considerable extension of the circulation could at all be expected, otherwise than by adopting them as legal tender. He also, like Lushington, proposed to divide the country into Circles and the notes were to be payable only in the Circle of Issue. Another wholesome provision in Wilson's Bill was the issue of notes of small denominations. He proposed notes of Rs. 5, Rs. 10, Rs. 20, Rs. 50, Rs. 100, Rs. 500, and Rs. 1,000. It may be noted that the act as passed empowered the issue of notes of Rs. 10 and upwards. The Select Committee was even less liberal in this respect ; their recommendation being denominations ranging from Rs. 20 and upwards. But in view of representations from various public bodies in the country and pressure from the Secretary of State, the Legislature had to give way. Sir Bartle Frere even proposed to bring down the lowest denomination to Rs. 5 notes, but his amendment was negatived on a division of 6 to 2.

With the death of Wilson, Samuel Laing became the new guardian of the bill. His ideas were diametrically opposed to that of Wilson. It is difficult to say which school of thought he belonged to. Perhaps he belonged as much to the Banking as to the Currency School. He has stated his views about note issues quite clearly in one of his Minutes (1862). ' A Government,' he says, ' cannot undertake this work which is the legitimate business of a private banker without immense risk both of losing its investments and of not being able to maintain the convertibility of its notes in times of difficulty.' Such being his ideas, if he had his own way he would have probably recast the whole of the Bill. But as it was, he had to be content with only making some amendments in the constitution of the Act. The main framework of the Bill he had to accept, yet his amendments were important, and to a great extent changed the nature of the Bill. Being in favour of associating the banks in one way or another with the issue, his first reform of Wilson's Bill was to introduce a clause empowering the Government to appoint banks as agencies for superintending and managing the issue. The issue was to be owned and directed by the Government, but the banks were to conduct it, on payment of a small commission. The Secretary of State, Sir Charles Wood, who was out and out a follower of the Currency School, at once opposed the idea, and after a fight lasting several years and filling a good many despatches and counter-despatches, he won his point. Other changes, introduced by Laing, were equally fundamental. He threw out the scheme of basing the issue on a proportional reserve of specie and substituted for it a much more rigid system. A maximum fiduciary issue was laid down, and beyond that, true to the Bank Charter Act of 1844, every note was to be a mere metal-certificate. On this point, Laing's ideas inclined towards the views of an orthodox member of the Currency School. 'The first condition of a sound paper currency,' he writes in a Minute, 'is that it shall represent coin and not credit,' and consequently he would allow only a very small and fixed proportion of the reserve to be invested in securities. The Secretary of State's ideas on this point being of a similar nature, a clause prescribing a maximum fiduciary limit was put into the Act. Another important clause which was incorporated in the Act provides for a limited issue against gold. It was wholly Laing's contribution. Wilson had not contemplated any such thing. But Laing had far-reaching ideas about the reform of India's monetary standard and he wanted to leave the door open for a possible introduction of a gold standard in future. Accordingly power was taken to issue a small amount against gold, which was not however to exceed one-fourth of the total metallic reserve. In this also, the principle of the Bank Charter Act was borrowed, only the metals were reversed. The Bank of England could keep one-fourth of its specie reserve in silver—in India it was gold that was not to exceed this fraction. The clause was a permissive one. Laing said, in explanation of it, 'the provision in the Act relating to the issue of notes against gold is only permissive and we have no present intention of acting upon the clause in question.' However the intention was not long in arriving. From 1865 onwards gold appeared to figure in the accounts of the Paper Currency Reserve.

Such important modifications in the framework of the Bill necessitated corresponding alterations in the machinery of administration proposed. As the Select Committee observed, when the

'.function of the Currency Commission was reduced to the simple one of giving notes for specie and specie for notes,' it was obviously unnecessary to provide for an expensive staff or to make them independent of the Government. Laing's scheme, as embodied in the Act therefore makes the Department of Paper Currency entirely subordinate to Government. Laing's view with regard to the question of Circles was to make them as large as possible. His aim was to have a uniform circulation over as wide an area of the country as possible. He would make the notes payable as of right only at the centres of the Circles. But they would be—as far as funds permitted—cashed by the Presidency Banks and their branches, as well as by the Government Treasury Offices. Here also, his ideas came into conflict with that of Sir Charles Wood who was for ensuring absolute convertibility even if the number of circles was increased, each of them covering a smaller area, rather than qualified convertibility with uniform notes over wider and fewer circles. With regard to denomination of the notes, Laing wanted the lowest to be Rs. 20.

Sir Charles Wood's share in moulding the Act of 1861 in its final form, was, as we have said, perhaps the least obvious, though the most potent. His ideas about paper currency were thoroughly conservative. A more determined opponent to bank issues has never been seen. He was in a perpetual dread of the banks taking any part in the note issue in any manner, and in this he went so far as to frequently imagine such association where there was none. He laid down his principle in his very first reply to the Government of India (26th March, 1860). 'What is to be done by the Government establishment in India is simply what is done by the Issue Department of the Bank of England.' Then in another part of the letter he wrote, 'The sound principle for regulating the issue of paper money is that which was enforced by the Act of 1844.' Having thus early formulated his principles, Sir Charles, be it said to his credit, stuck to them unflinchingly from first to last. Accordingly he was against introducing any elasticity in the note issue. He supported Laing's policy of a maximum fiduciary issue and every single note beyond that was to be backed by an equivalent in specie. He was however doubtful of the merits of the permissive clause for the issue of notes for gold, but he did not insist on its removal. He was a masterful personality. He carried nearly all the points that he insisted upon except his suggestion for fixing the lowest denomination of the notes at Rs. 5. His argument for such low denomination was that since 'notes were meant to replace metal as economically as possible,' they should be made available for all transactions, great and small. Except this minor defeat, Sir Charles had the satisfaction of seeing nearly all his ideas literally reproduced in the Act of 1861.

§ 5. The Act, which will be found in full in Appendix A, is a carefully drawn-up document. It starts by making the issue of paper money henceforth a complete Government monopoly. It provides for the establishment of a Department of Issue, subordinate to the Governor-General in Council. Power is taken to appoint banks or any other extra-governmental institutions, agents for managing the issue, although in no sense affecting the control of the issue. Notes are to be issued against silver coin or bullion and of the total specie reserve one-fourth may be held in gold. The maximum security-covered issue is put down at Rs. 4 crores, and all notes beyond that amount to be backed by full specie reserve. The interest accruing from the securities in the reserve, is to be regarded as part of Government's revenue under the head 'Profits of the Note circulation.' The country is to be split up into a number of districts or circles of issue and notes to be made legal tender and payable only within them. They were to be issued in denominations of Rs. 10 and upwards. Such was in outline the Act XIX of 1861. It was passed by the Legislative Council on the 13th July and received the assent of the Governor-General on the 16th. It came into force practically 'on and after the first day of March, 1862' from which time onwards the Presidency Banks were to cease issuing promissory notes. As already noted, it was a joint-stock production. The principal persons in the drama, whose views we have noted above, were Laing, Wilson and Wood. Apart from them, there were others who collaborated with them at various stages in the passing of the Act. There was, for instance, Sir H. B. E. Frere who has been mentioned once before as moving for the adoption of the Rs. 5 denomination of notes. He has left us a valuable Minute, dated the 2nd February, 1861. He advocated a proportional reserve, like Wilson, although it would not necessarily mean Wilson's one-third system. In an almost prophetic sentence he warned of the futility of any self-imposed limitation about fiduciary issues. He said, 'that in the course of years there will be great temptation to raise the limit, cannot, I think, be doubted......... Unless we have fixed some limit proportional to the total note-issue of the day, is there no danger that we may be tempted to overstep the really safe limit, whatever that limit may be ?' Besides Sir B. Frere, the Council included Laing, H. B. Harrington, H. Forbes, A. Sconce and C. J. Erkskine some of whom took part in the discussion on the Bill.

§ 6. How was the Act received in the country ? To judge by the comments made upon it by officials as well as non-officials, it is possible to say that on the whole the measure was well received. It was generally greeted with approval, although it was a qualified approval. Even among the ranks of Government officials, much difference of opinion as to the detailed provisions of the Bill was noticeable. The comments of some contemporary high officers are interesting reading. We come across, for instance, a long and well written Minute on the Act by Sir C. E. Trevelyan, K.C.B., who, with certain reservations, supports Sir Charles Wood. Some of his lines are well worth quoting, if only for their rhetoric. 'I hold,' says he, 'in the strongest manner the opinion that absolute, instant, never-failing convertibility is essential to a Government paper currency.' Then again, if the plans of Wilson and Sir Charles Wood were carried, the Government 'currency system would stand like a house founded upon a rock, whatever floods come and winds blow and beat upon the public finances and upon Banking and Commerce.' We meet with Minutes by Sir R. Napier, Viceroy and Governor-General of India, who was in favour of the existing arrangement, although ready to follow the Secretary of State's wishes on any point, and by H. B. Harrington who echoes the Viceroy ; by H. S. Maine, who had a very 'strong opinion on the desirableness of severing banking from issue'; and also by W. Grey, who approves of the Act. Against the Act also voices were raised in certain quarters. C. N. Cooke, for instance, in his Banking in India (1863) says, 'We are not prepared to admit that the substitution of a Government paper currency in lieu of that of the leading Bank of India is a move in the right direction ; in fact we doubt whether it is not a grave mistake.' Perhaps an impartial and representative estimate of the Act was what appeared in the *Calcutta Review* of 1863 (Article on Indian Paper Currency). There the scheme is given a general measure of support and an attempt is made to analyse after a very long study (almost too long) of the theory and practice of note-issue in England, the principles underlying it. In the first place, it is plainly recognised that the substitution of the precious metals by paper as money, is most beneficial to the community and profitable to the issuers. Since the substitution is a gain, it should be carried on as far as is consistent with safety. Safety means nothing but convertibility. The high specie reserve and the rigidity of the issue are to be explained by the peculiar conditions of India, such as mistrust of the people, etc. It is not known who wrote this article, but that it represented faithfully the viewpoint of the authors of the Act may be quite safely assumed.

§ 7. The Act of 1861 is the starting point. Since then a large number of Acts have been passed, modifying from time to time the regulations as to the issue of paper currency in the country. As needs arose, the different parts of the system had to be more or less changed, to suit the new conditions. Sometimes alterations have been made in the regulations governing the reserve ; at other times other parts of the Act have been touched. But though the changes made have been in some cases important and noteworthy, the principles embodied in the Act of 1861 still predominate. If the provisions of the Act can be arranged into three main classes, namely, (1) those that deal with the Agency of Issue ; (2) those that deal with the mechanism of the Issue, and (3) those that concern the Cover of the Issue,—they also indicate the lines along which the future history of the Issue may be most conveniently studied. The problems of Indian paper currency since 1861 belong to one or other of these three heads. All the later developments can be grouped under them and are most usefully studied under these classes. There are first, questions relating to the Agency of Issue such as, who is to direct the issue, and whether banks or any other extra-governmental agency is to be associated with it. Secondly, the Mechanism of the issue opens up a series of questions regarding the practical administration of the issue ; whether the circle system is good or bad ; how far the notes may be universalised and facilities for encashment provided and so on. Thirdly, there remains the subject of the Cover of the Issue, under which come the questions relating to the amount, location and distribution of the reserve, and other related matters. I propose to study the future history of the paper currency—the progress of ideas and facts in connection with it,—under these three heads. Last of all, a statistical chapter will be added dealing with the growth of the issue since 1861. Thus the whole period from 1861 up to the present day will be treated as one period. In spite of many developments and many interruptions, there is an unbroken continuity in the history of the last fifty years. Act XIX of 1861 still serves as the basis of the imposing and complicated superstructure that has been built upon it during this period.

CHAPTER IV.

THE AGENCY OF ISSUE.

§ 1. Presidency Banks made agents for the management of the Issue, p. 55.—§ 2. The Wood-Laing controversy. Laing's case for enlisting the co-operation of the Banks and Wood's objections, p. 58.—§ 3. Wood's victory and the final dissociation of the Banks from the Issue, p. 65.—§4. Fresh attempts to connect banking with the Issue, early in the 19th century, p. 67—§ 5. The Imperial Bank and the question of the transference of the Issue to it, p. 70.—§ 6. The proposal of the Hilton Young Commission for a Central Bank Issue, p. 74.

§1. The avowed object of the Act of 1861 was to transfer the issue of paper currency from the banks to the Government. But the banks were not to be deprived of their long connection with the note issue so easily. They were ostensibly removed from the stage, but they practically remained there under a different name and in an humbler role. Their cause was far from being entirely lost. In Samuel Laing, as we have seen, they found a stout champion right inside their enemy's camp. Thanks mainly to his sympathies for banks, in the legislation of 1861 the door was left open for associating them with the note-issue in a somewhat indirect way. Clause IV of the Act empowered the Government to make arrangements with "any persons, banks or bodies corporate, either at Calcutta, Madras or Bombay or elsewhere, as may be required to regulate and facilitate the issue and payment under the provisions of this Act of promissory notes of the Government of India." Samuel Laing was none too slow in availing himself of the provisions of this Clause. The Presidency banks were made agents for management as distinguished from agents of issue. They were thus made to retain some connection with the issue in however disguised a form it might be. Sir Charles Wood who had no love for banks, was as quick in opposing the arrangements as Laing was in making them. A great battle in despatches followed between these two mis-matched reformers of Indian Currency. Although at last, after a severe tug of war, during which neither party was too sparing in outspoken expressions, Sir Charles won his point, and the banks were completely dissociated from the issue, still the question could not be said to have finally rested in peace. In later times, *pari passu* with the progress of banking and the development of the paper-currency, the question of using the agency of banks in some form or other has oftentimes been revived. It cannot be said to be still dead. Whether Laing's view-point rejected in the sixties of last century mainly by the efforts of Sir Charles Wood will not yet carry the day—whether, in a word, banks will not in future be reinstated with a share of the responsibilities of the note-issue—time has yet to show.

Clause IV of the Act was the thin edge of the wedge. Not long after the passing of Act XIX, in the same year, another Act, Act XXIV of 1861 was passed, which authorised the Secretary of State to enter into agreements with the Presidency Banks "for superintending, managing and becoming agents for the issue, payment and exchange of promissory notes of the Government of India and for the carrying on of the business of an agency of issue."

On the strength of this Act, either honestly misunderstanding the intentions of the Secretary of State, or pretending to misconceive them while the object was perhaps to disregard them, extensive and elaborate agreements were made with the Presidency Banks, one after another, constituting them the agents for the management of the issue for a period of five years. The terms and conditions of the contract with the Bank of Bombay may be given here. They will illustrate the exact nature of the agency work entrusted to the banks. The other agreements were of a similar kind. Article 7 of the agreement with the Bank of Bombay provides that "an agency of issue shall be established in the Bank as the agency for the Circle of Issue (Bombay Circle)......and the said Bank shall and will act as Government agents in and for the issue and circulation of Government currency notes and in the payment and cashing of such notes and in all things required to be done by such agents." This was followed by Article 8 which said that demand for currency notes might be made at the said agency and the bank was bound to meet this demand by the issue of currency notes which it might obtain from the Circle Commissioner. At its head office, the bank was bound to redeem all Circle notes presented to it, in the same way as the Department of Issue itself was. It was proposed to locate the office of the Department in the premises of the Bank. As regards new branches, the Directors had the power to enter into arrangements with the Government for the agency of the local issue. When the Bank of Bengal opened branches within the Calcutta Circle of Issue arrangements on similar terms were entered upon for the transaction of currency work at those places. It must be noted that though the notes were always to be available in exchange for cash at these branches the obligation to pay cash on demand in return for notes, was not made absolute. The words of the agreement left no doubt on the point. It said, "that the said Branch Bank shall and will *to the utmost of its power* pay and satisfy on demand to the holders of notes" the value of the notes in cash at the offices of the Bank. It is important to note this qualified encashability, as most of Sir Charles Wood's objections centred round this point. However much the notes were encashable in practice, there was no legal right to demand coin for them at the branches. By way of remuneration a "commission calculated at the rate of ¾ths per cent. per annum on the daily average amount of Government currency notes outstanding and in circulation through the said agency" together with any special expenses incurred by the Bank in the way of offices, etc., was to be paid to the Bank. These were the main points of the agreement. They were to hold good for a period of five years up to 1867.

§ 2. In this way Laing sought to enlist the help of the banks to facilitate the growth of the issue. He made it quite clear that in no case was it proposed to make the banks the Commissioners for Issue. (Government of India letter No. 71 of 1862, May.) But that the result of the arrangements was to mix up the banks with the issue in some important ways remains undoubtedly true. They were not however, as Brunyate supposes, " almost completely identified with the department of Issue." A subtle but important distinction had emerged between an agency of issue and an agency of management, or an agency for circulation after issue, as the Government of India defined it (Letter No. 1 of 1863). The Secretary of State found himself unable to appreciate this distinction. According to Laing's proposals the banks would have no share in the policy or control of the paper currency, but they were simply to carry out the administration part of it. How far the administration part could be divorced from the policy and direction of the system without jeopardising the basic principles of the Act was the crucial question. To Sir Charles Wood they appeared inseparable one from another. If convertibility was what was mainly sought to be assured by the framers of the Act of 1861, bank agency, in so far as it weakened this absolute convertibility, certainly militated against the spirit of that piece of legislation. But, on the other hand, there was no reason why, subject to the provisions of the Act, the banks should not have done the clerical part of the business with greater efficiency than the Government. On this point Laing's pleading of his cause was as powerful as it was unheeded by the Secretary of State. Both showed an obstinacy that bred lively passages in their correspondence but did not contribute much to any impassioned solution of the difficulties. In his letters we find Laing was complaining that " it was evident that the arrangements entered into in India had never been properly understood at Home." Once he wrote bitterly, " It is a good illustration of the impossibility of dealing with practical details at a distance of ten thousand miles." (Minute, March, 1861.) In his letters the Secretary of State is found constantly repeating the accusation that his instructions were not being acted up to. The controversy is an interesting disclosure on the tone of official correspondence. It is full of lessons about the difficulty of financial administration from two different places, by two different authorities.

As far as can be gathered from his despatches, Laing's arguments for bringing in the Banks to take a subsidiary part in the note-issue were four in number. In the first place he preferred uniformity in the note-issue, to absolute convertibility in it. Not that he did not want convertibility. But he would sooner make a note current over a larger area than too scrupulously safeguard its convertibility by making it current only in a smaller area. He misread Wilson's plans and thought, until in this he was corrected by the Secretary of State, that they involved the division of the country into forty or fifty different currency Circles. He feared there would be then no uniformity in the issue. The result would be, as he said, that travellers would have to, as before, carry bags of rupees with them. The Government "could scarcely make its notes a legal tender at Delhi without making any provision of cashing them nearer than at Calcutta." To this end, banking agency was necessary. The Government could not do without an intermediary. The notes would be cashable at all the branches of the banks, and thus a uniform currency could be secured over a large area. Although the accommodation granted to the public of cashing notes in the country would strictly be a matter of convenience and not of legal right, still every attempt would be made to safeguard unfailing and immediate convertibility. The Government retained certain powers over the branches of the banks and these branches were to keep reserves of specie for the purpose of cashing notes. It was hoped, no notes would be refused conversion. Besides, the Government owned Treasuries all over the country ; they would always assist the banks in all possible ways. Everywhere the notes were to be received at par in payment of Government dues. Thus with the banks and the Treasury offices as two successive lines of defence, Laing hoped to make the convertibility of the notes virtually perfect in practice if not in theory. How far his anticipation would have come true it is difficult to say. The arrangements were all cancelled in 1866, before they had received a fair trial. But the fact remains that by that year the circulation had grown only on a very small scale. Imperfect convertibility was certainly one of the causes for this. Sir Charles Trevelyan, the third Finance Member of the Viceroy's Council (1863-1865) wrote that " even the notes of the Head Office of the Calcutta Circle were charily cashed at the branch banks within the Circle and were altogether refused if apparently employed solely for purposes of remittance." A uniform currency is certainly an inestimable boon, but a currency must first pass current. For lack of facilities for conversion, practically no paper currency, by 1866, existed in the country, as distinguished from the Presidency towns. In that year we find W. N. Massey, the fourth Finance Member of the Governor-General's Council, testifying that at a distance from the Circles, the note ceases to pass current and when it is tendered in payment of a debt it is usually cashed at a discount in the bazaar. The instructions of the banks to their branches were for what the Indian Fiscal Commission would have named "discriminating" convertibility. A section went thus :—"Though you will in the exercise of your discretion take care to counteract any attempts on the part of the Mahajans to throw the burden of the internal exchange on the bank and the Government, by, for instance, having a large sum of head office notes remitted to your station and demanding cash for same at your branch, in lieu of taking a bill on you from head office at the ruling exchange, yet in every case, as a rule, you will, as far as you can, give your assistance to promote the circulation." It is doubtful how far the spirit of these instructions was obeyed. For one thing, it was contrary to the interest of the bank to cash notes freely. To the extent that it cashed the head office notes at the branches, to that extent it lost the profits of its internal exchange business. The agency work for paper currency thus collided with the other operations of the bank. There was a further danger which the arrangements implied, and which the Secretary of State pointed out. That was that the chances of conversion, already too few, were still further reduced by these arrangements. He pointed out, quite rightly, that the banks, under temptation of earning the three-fourths per cent. commission had "every inducement to hold as little coin and as large an amount of notes as possible in its reserves." Since the commission was to be paid for all notes for which the Bank had given coin or bullion,—it was payable only on *notes* kept in reserve by the Bank while on *coin* so kept it would receive nothing. The bank would be tempted to keep as few coins in reserve as possible. This would hardly promote safety. Its effect would be that the cash reserves would stand at a very low amount, seriously endangering convertibility. In the choice between convertibility and uniformity, the Secretary of State clung to the former, while Laing was prepared to sacrifice it to some extent.

Laing's second argument was that the banks could more efficiently manage the issue than the Government could ever hope to do. The banks were intimately connected with the money market and could feel its pulse more accurately than the officials of the Government. Consequently they knew what exact amount of reserve should be kept and how it should be distributed between different seasons and different places. The banks had past experience to guide them, while the Government was only new to this kind of work. For the three-fourths commission the banks undertook the whole retail work of issuing and cashing notes, the whole correspondence as to notes lost and stopped, and all risks of loss from forgeries. Laing could thus plead economy for his proposals. Government could not have possibly established Commissions of Issue of its own for anything like the sum which it paid to the banks. The banks also undertook "to establish branches wherever desired by the Government and to provide at them at their own risk and cost the means of cashing all Government notes " (Laing's Minute, 1862). Besides, there would be great convenience to the public in being able to cash or obtain notes at the place where ordinary business was transacted. Here were all weighty advantages which the Secretary of State simply brushed aside.

Thirdly, Laing argued that it was expedient to hand over the management to the banks as in that case the consequences of any postponement of conversion would be far less serious. Even if the banks refused payment the credit of the Government would not be directly touched, but if once the Government had to refuse encashment the effect upon the credulous people of India would be disastrous for the future success of paper currency. This argument of course had another side to it, which Sir Charles Trevelyan pointed out. He said that if the Government's own agents set the example of refusing to cash the notes there would be no length to which other people might not go.

Laing's last plea was that some compensation should be paid to the banks when the issue was being taken away from them. They had done the work so long entrusted to them to the best of their ability. About the Bank of Bengal, for instance, Laing wrote—" the Bank having been chartered by the Government and in effect called into existence by it as the sole bank of issue for Bengal, and the Government holding shares and being closely connected with it in public opinion, it was felt that it would neither be morally right nor politically expedient......withdrawing the note circulation of the Bank without a fair equivalent." This was perhaps one of the trump cards in Laing's hands as the idea of fair play was very attractive. But if at all, any compensation was due to the Presidency banks for parting with the note-issue, it certainly could have been given in many other ways than by trying to link them still with the issue in some form. It amounted to paying back half a loaf for a full loaf taken away.

§ 3. To many of these arguments the Secretary of State did not fully reply. To all of them he turned a deaf ear. He was entirely against the idea of the banks having anything to do with the issue. At first he was under the impression that in each circle the Presidency Bank was going to be made the sole agent for the issue. He strongly objected to " any banker at any circle of issue being the only place where coin may be issued for notes and notes for coin." Laing in reply wrote, ' How a banker can be a place is certainly not very clear, but the Commissioner having an office in the Bank, set apart for him under the same roof as the Bank, the arrangements thus enabled any person who chose to obtain notes for coin or coin for notes altogether independently of any Bank. What the Secretary of State means is perhaps that the Bank should be distinct from the Commissioner of Issue, which they are."

It must be remembered that persons who wanted to apply direct for notes, instead of at the Bank, had to ask for notes of the value of Rs. 2,000 or more and had also to give one clear day's notice

9

for it. The facilities for independently receiving the notes were thus, for all Laing's earnest pleadings, limited to certain extent.

However, the Secretary was still hard to please. As a matter of fact his objection was not only against making any bank the *sole* agent of issue within any circle ; he would not employ the banks on any terms whatsoever. His favourite slogan was that the banks must be totally separated from the issue of paper currency. Although he did not wish to disturb the arrangements already entered into, he kept on repeating the slogan until finally the agreements were all revised. He maintained that if the notes were sound as currency the banks themselves would help in their circulation in the ordinary course of business. "I am certain," he wrote, "that in the exercise of its legitimate functions, the Bank (of Bengal) would essentially promote the circulation of notes." There was therefore no need of employing them as agents. He was for looking first and last to the convertibility of the notes—if that was assured the rest would take care of itself.

Meanwhile the resignation of Laing, which was the natural sequence of his difference with the Secretary of State on a number of vital points, on the 12th of July, 1862, and the succession to the Finance Membership of the Council of Sir Charles Trevelyan—whose views on paper currency were very similar to those of Sir Charles Wood, radically altered the situation. It gave the Secretary of State a timely lieutenant in India. His victory was now assured. Trevelyan's lyrics about "absolute, instant and never-failing convertibility," have already been referred to. In a Minute he wrote (28th February, 1863), " Conditional convertibility is hardly to be distinguished from inconvertibility." Again, " banks are acted upon by too many deflecting circumstances to allow them to be made the basis of so delicate an instrument as a system of Government paper currency." Provision of absolute convertibility was what they owed to their subjects, to themselves and to society. Such being his views negotiations were not long in being entered into with the banks for some possible revision of the agreements. The upshot was that the old agreements were cancelled and new ones were made in their place with effect from 2nd June, 1866. The banks consented to be entirely dissociated from currency business " in consideration of receiving compensation calculated at $\frac{3}{4}$ths per cent. per annum on the value of the notes in circulation through their agency at the time the agreements were revised." This compensation was payable up to 1st March, 1867,—the date at which the agreements of 1862, that is, the original agreements, would have expired in the ordinary course. The banks had made some further demands in the way of compensation for thus releasing the Government—but the Secretary of State and the Government of India would not listen to them.

§ 4. Thus ended the chapter of the attempt to link up the banks with the issue,—the first to be made after the passing of the Act of 1861. Henceforward for many years the banks stood entirely aloof from the Government paper currency. But, as has been said before, the question never died out. Banks being the principal dealers of currency in a country it is impossible to separate them completely from the issue of paper currency. However much the Government may try to dissociate the one from the other, the commerce and finance of the country constantly bring them together in many ways. Each is constantly reacting upon the other. It is therefore not surprising that in 1900-2, when much of the early conservatism against the banks had worn off, the question of passing over the issue of paper money to the projected central bank was once again seriously revived. We have seen how the absence of a strong bank "of the magnitude of the Bank of England" (Wilson) was one of the telling arguments that led the Government to conduct the issue itself. If now the three Presidency Banks were amalgamated it would create a first-rate banking institution for India and Government could then safely contemplate handing over the note-issue to it. Indeed, in the discussion for a Central Bank in India, the transference of the paper currency has always figured prominently. The fact that when at last the long projected plans nearly materialised the paper currency still continued under Government hands, has to be explained by the peculiar circumstances left behind by the war. The transference of the note issue in some form or another to the Imperial Bank of India remained for years a possibility, although nothing more than a possibility.

The idea in 1900-2 was that the Presidency banks were to amalgamate on their own initiative and Government would then make over the management of the paper currency to the new bank, on terms mutually agreed upon between the Government and the Bank. It was however, not considered a vital part of the scheme for the Central Bank, but was generally looked upon as a corollary. Even if the note-issue was not to be handed over, Government was ready to proceed with the project (Government of India Letter, 18th January, 1900). But Government favoured the idea of the transference. "We are," they wrote to the Secretary of State, "of opinion, though not forgetting the objections that have been raised to such a course in India...... that there is nothing in the peculiar circumstances of India to prevent the note-issue being transferred to a Bank. We are moreover disposed to believe that it is through the agency of a Bank that the note-issue may have a larger development." The wind of official opinion thus between 1861 and 1900 completely veered round. The Secretary of State, to make assurance doubly sure, sent the following question to the Government of India (22nd March, 1900) : "Is it desirable to entrust to a bank the management of a paper currency, due regard being had to the principles upon which it was established in 1862 ?" To this the Government of India's answer was, "Our honourable colleague, Sir Edward Law, is of opinion that the management of the paper currency by a bank would be preferable to its management by Government, always provided that the bank to which this responsibility was entrusted was established on suitable lines and that Government had some control over its operations."

Sir Edward Law's opinions would certainly have shocked some of his predecessors in the Finance Department. That the proposals were quite advanced appears from the fact that at a Conference between the Government and the leading banks and Chambers of Commerce, detailed conditions of the transfer were discussed on the lines of an issue by a single bank, " the Government retaining the profit on the present currency investment, but indemnifying the bank for the cost thereof." (Speech by Dawkins, Legislative Council, 5th January, 1900). Unfortunately the proposals for the Central Bank themselves fell through. It is perhaps safe to say that, if instead of 1920, the Imperial Bank of India had come into being in 1902, our note-issue would have been a bank-issue by now.

§ 5. In the discussions over the formation of the Imperial Bank of India, the transference of the paper currency was always kept in view. But the bank was born in a most difficult time—the aftermath of the war—and rightly or wrongly that supplied a plausible excuse for withholding the transference. It is curious that although in the earlier stages of the negotiations for the bank, the transference of the paper currency was considered a part and parcel of the scheme, yet it was ultimately dropped without much discussion. The valuable memorandum by Mr. Keynes, on the proposals of a Central Bank, appended to the Report of the Chamberlain Commission, contemplated such a transference. His view was sufficiently clear. " If the Central Bank," he wrote, is to be useful, it must have the management of the Government balances and of the note-issue." It is to be noted however, that a Central Bank, built on Mr. Keynes' suggestions, would have differed in some important respects from what we now find the constitution of the Imperial Bank to be. He aimed at a State Bank, the higher executive officers responsible for the policy and administration of the bank being appointed by the Government, and resting under its ultimate authority. In the Imperial Bank to-day the shareholders have quite a considerable voice in the affairs of the bank. If we look to actual facts, apart from ideas, we find that even before 1914 the services of the Presidency banks had been already utilised for furthering the note circulation in some minor ways. In 1913-14 for instance, " arrangements had already been *made* with the Bank of Madras for taking over the Treasury work at certain Treasuries and simultaneously arranging for the issue and free encashment of notes from their branches in these cases " (Controller's Report for 1913-14). A similar arrangement was made with the Bank of Bengal in the case of Delhi. " The possibility of extending " the Report concludes, " these arrangements will be steadily kept in view." These were but stray cases of the employment of bank agencies. Although they were not undertaken with any set or formal plan of gradual enlistment of bank support for the paper currency, yet they sufficiently indicated the swing of the pendulum. Before the 1914 Commission, evidence was not wanting in favour of the introduction of some bank agency. Mr. Hunter of the Bank of Madras thus supported the cause of the banks :—" We have direct dealings with the trading public and can induce our constituents to take notes instead of silver by offering them more favourable rates,—means which Government cannot employ.'' In all these developments, the War came as a violent and sudden interruption. The hands of the clock underwent some swift turnings. When the Imperial Bank of India was established, it was found premature to transfer the note-issue to it. To-day, when the Imperial Bank has been in existence for nearly five years the idea of transference still continues to be "premature." The latest official pronouncement on the subject seems to have been made on the 15th September, 1924, when Sir Basil Blackett in reply to a question asking "what steps the Government was taking to transfer the control of the currency to the Imperial Bank of India" stated that "the Government regarded this suggestion as premature for the moment.'' The reasons that in 1920 influenced the Government in its decision to retain the paper currency in its own hands (and the same reasons evidently have full force still) may thus be restated through a semi-official mouthpiece, that of H. F. Howard. He writes, "As regards the note-issue, with the whole currency arrangements of Government still deeply affected as the result of War conditions, it would manifestly have been impossible for the new bank to contemplate the undertaking of this responsibility. The Government of India, however, indicated, when placing the scheme before the Secretary of State for India, that when a stable position had been reached and currency conditions have settled down, it may be anticipated that the management of the paper currency in India will consist of a more or less routine application of authoritatively accepted principles, and in that case the question of the employment of the bank as the agent of Government in the matter may in the future need further consideration."* Thus the introduction of the bank agency, once again coming very near realisation, has had to be shelved. It is immaterial to examine the excuses set out by the Government for this indefinite postponement. They may or may not hold water. A bank agency has its merits, as well as its demerits. In a country like India the credit of the note-issue stands on a delicately poised balance. The Government must think twice before making any attempt at connecting the note-issue with private banks. But the banks cannot be entirely divorced from the issue. That is the lesson of experience. Already, in introducing elements of elasticity into the note-issue, their help has had to be taken to some extent. The new elasticity operates only through loans made to the Imperial Bank of India at fixed rates of interest. Properly used, the banks can give a great amount of assistance as intermediaries, but the exact relation in which they are to stand to the issue has yet to be solved. At present the Imperial Bank serves as a distributor of the temporary loan, made on the security of short-term bills, from the paper currency. It is thus with the temporary or seasonal circulation of paper currency that the bank is connected to some extent. The more permanent part

* Howard, Article on the Imperial Bank of India, *Economic Journal*, 1921.

of the circulation is independent of any such connection. To the present writer this indicates a theoretically sound line of bank connection, which is full of prmise. The policy with regard to the permanent part of the paper currency, is more or less a routine policy. Sound finance will always base that on the price level of the country. The policy with regard to temporary or seasonal increase or decrease of the paper currency cannot be worked efficiently without enlisting the support and co-operation of the banks. Here only is the proper province for the employment of bank agency. That part of the paper circulation which aims at mitigating the seasonal glut or stringency of money in the market, as distinguished from providing for the country a sound and stable currency over long periods, must work through loans made to banks and must count on their co-operation.

§ 6. The question of a Central Bank and its relation to the Paper Currency has once again come to the fore, with the publication of the Report of the Royal Commission on Indian Currency (Aug. 1926). That Commission, among other far-reaching proposals, advocate a full-fledged Central Bank for India and a wholesale transference of the Issue to it. A detailed description of the proposals cannot be given here for want of space. Neither again is it easy or fair to isolate the specific recommendation regarding the handing over of the Issue to the Bank and deal with it separately from the totality of the Commission's recommendations. In India the long-established connection of the Government with the Issue and the faith that such a connection inspires in the mass of the people, both militate against the idea of a sudden and complete severance of the connection. The Commission seem clearly to realise these difficulties. They propose a Bank Issue, but consider a Government guarantee of the notes indispensable. The necessary implication of such a guarantee, is some amount of Government control, if not in normal times at least in emergencies. A Bank-Government partnership, in the peculiar circumstances of India, is more or less inevitable. The Commission have tried to minimise, as much as possible, the share of the Government, but cannot claim to have devised an absolutely independent Bank of Issue for India. Absolute aloofness is desirable, yet the value of the Government connection is important in view of its bearing on the credit of the notes. It is doubtful if the terms of separation, as suggested by the Commission, really make the formal transference of the Issue to the new Bank, much worth while. In many important respects, the Bank will be tied down by legislation, while the Government guarantee of the notes will carry with it the promise or the threat of Government interference, in exceptional circumstances. Much of the independence of the new Central Bank will thus be of a shadowy nature. It would not have perhaps done much harm if Government had retained the Issue in its own hands, or what would have practically amounted to the same thing, transferred it to a State Bank,—rather than hand it over to a private institution. Still it is perhaps the only line of progress that could be suggested, and the scheme of the Bank Issue is full of promise.

Whether, after all, India will accept the Commission's recommendations and entrust a Central Bank with the monopoly of the note issue, thus bringing to a close the long but instructive chapter of Government Issue, will be settled in the not very distant future. The wind seems to blow in that direction.

CHAPTER V.

THE MECHANISM OF THE ISSUE.

§ 1. The building up, in stages, of an independent Paper Currency Department under a Controller of the Currency, p. 77.—§ 2. A glance at the office work and the officers in a Currency Office, p. 82.—§ 3. The designing and the printing of Currency notes, p. 85.—§ 4. The denominations, p. 87.—§ 5. The Circles and the Sub-Circles of Issue, p. 89.—§ 6. Other subsidiary establishments—Currency Agencies, Currency Chests, Mint Chests, p. 94.—§ 7. The process of universalisation, p. 97.—§ 8. The question of legel tender and of facilities, legal and extra-legal, for convertibility. The War-time crisis and the steps taken to meet it, p. 103.

§ 1. In this chapter I propose to deal with the organisation of the Department of Paper Currency;—how the country has been divided into circles for the purpose of administration and working of the system—what arrangements have been made to ensure the convertibility of the notes, the denominations chosen—and various other questions relating to the technique of the issue. There is not much of theory involved in this part of the discussion, most of it being the province of practical administration, but some light on the methods of working the issue is essential for the proper understanding of the system. The Government took over the management of the issue without any previous schooling for the task. For some time indeed the banks were assisting it. But ultimately, by 1867,*

* The agreement with the Bank of Bengal expired on the 31st December, 1865 and those with the Banks of Madras and Bombay, on the 28th Februrary, 1867.

as we have seen, the last semblance of bank connection had disappeared, and henceforth the Government was called upon to carry on the management as best as it could. How it has acquitted itself in this work, we shall presently have an opportunity of examining.

The Act of 1861 provided for the establishment of a ' department of public service to be called the Department of Issue either in connection with the Mints or otherwise, for the issue and payment of government promissory notes ' (Clause III). Accordingly the first Department was organised with the Master of the Mint at Calcutta as the Head Commissioner of Issue, and the Mint Masters of Bombay and Madras as Commissioners of the Department of Issue under him. The whole Department was to be under the Government of India. In the legislation of 1861 Government had also taken powers to establish districts to be called ' Circles of Issue,' three of which were to include the towns of Calcutta, Madras and Bombay respectively. If necessary, Government could later create other circles of issue under persons to be called Deputy Commissioners of Issue. These provisions were soon availed of. The Calcutta Circle was the first to be established. It was opened on the 3rd January, 1862, with its office in the Bank of Bengal. The first Department of Issue in India was thus housed in the premises of a private bank. Any one who wished to apply directly to the Mint for notes could do so, provided he wanted notes worth at least Rs. 2,000. Almost simultaneously the other two curency offices of Bombay and Madras were also started. These three offices of Issue at Calcutta, Madras and Bombay could be regarded as the head-quarters of the Department, other circles and sub-circles came later on, together with such distant feeders as currency agents, currency chests at Treasuries and so on. But in spite of all its growing paraphernalia, the Currency Department mainly stood as an annexe to the Mint. It had no independent existence of its own. This arrangement continued up to 1870. But it was hardly an arrangement that could be said to conduce to efficiency. The double duties of looking after the affairs of the Mint as well as those of the Paper Currency, that his double rôle of Head Commissioner of the Currency and Master of the Mint imposed upon him, made the first bearer of these offices himself protest against the system. The Commission to enquire into the operations of Act 19 of 1861, realised the evils of the system and recommended the separation of the two offices. At last in 1870, steps were taken to remove the anomaly. By a Resolution on the 31st August in that year the Government wisely separated the Paper Currency Department from the Department of the Mint; but instead of freeing it completely they linked it now to another, *viz.*, the Accounts Department. Henceforward the Comptroller-General of Accounts, instead of the Mint Master of Calcutta was to be the ex-officio Head Commissioner of the Issue, and the Accountant-Generals of Madras and Bombay, ex-officio Commissioners. The Resolution thus set forth its grounds for this change of arrangements :—' Colonel Hyde (the Head Commissioner) himself was one of the first to urge that the proper duties of the Mint Master are sufficiently onerous and important to occupy his whole time.........The Governor-General in Council observes that prolonged experience has only strengthened Colonel Hyde's opinion that the Master of the Mint ought not to be the Head Commissioner of Paper Currency.' Then the Resolution went on to say that the Accounts Department had a specially trained and widely distributed body of officers. That would form an agency ' well qualified to undertake the management of the Paper Currency.' It was overlooked that the Paper Currency Department demanded not only special training, but also whole-time service from its officers. No ex-officio governor from the Accounts Department, any more than one brought from the Mint, could properly serve the interests of the Department. However the transference was an improvement. It relieved the Mint as well as the Paper Currency. For a long time this arrangement worked satisfactorily. But as the paper circulation grew and the work of the Department also increased considerably in volume, the need was felt of giving the Paper Currency an independent entity. But it took a long time before a move was made in this direction. In 1913 the first step for the new reform was taken. Prior to that, the paper currency, resource operations, the public debt, and a whole host of other businesses belonged to the Comptroller and Auditor-General. In that year a separate officer called the Controller of the Curency was appointed in charge of the Paper Currency specially, and certain other functions. He relieved the Comptroller and Auditor-General in the capacity of Head Commissioner of the Currency, though the corresponding work in the Provinces continued to be performed by the Accountant-Generals working under the orders of the Controller of the Currency. Further provincialisation was carried out in 1919. A Deputy Controller of the Currency was then appointed in Bombay whose duties comprised the supervision of the work of the two Currency Circles of Bombay and Karachi, and the resource operations and securities work of the Bombay Presidency and the Central Provinces. In 1921 a second Deputy Controller of the Currency was appointed in Calcutta, thus contributing more and more to the evolution of an independent Currency Department. The Deputy Controller, says the 1920-21 Report of the Currency Department, exercises general supervision over the Calcutta Circle and has relieved the local Accountant-General of the resource and securities work of Bengal, Behar and Orissa, and Assam. 'It is intended,' we read, 'to develop the organisation by the appointment of a Deputy Controller of the Currency for Northern India* who will be in charge of the Currency Circles of Lahore and Cawnpore and will undertake the resource and securities work of the United Provinces, the Punjab, and the North West Frontier Province. The remaining Currency Circles of Madras and Rangoon remain for the present under the control of the local Accountant-General.' Thus appears a sort of

* It was found possible to appoint a Deputy Collector for Northern India in the same year. (1921).

duality in the organisation of the Department of Paper Currency, most of it being constituted an independent Department, but some part of it still being an appendage to the Accounts Department. The officers in the Department have, since some years, been re-christened. We have now Controllers and Deputy Controllers, instead of the imposing but clumsy titles of Head Commissioner and other Commissioners. Paper Currency, it may be noted, is controlled by the Department of Finance of the Government of India.

§ 2. So much about the framework of the Department. Next may be given a picture of the arrangement of the work within the Department. If the roof is taken out of any Currency office it will disclose two main departments between which all the work is divided. First, there is the Treasurer's Department which includes (*a*) the Exchange Branch which arranges for the receipt and examination of notes and coins from the Banks, the public currency chests and Treasuries, and for the sorting and testing of defaced notes in the cancellation section. (*b*) The Issue Branch, which deals with invoiced and foreign circle notes (that is, notes cashed in other circles and sent to the particular office of origin), arranges for the receipt and custody of fresh notes and for the stamping of the signature on such notes, and takes over cancelled notes from the Cancellation section pending their verification by the outside Audit Department. Secondly, there is the General Department doing all sorts of miscellaneous work. Among them may be noted (*a*) the Registration Branch which attends to the posting of cancellations in the Issue Registers and to the proof of the circulation balance, (*b*) the cancelled note vault which takes over cancelled notes from the verifying officer and arranges for their safe custody and eventual destruction, (*c*) the Claims Branch attends on mutilated, mismatched, altered, half, wholly lost or destroyed and forged notes. Claims are not admitted as a matter of right, but are dealt with according to individual cases. No claims are entertained regarding notes up to the denomination of Rs. 10 when they are wholly lost or destroyed; (*d*) the Accounts Branch, (*e*) the Record Branch. Besides these, the Currency offices have to perform some work in connection with the so-called Exchange Treasuries,* the issue and receipt of small silver and copper and bronze in the small coin Depôt, though these duties formed really no part of the work of the Currency Department itself. The Balances under the Gold Standard Reserve are also held in the Currency Offices under orders issued from time to time by the Controller of Currency. The Currency Officer is in executive charge of the office. He is responsible for the work in the Department. When the Currency Officer is provided with quarters, he may never be absent at night without the permission of the superior officer and without arranging for some other officer to sleep in the

* These may be looked upon as the descendants of the former Reserve Treasuries in the Presidency towns, abolished since the creation of the Imperial Bank. Apparently, the Bank has not been able to supplant the Reserve Treasuries wholly

premises. The principal ministerial officer is the Treasurer. He is personally responsible for the whole of the balances and valuables of the Department. Vaults are provided for the storage of notes and coins. A portion of the Reserve coin are ordinarily held in Vaults in the local Fort or Castle. This is all the information that we need have about the internal organisation of a Currency Office in a Circle.* (For details see Paper Currency Manual, 1920.) Besides Circle offices, a number of other offices, having more or less to do with the issue and payment of Currency notes, also come under the purview of the Currency Department. We have currency chests attached either to Treasuries or to branches of the Imperial Bank. Almost the same organisation under a different name was the Currency Agency, now given up. There are also two Mint Chests at Calcutta and Bombay. Their work will be described later on. The Currency Department to-day is thus a ramified organisation with main offices at its present seven Circles and its tendrils sent out far and wide in all directions. It has been allotted a more independent and distinct existence than it ever had before. But there is still room for further improvement. The importance of the work that it does requires its isolation from all disturbing influences. Another question is whether the Department is being worked economically or otherwise. On the 17th March, 1922, a motion was carried in the Legislative Assembly reducing the grant to the

* Such was also the organisation in Sub-Circles. There are no Sub-Circles now, the last having been abolished in 1910.

Department on grounds of enforcing economy. To judge by this adverse vote, there seems to be a necessity for setting up an enquiry as to how far retrenchment can be carried on within the Department.

The business of the Currency Department briefly is the issue and payment of notes and the management of the reserves kept against the notes,—together with some other allied work. Notes are now issued against gold and silver coin and bullion at fixed rates. Up to 1893 only a limited amount of notes could be issued against gold. In that year the limitation was removed. Although since then notes may be equally demanded for gold as well as for silver, the issue has been predominantly against silver. From 1898 onwards gold has become a legal tender money of India, and notes are now both issuable and payble for the yellow metal. But the rates are settled by the Government, and often they are so unsuitable as to make the provision with regard to gold practically a dead letter. Apart from gold and silver, an amount of notes is now issued also in special cases and to a selected bank, in exchange for selected bills of exchange. A charge is made for these issues. The notes are printed in England on behalf of the Government of India.

§ 3. A word may be said here about this rather technical question of the printing of notes. James Wilson's idea was to manufacture the notes in India, but on ground of safety the Government of India was persuaded to import them from England. Since then the lack of printing facilities for such fine workmanship as of currency notes, coupled with the climatic difficulties of India, made it impossible for the Government to look for their production in this country. Indian opinion has been averse to importing them from a foreign country. In their evidence before the 1919 Committee, the Indian Merchant's Chamber and Bureau for example urged that the art of printing was now sufficiently developed in India to enable the notes to be printed here. This view was echoed by Sir Dabida Dalal in his Minority Report. The Government itself was not apathetic to the proposal. For a long time it had been considering the feasibility of the scheme and had special enquiries being made by its own expert officers. On the 4th February, 1924, in reply to a starred question by M. A. Jinnah, Sir Basil Blackett announced that the Government of India had made arrangements for an experimental press to test the practicability of security printing in India. This, if successful, would then be extended to the printing of currency notes, as well as stamps and stamped paper. The latest information is that preparations are well-advanced for starting a Government Security Press at Nasik. The Government however cannot yet print any notes in India, since the existing contract with the Bank of England, whereby the Bank supplies the notes to the Government, will not expire before June, 1929. It is, however, possible to terminate the contract earlier and this is what the Government seems to have done. The Controller's Report for 1925-26 says that it has been arranged to terminate it on the 1st

January, 1928. India thus will be using home-made ntoes in the near future.

The design and format of the notes remained unaltered ever since their introduction but recently a change has been made. Even before the War the Government had decided to introduce certain alterations in the design and form—in order to make the notes more forgery-proof and better to handle. The War however interrupted the plans, and it was not until 1923 (May) that a beginning was made. In that year the first ten-rupee notes of the new design were put into circulation. The most prominent feature of the new pattern is a ' clear window or space left on both sides through which a distinctive water-mark can be easily distinguished.' These notes proved to be very popular at once and within a year of their introduction they had practically replaced the old ten-rupee notes. ' The alteration of the five, fifty and hundred-rupee notes on similar lines with different sizes has also been undertaken and it is hoped that supplies of the first of these will shortly be available.' (1923-24 Report of the Currency Controller)*

§ 4. The denominations in which the notes have been issued have varied from time to time. The Currency Act of 1861 authorised a minimum denomination of Rs. 10. We have noticed before the struggle that took place over the question of a further lowering without any success. After the pas-

* The new pattern five-rupee notes were first issued to the public in October, 1925. At the same time some change was made in the design of the ten-rupee notes.

sing of the Act, notes were issued in amounts of Rs. 10, 20, 50, 100, 500 and 1,000.* But it was evident that without a smaller denomination whereby the notes might enter into the transactions of the poorer classes of the people, it was hopeless to look for a growth of the circulation. The logic of events converted both official and non-official opinions slowly in favour of a five-rupee note. In a tract written in 1864, a writer under the pseudonym of 'Indopolite' advocated the issue of five-rupee notes (India Office Tract, No. 339). In his memorandum before the 1866 Commission we find the Finance Member of the Government, W. N. Massey, also favouring the issue of lower denominations. The majority of the Commission, however, although recording a preponderance of opinion in favour of the five-rupee note, did not favour its issue, and invited particular attention to the evidence of one Ram Gopal Ghose, a notable merchant in those days. In reviewing the Report of the Commission a writer even went further than five-rupee notes. He suggested in agricultural districts the issue of two-rupee notes. This is perhaps the earliest suggestion for so low a note in India. (A Simple Plan for a State Paper Currency, etc., by Aliquis, 1869, G.L.) In 1871, at last, Government took courage in both hands, and by Act III of that year lowered the minimum denomination to five rupees. In 1910 the twenty-rupee note was discontinued, as it was not much in demand. The

* The Rs. 10,000 notes, which are used more as reserve by banks than as a medium of circulation by the public, were issued later in 1872.

next development in the history of the denominations is the issue of one-rupee notes in December, 1917 and of 2½-rupee notes in January, 1918. Not only that there was already a demand in the country for notes of smaller denominations, but the silver famine of 1817-18, with the consequent dangers about the convertibility of an inflated note issue, compelled the Government to take measures for the conservation and economy of silver. It was with this end in view that the 1 and 2½-rupee notes were at first issued. Unfortunately both of them were destined to be rather short-lived. The 2½-rupee note was retired for want of popularity, while the one-rupee note, although in popular favour fell a victim to the 'axe' of the Inchcape Retrenchment Committee. It was declared to be too costly. Both denominations have been discontinued since January, 1926. The re-introduction of the one-rupee note however has been strongly recommended by the Hilton Young Commission. The earliest suggestion, it may be noted, for the rupee note for India, was perhaps made by Sir R. West, K.C.I.E., LL.D., before the Herschell Committee. He advocated the temporary introduction of such notes. The existing denominations, to recapitulate, are Rs. 5, 10, 50, 100, 500, 1,000 and 10,000.

§ 5. Of these, all notes up to Rs. 100 are universal currency notes, that is to say, from whichever place they may have been issued they are convertible into specie at all Currency offices in India. The word universal,' in this particular sense, was perhaps first used by the Commission of 1866. A more shy Commission has never reported on currency matters. Almost on all issues the Commission was content with summarising the evidence received, rather than give its own decisions. In this case also, as was to be expected from them, the members recorded a 'preponderating opinion' in favour of such a universal or all-India note. Conversion facilities over the whole of the country did not exist for any notes then. After the passing of the Act of 1861, the country was divided into three distinct Circles of Calcutta, Madras and Bombay, and notes issued from any of these Circles were not legally encashable outside their respective areas. A Circle was thus a self-contained Currency district. In 1864 Circles, or rather sub-Circles, were established at Allahabad, Lahore, Calicut, Trichinopoly, Vizagapatam (afterwards termed Coconada) and Nagpur. By 1865-66 'Kurrachee' was added to the list. The notes of these sub-circles were payable not only at their places of issue, but also at the Circle office of the Presidency to which they belonged. Thus Nagpur notes were payable at both Nagpur and at Calcutta, the head-quarters of the Presidency to which Nagpur belonged. The boundaries of these Circles were as follows in 1866:—(1) The Calcutta Circle comprised the territories of the Lieutenant-Governor of Bengal. (2) The Allahabad Circle, areas under the Lieutenant-Governor of North Western Provinces and the Chief Commissioner of Oudh. (3) The Lahore Circle comprised the areas under the Lieutenant-Governor of the Punjab. (4) The Nagpur Circle—all territories under the Chief Commissioner of the Central Provinces. (5) The Madras Circle—the districts of Madras, North and South Arcot and Salem. (6) The Calicut Circle,—the districts of South Canara, Malabar and Coimbatore. (7) The Trichinopoly Circle, the districts of Tanjore, Trichinopoly, Madura and Tinnevelly. (8) The Vizagapatam Circle,—the districts of Ganjam, Vizagapatam, Godavery and Kistna. (9) The Bombay Circle,—the districts of the Presidency of Bombay proper. (10) The Kurrachee Circle embraced the province of Sind. (Major Hyde in 1867.) The increase in currency circles was partly due to the discontinuance of the banks as currency agents. Later as paper currency increased in circulation more Circles were created. Akola was established in 1868-69.—(See Chalmers' Colonial Currency.) By 1876-77 some shuffling had been done with the circles,—but their number stood at ten. They were then—Calcutta, Madras, Bombay, Allahabad, Lahore, Calicut, Coconada, Nagpur, Kurrachee and Akola. In the next ten years they had not remained further unshuffled. In 1887, we find their number reduced to seven, *viz.*, Calcutta, Bombay and Madras as the principal Circles and Allahabad, Lahore, Karachi and Calicut as the sub-circles. Of these, the first two belonged to the Calcutta Circle, and the next two to the Bombay and Madras respectively (Manual of Indian Paper Currency Notes, compiled by W. T. Piercy, 1887, B.M.L.) Later the Currency Office at Allahabad was shifted to Cawnpore, a more industrial town. By Currency Act of 1910, the sub-circles were abolished. Calicut was absorbed in Madras, and the others were made into separate circles. The sub-circles were valuable in furthering the growth of the issue, but with the progress of universalisation of the notes, they became practically redundant. They might be said to have lived out their purpose. Their relation with the parent Circle indicated that they were established with the double aim of taking the note into the interior of the country at a distance from the circle and at the same time maintaining the uniformity of the notes as far as possible. Notes of the sub-circle were cashable at the Circle Offices but circle notes were cashable at the sub-circle only under special circumstances. Sub-circle notes were thus 'universal' within the boundaries of the Circle. The issue of all-India universal notes made the sub-circles unnecessary. Only for administrative purposes some were retained as Circles. In the meantime by Act XX of 1882, Burma, which was hitherto outside the scope of the Paper Currency Act, was brought within it, but it was some years before a Circle Office was established at Rangoon. That came about in February 24, 1893, by a Notification of the Government of India (see General Statutory Rules and Orders, 1915 edition, India Office Record Department). Ever since 1910 the Currency map of India has remained practically unchanged. The present Circles as given in the Government Resource Manual of 1921 have their boundaries as follows:—

Calcutta :—All territory under the Governor of Bengal, Governor of Behar and

Orissa, Governor of Assam, Superintendent, Port Blair, Chief Commissioner, Andamans and the Bikanir State.

Cawnpore :—Areas under Governor of U. P.—Cantonment and Civil Lines of Nowgong, Sambhar, and the Bharatpur and Dholpur States and some other lands.

Lahore :—Areas under Governor of the Punjab, Chief Commissioner North West Frontier Provinces and the Chief Commissioner at Delhi.

Bombay :—Bombay Presidency proper, the C. P., all districts in Ajmere-Merwara and the areas in the Hyderabad (Deccan) State in which the Governor-General in Council exercises jurisdiction through the Resident, the Cantonments of Baroda, Mhow and others, Indian States in Rajputana except the Bikanir, Bharatpur and Dholpur States and some Railway lands.

Karachi :—Providence of Sind and Beluchistan (British and Agency).

Madras :—All the districts of the Presidency of Madras, the territory administered by the Chief Commissioner of Coorg and the Civil and Military Station of Bangalore.

Rangoon :—Areas under the Governor of Burma.*

§ 6. Mention has already been made of other subsidiary establishments except sub-circles meant to further the work of the paper currency. Currency Agencies were one such class to be early started. With the object of facilitating the encashment of notes, the system of currency agencies was introduced in 1871 (1913-14 Report). These agencies were opened at important stations to afford facilities to the public for exchanging coin for notes and notes for coin (1891-92 Report). Defining these facilities Mr. B. N. Mitra said, (evidence before 1924 Commission), that notes issued by the agency were freely encashed at that agency and other notes were also encashed, if possible. The currency agencies were an humble edition of the sub-circles in reality, with this difference, that while the sub-circles were bound to issue notes on the tender of proper coin, the Currency Agent might issue notes 'if he thought fit.' (*cf.* 1882 and 1905 Currency Act) They were a sort of unofficial sub-circles. Towards the nineties the number of these agencies had grown to a respectable figure,—which is proof enough of the success of the experiment. The whole country was dotted over with agencies. The Calcutta Circle had 24 agencies; Allahabad counted 8, Bombay 1 (Nagpur), Madras 2, (Vizagapatam and Coconada) and Rangoon 9 (1891-92 Report). Regarding the

* The officers looking after these Circles are, a Deputy Controller for the Calcutta Circle, a second Deputy Controller for Cawnpore and Lahore combined and a third for Bombay and Karachi combined. In the two remaining Circles, the local Accountant-Generals are ex-officio Deputy Controllers.

working of these agencies we read, ' The only Province in which the Currency Agency System properly so-called is at all thoroughly worked, is the Punjab. The issues from agencies form a very large proportion (18 per cent.) of the total issues in this circle. The other so-called agencies are really currency chests established with the object of more conveniently and rapidly effecting the resource operations of government.' (1894-95 Currency Report.) This is quoted almost verbatim in some of the subsequent reports. With the progress of the universalising process, and the growth of Currency Chests at Treasuries which took away much of their work, the value of these agencies considerably fell in importance. Still they were a link in the chain of paper currency organisation, although none of them, I understand, exist to-day.

Apart from the agencies which were practically sub-circles under another name, there were also established what has been called ' Currency Chests ' at Government Treasuries for facilitating the issue. This meant simply the opening of a separate Currency account at the Treasury, the funds wherefrom could be conveniently exchanged for the general Treasury balances—a corresponding exchange from Treasury to Currency Chest being made at some other place. The equation of mutual exchange may be thus shown by means of arrows—

Treasure Balances ⤨ →Treasury Balances
Currency Chest ⤨ →Currency Chest.

'Currency Chests' says the 1920 Paper Currency Manual, 'are opened at Treasuries for the convenince of resource operations and also in order to facilitate the free issue and encashment of currency notes. In order that Treasuries may at all times be adequately supplied with funds, surplus balances are collected at convenient and accessible points and transferred to the Currency Chest. Remittances are made from those places to Treasuries requiring funds. Actual remittances can often be avoided by allowing a Treasury requiring funds to draw upon the balances of the Currency Chest attached to it. The equivalent must in such cases be transferred from some other Treasury to its Currency Chest in order that the total balances of the Currency Department may not be affected.' The balances of the Currency Chest whether in notes or coins must of course be always kept distinct from the Treasury Balances.

It must be remembered that although the Treasuries were thus utilised for assistance to the paper currency, the Government had no legal obligation to cash notes at Treasuries. Only when funds permitted did they usually give this kind of accommodation to the public. At present at places where the Imperial Bank of India is taking over the Treasury work of the Government, the providing of these extra-legal facilities are gradually devolving upon the branches of the bank.

Apart from Treasuries the latest development in connection with the resource operations is the opening of currency chests at Sub-Treasuries. The new arrangement which aims at further economical handling of the Government balances, dates from only a few years back and has been increasingly used since 1920-21. In that year the number of such Sub-Treasuries possessing Currency Chests was increased from 342 to 423. ' The device ' says the Controller's Report for that year, ' enables the rapid transfer of surplus funds through currency, especially during the seasons of heavy revenue collection, to the Central Government balances and reduces the amount which has to be kept at out-stations to meet the ordinary day-to-day Treasury transactions, since a re-transfer of funds from Currency Chest to Treasury can, if required, be made at short notice.' By March, 1926, the number of such Sub-Treasury Chests had increased to 1013, perhaps the limit of useful expansion.

A passing reference may here be made to another institution in connection with the paper currency, which is wholly due to convenience of practical administration. This is the Mint Chest. A Currency Chest is opened and maintained at each of the two Mints at Calcutta and Bombay. ' No notes are held at these chests and they are intended to serve as a convenient method of acounting for bullion and coin held in the Mints as part of the currency Reserve.' (1920 Manutl)

§ 7. What with the Circles, Sub-circles, Agencies and Currency Chests at Treasuries, Government seemed to have spared no pains in carrying the currency irrigation of India to a very high degree of perfection. Still parts of the country remained backwaters.

Mr. Dunbar, for example, giving evidence before the 1914 Commission, deplored the absence of any Currency office at Dacca, a circumstance that was responsible for the small use of notes in East Bengal. The reason seems to have been that the financing of the jute crop required considerable amounts of silver rupees, rather than notes, and a currency office there would not have been paying. Mr. Dunbar said that during the jute season the Presidency Bank of Bengal used to send nearly 7 crores of rupees to the Dacca District and the cost of sending it was large. Government found that the opening of the currency office at Dacca would throw over the cost of remittance entirely on itself. It is this bogey of taking over the costs of remittance upon itself that eternally stood in the way of the Government's enlarging the boundaries of the Circles and making notes universal for all India. Universalisation meant obliterating the artificial currency boundaries. The utility of a universal note was very early appreciated by the Government as well as by the people of the country. We have seen how the shyest of the Currency Commissions—which are usually the anthesis of shyness, readily recognised in 1866 the demand for one such note in the country. Aliquis, in his pamphlet in 1869, commenting on this shyness writes, 'The Commissioners are very shy. They do not like the present Circle system, but shrink from discussing the universal note.' The first difficulty in the way of a universalisation was the cost of remittance. He rightly accuses the Commission of over-sight ' in not gathering the rates of exchange between different places in India now as well as in the past.' It would have shown the Government its responsibilities, if the universal note displaced bills of exchange. We have no means of knowing now what the internal rates of exchange were between different localities in the country; that would have enabled us to judge whether the fears of the Government were well-founded or not. They could not have been very far from the par with the rapid increase of cheap transport facilities and highway robberies almost becoming an extinct profession. It is curious that even after the universalising of the five-rupee note in 1871, and after its success was undisputed, the Government was still under the influence of the spectre of being saddled with the enormous costs of remittance. With a little less nervousness it could have felt perfectly easy at heart. The throwing open of the whole country to a note, convertible everywhere, might have at the outset thrown some cost of remittance upon the Government. But it was absurd to suppose that the demand for remittance would be only one way. With the opening of the sluices of paper currency remittance the local price-levels were bound to be equalised everywhere and there was no reason why more money should have flowed towards Dacca from Calcutta than from Dacca towards Calcutta. Once the reserves had been adjusted according to local needs the universal note would have no more added to the costs of remittance of the Government than later events proved it did. Government actually felt no excessive pressure of remittance after it universalised the five and the ten-rupee notes. The attitude of the Government was over-cautious and that explains the rather halting progress made with the idea of universalisation. It was a short-sighted policy to fear initial costs and neglect ultimate benefits. The cost view as well as the profit view, has been the bane of the Currency policy of not a few nations. The provision of a currency, mobile throughout the country, without the least possible hindrance, is as important for the economic prosperity of a country as mobility of labour or mobility of capital and goods. The Currency Circles acted as a bar to the free mobility of purchasing power from one place to another and hampered the free working of the economic forces.

In 1903 the five-rupee notes were universalised for all India excluding Burma. By Act II of 1909 this reservation as to Burma was removed and India for the first time had a note current and convertible everywhere. The words 'Indian Paper Currency' could now be correctly made use of. Hitherto there was no Indian, but only sectional paper currencies. The next move in this direction was made in 1910. Act II of that year carried universalisation still further to ten-rupee and fifty-rupee notes. On the All Fools' Day next year the Government did a wise thing. It issued a notification declaring the hundred-rupee note also universal legal tender. Here the victorious course of universalisation has come to a stop. The reasons assigned by the Government for not carrying the process higher up may thus be summarised in the words of Lord Meston. 'In the first place,' Meston explained before the 1914 Commission, 'notes above the hundred-rupee are unfamiliar for ordinary hand to hand purposes. The larger notes are really used as stores of value in the banks and other places.' He had himself never seen a Rs. 10,000 note except at head-quarters in the Reserve Treasuries. Secondly the internal remittance business was in the hands of the Government who worked it either by Treasury transfers or by the medium of the post office. In these ways a certain amount of revenue was earned which the Government would be sorry to lose. But the main argument was that after universalising the higher notes the costs of moving funds would be thrown very greatly upon the Government. It will appear from these arguments that even after the satisfactory experience of universalising notes up to Rs. 100, the Government had not yet been able to shake itself free from the costs of remittance idea. Before the 1914 Commission a formidable array of evidence was recorded in favour of abolishing the Circles and carrying the universalisation process still higher. Every one except a few officials seemed to argue that the time had come when the country could be thrown open safely to the Rs. 500 note. Mr. Newmarch, an official, in reply to a question by Mr. Keynes, agreed that, now that the hundred-rupee note was made universal legal tender it would make very little difference to universalise all other notes. The Commission's recommendation was for the immediate universalisation of the 500 rupee note. They hoped that 'with the experience so gained it might be found possible to carry universalisation still higher.' Extra cost of remitting specie from place to place would, according to the Commission, be negligible, except at the outset. The interruption of the war, and possibly a still lurking fear of shouldering the costs of remittance have prevented the carrying out of the recommendation. But it is to be hoped that it will be acted upon in the near future. Meanwhile, the existing universalisation up to Rs. 100 means considerable progress and even if the Government delays and nurses its pet theory of 'costs of remittance' the country can afford to wait.

A development that arose early in connection with the universalising process and which, in a sense was its result, was the provision of remittance facilities through the currency. As universalisation progressed currency notes were more and more used as a remittance medium. In order to reduce the pressure in that direction, the Government thought it wise to open out a new outlet for remittance by means of telegraphic transfers through the currency. These T. T's, as they are called, provide a method of remittance for banks and other private parties. On payment of the prescribed premium and the costs of the necessary telegram, arrangements are made under certain conditions for money deposited at one place to be paid to the depositor's representative or agent at some other place. T.T's, it is to be noted, are offered through Currency only. 'Such transfers are always in the form of telegraphic transfers' (1920 Manual) and may be made anywhere between Currency Offices and Currency Chests local and foreign. Many people avail themselves of the offer since the costs are usually low. Sending Currency Notes through the post entails some loss of interest during the time of sending the two halves. Apart from all this the currency offices have been utilised also for other non-paper-currency affairs. They form an organic part of the general financial machinery of the Government and hence are often made to do other work such as in connection with the maintenance of exchange, etc., which cannot be strictly called paper currency work. But no discussion about them can be entered into here.

§ 8. We may next pass on to the question of legal tender. The history of this aspect of the mechanism of issue is also full of interest. It was the intention of the Currency Act of 1861 to make the Currency Notes legal tender only within the Circle of origin. Within the Circle they were valid for all payments except by the office of issue. Although thus legally, lines were drawn about the area of usefulness of a particular note, in practice the provisions of law were quite liberally interpreted. Notes were usually accepted as valid tender, within and without the circles in payment of all dues to the Government, for Railway charges etc. (Vide the officially published Paper Currency Manual, 1887, B.M.L.). Gradually, the spread of universalisation extended the legal tender validity of the notes. Universalisation meant making the note legal tender all over the country. At present therefore notes up to Rs. 100 are legal tender at any place in British India; others only at places within the Circle from which they were issued. No currency note is legal tender at any office of issue (cf. Clause 14 of 1923 Act).

Lastly remains to be discussed the question of facilities for encashment legal and extra-legal, for the note issue. The net-work of Circles, Agencies and Treasuries provided a multiplicity of points for conversion, but in many of these establishments the accommodation was more nominal than real. On the whole it was complained that the facilities for conversion were not adequate.

First about Circles. It has been seen how the Sub-circles only cashed the Circle notes by courtesy. Government was legally bound to cash notes only at the office of the Circle of Issue or at the currency office of the corresponding Presidency town. Regarding cashing at other circles the early instructions were, 'foreign notes are cashable only where there is a balance of cash available, that is, when the cash reserve at the time exceeds the difference between the note circulation of the Circle at the time and the fixed minimum circulations.' (Brunyate) 'But,' the instructions continued 'in the following cases foreign notes to a reasonable amount may be cashed irrespective of the cash balance,—(a) for bonâfide travellers on a certificate of receipt (b) hotel-keepers, (c) shipping agents, and (d) shopkeepers' agents. Foreign notes paid on Government Account into the Presidency Banks are cashed without restriction.' (Brunyate). Regarding extra-legal facilities at Treasuries, a great claim is made by the Government that notes are always, as a matter of practice, cashed there. But evidence on this point seems to be conflicting. Lord Meston as the official spokesman before the 1914 Commission, said, ' in point of fact it was nearly always possible to get a note encashed, except large notes ' at the Treasuries. This was also the testimony of a young and rising officer, Mr. B. N. Mitra, who ought to have known the ins and outs of the Currency Department. On the other hand Sir Dabida Dalal pointed out that ' in 1910 according to Government statement there were still 16 Treasuries where encashment of notes were generally refused! He said that the Comptroller-General in the 1910 Report frankly acknowledged that traders knowing that it would be useless to ask for large sums in silver in exchange for notes, did not make such attempts at all. If that was so, the Government had certainly failed in the task of providing adequate extra-legal facilities for encashment. The case of the Sub-Treasuries were of course different. They were meant for other purposes than encashment of notes and they generally did not pretend to do so. On this point also the evidence is not clear. In answer to a question if currency notes were ever cashed for the convenience of the public at Sub-Treasuries, Sir B. N. Mitra unequivocally replied ' No. The nature of the Sub-Treasuries is different. They are mostly revenue-collecting centres.' In the teeth of this statement when Mr. Sundara Iyer was told by the Commission that they understood that currency notes were never cashed for the public at Sub-Treasuries, he answers, ' Notes are cashed. I have taken notes there and got them cashed.' Lord Meston thought that any large presentation of currency notes at Sub-Treasuries was unlikely. But he recognised it to be a natural thing for a person to go and ask for the encashment of even a fifty-rupee note and generally get it changed. Apart from sub-treasuries, and treasuries, the Post Offices were also mentioned by some witnesses,—not too impractically,—for serving as additional stations for encashment, as far as possible. In its report, the Commission put in a strong plea for the extension of extra-legal facilities for convertibility. But before the ink was dry on the recommendation, the country found itself in the midst of a war which put off all reform for an indefinite period. During the war the opportunities for convertibility had to be very seriously reduced. In the very first year of the war the Controller of the Currency could not help feeling considerable doubt whether in many places the facilities had been really more than nominal (1914-15 Report). He was referring to District Treasuries. In the big towns the credit of the notes was perhaps still undamaged. But later on, the watering of the issue reducing progressively the percentage of metallic backing from 78 per cent. on the 31st March, 1914 to 70 per cent. in 1916, 43 per cent. in 1917, 38 per cent. in 1918, down to 35 per cent. in 1919, the lowest point ever touched,—together with the heavy absorption and demand for silver coins in the country, brought the issue almost on the verge of inconvertibility. This was not, of course, the first time that the convertibility of the issue was in serious danger. A similar situation but far less acute, had arisen in 1900. In that year, due to the operation of the Gold Note Act of receiving gold in England and issuing excessive amounts of notes in India, ' the additional issue of currency added to the drain on the rupee reserve of the Government of India.' (Report of the Currency Department, 1914.) Government in its difficulties sought to force sovereigns into circulation. The Currency offices were instructed to offer sovereigns to the presenters of notes, while giving rupees to any one who objected to receive sovereigns. The experiment was not successful; most of the gold coins soon after made their way back into the hands of the Government, and the ' Government found themselves unable to cash currency notes in rupees, not only at Cawnpore and other Treasuries in the North West Provinces (where, though not legally bound to do so, they had been in the habit of encashing notes), but on the 11th April, 1900, at the Head Office in Calcutta itself. Notes became subject to a discount of as much as $\frac{7}{16}$ths per cent. in Cawnpore and there was a serious danger of a failure of confidence in the paper currency'. (Report, 1914). The crisis was met by feverishly coining more rupees. The war-time crisis was a more difficult problem to tackle. Government had no silver to hurriedly coin into rupees and no silver was available in the market. Meanwhile, to quote the Report of the 1919 Committee, ' unfavourable war news in March and April 1918 caused a run on the Bombay Office for the encashment of notes, and this was followed by similar difficulties elsewhere, notably in Lahore. Inconvertibility appeared to be inevitable and was only averted by the energy and resource of the officers responsible and by the timely announcement of the acquisition of the Pittman silver.' This was an Act passed by the U. S. A. Congress on April 23, 1918. It authorised the U. S. A. Treasury to melt and sell as bullion silver dollars not in excess of 350 million. India was then able to purchase silver from the U. S. A. Treasury. Of the total amount of 270 million fine ounces, melted down under the Act, India's share was 200 million fine ounces. From July the delivery of the Pittman silver commenced, a not-too-early arrival considering that in the first week of June the rupee balance of the Government of India had fallen to little more than 4 crores. However, the Pittman silver saved the situation. After that, the situation gradually improved, but the necessity for conserving their reduced stock of rupees had forced on the Government a reversal of their previous policy. 'Facilities for the encashment of notes at District Treasuries were in a large degree withdrawn. The conveyance of specie by rail and river-steamer was prohibited and an embargo was placed on its transmission by post. Later, in January 1919, owing to the practical administrative difficulties of dealing in full with the demands for encashment at the Currency Offices during the busy season, the daily issues of rupees to single tenderers of notes were limited to a figure which made it practicable to satisfy large demands in part and small demands, as a rule, in full. The result of these restrictions was the substitution to a large extent of notes for rupees as the common circulating medium. There was in many parts of India a considerable discount on notes, especially the new Rs. 2½ and one-rupee notes, when they were first issued in large quantities to replace rupees. Discounts as high as 15 per cent. and 19 per cent. have been reported; but the discount rapidly diminished when it was seen that the notes were freely accepted in payment of the Government dues and when small coin was made available in large quantities. The reports received by the Government of India in the year 1919 do not show any discount on the notes as compared with silver coin exceeding 3 per cent. (Report of the 1919 Committee, pp. 13-14). The greatest crisis in the history of Indian paper currency was thus tided over. The crisis was due mostly to what Sir Dabida Dalal called 'simply watering the note issue in its worse form,'—*i.e.*, issuing notes without any adequate metallic backing, although the high price of silver and other factors beyond the control of the Government contributed materially to bring it about. There is a tendency of course, as in most things during the war, to speak about it in a passive voice. It is said to have been caused by the War—as if no one was responsible for it. It is well to remember that it came about at the tail end of the War, when faith in British victory was stronger than ever, and it persisted even after the armistice. By 1919 the worst of the storm had passed over. But still on the 1st March, 1920, the situation had not returned wholly to the normal. Sir Malcolm Hailey said then that the Government was 'still unable to contemplate any return to the free and unrestricted issue of rupees or encashment of notes at District Treasuries throughout the country.' In June the position looked much better. Government then hastened to remove all the then existing restrictions both on the encashment of notes and on the ultimate movement of coin by rail and steamer. In consequence in 1921, reports of notes going to a substantial discount, were no longer heard of. The facilities for cashing notes at Treasuries which were fully restored in the year 1920-21 continued throughout the next financial year (Currency Report, 1922-23). The story of the war cirsis, has, of course now passed into history, but it is a history full of interesting lessons. It showed, among other things, the extreme capacity of endurance of the machinery of paper currency evolved by the Government; it showed how shock-proof it was. It is doubtful if any private bank could have at all weathered so severe a storm, if it had been in charge of the note issue. The handling of the crisis of 1918 'saved by the energy and resource of the Department' is a tribute to the Government management of the paper currency, but its causes do not all reflect credit on that management. Its detailed history, in view of its importance, needs no apology.

In the development of extra-legal facilities, to summarise, three distinct stages are discernible. First, there is the period up to 1914, when the legal right to convert notes was confined to a few places, but extra-legal facilities were steadily being enhanced. Secondly, during the War drastic reductions were made in these facilities which did not entirely disappear until 1921. Then, there is the third, or the present period, when facilities have been once more installed and are being added to. It will be noted that in many places the Imperial

Bank of India has taken over the work of the Treasury. In these stations, the old tradition of trying to encash the notes whenever presented, as far as funds permit, is being maintained. Payment for notes can be made either in gold or in silver coins, which are legal tender in British India. Up to 1899 gold was not legal tender in India, and then no one was bound to receive gold coins in exchange for notes. Although at present both metals are valid for payment, usually the rupees are preferred.

This Chapter, which has now grown quite long, may be closed with a slight reference to the rules governing the payment for lost or mutilated notes. The principle underlying these rules is that while the Government does not take upon itself any obligation for making good the value of the notes lost, as far as possible, payments are made for them. For this purpose bonds are entered into between the Government and the party claiming payment. No claims are entertained for notes up to Rs. 10, which are wholly lost or destroyed, as no issue registers are kept about them, and there is no means of stopping them being re-cashed if they are found later. These and other rules regarding stopped notes will be found in detail in the Paper Currency Manual (Official Edition) of 1920.

CHAPTER VI.

THE COVER OF THE ISSUE.

The Paper Currency Reserve, its functions, its location and its relation to other Government Reserves.

§ 1. The functions of the currency reserve exceed mere convertibility and are rather undefined, p. 112.—§ 2. The influence of the two main schools of elasticity and convertibility on the history of the reserve, p. 114.—§ 3. Various non-currency uses of the currency reserve Some early instances of such unorthodox use, p. 118.—§ 4. The inseparable connection between the currency reserve and the gold standard reserve, p. 124.—§ 5. The case for amalgamation of the currency and the gold standard reserves, p. 132.—§ 6. The location of the re serve. Beginnings of the system of holding parts of the reserve outside India, p. 133.—§ 7. Further widening of the area of holding of the reserve during the War and after, p. 138.

§ 1. We have to take up now the question of the cover of the issue, that is to say, of the reserves metallic and non-metallic, that have to be kept against the notes. It is a very important question. It has figured always very prominently in the history of our paper-currency,—nine-tenths of that history being nothing but the story of the reserves. There is nothing surprising about this emphasis. Paper Currency was a new experience to India and its success depended more than anything else on its convertibility. The reserves which guaranteed this convertibility had therefore always to be carefully looked after. One has only to remember this to understand why far greater attention has been paid to the question of the reserves than to any other matter connected with the paper currency. Then, again, the problems arising out of the management of the reserves have been the most difficult of all to settle. There has been first the question as to what exact amount of them should be in metal and what in securities. Secondly, the location of the different parts of the reserve as between India and England, has been for a long time the subject of controversy. Of the metallic reserve again, it has been asked, how much should be in gold and how much in silver? Regarding the investment portion, the question naturally arises, what kind of securities should be allowed there,—permanent or temporary,—securities of the Government of India, or of the British Government?

These questions can only be answered with reference to the objects for which the paper currency reserve is kept. It is hopeless to try to examine the methods employed without first ascertaining the purposes they endeavour to fulfil. In this respect the history of our paper currency affords some instances of fighting at cross-purposes. Although ostensibly and primarily the aim of the paper currency reserve has been to provide for the payment of notes, various other subsidiary functions have been ascribed to it from time to time. At times it appeared as if these subsidiary functions had become more important than the primary one. Convertibility has been the guiding consideration, but linked to convertibility,—allied to it in certain respects, and hostile in some others,—there has grown up a number of other considerations too. The changes that have been made from time to time in the provisions regarding the reserve in the successive Currency Acts from 1861 onwards, show sufficiently the growth of these extra-convertibility aims. The motive of the Act of 1861 was perhaps to utilise the reserve solely and wholly for the purposes of conversion of the notes. But very soon it began to be utilised also for the resource operations of the government. In time, other non-currency uses also developed. As ideas changed, the regulations about the reserve were more or less tampered with. To-day it is readily recognised that paper currency reserve has some purposes which are not strictly connected with the convertibility of the notes. It is used for the maintenance of exchange and for assistance to trade and commerce. It is sometimes looked upon as inseparable from the other reserves and funds of the Government of India. It is freely interchanged with these other reserves and helps them as often as they also help it in their turn. The whole matter seems to be now shrouded with much uncertainty. And consequently the question of the location and composition of the reserve gives rise to considerable differences of opinion. We have only to compare the provisions of the Act of 1861 with those of the Act of 1923, to discover the remarkable contrast that has grown up. The key to understand the changes lies in the ever-broadening conception of the purposes the reserve.

§ 2. There has been no lack of views with regard to the objects of the reserve. Briefly, two contending principles seem to have striven all along for mastery. One of them is safety, and the other is elasticity. Safety has been rather narrowly interpreted only in terms of convertibility of the notes into coins. and not much has been thought of their ultimate convertibility into commodities. This view has sought to safeguard convertibility beyond anything else. The advocates of elasticity on the other hand, have aimed at increasing the size of the circulation permanently or seasonally. They have been wise with a philosophy of profit and loss. The growth of the issue, according to them, would not only help the trade and commerce of the country, but a growth on the basis of fiduciary issues would mean more revenue to the Government of the country. They have thus tried to benefit the tax-payer without considering the harm done to him indirectly by putting up the prices of his necessaries. It is obvious that the preponderance of one or other of these views would correspondingly affect the location and composition of the reserve. Both views are very attractive, but the convertibility doctrine seems to have had the greater amount of influence in the preparation of our paper currency regulations. We have seen how, originally, the note issue was made perfectly rigid by the Act of 1861, the notes being practically bullion certificates. It was a triumph for the convertibility school. But later, with the transformation of the monetary system of India from a silver monometallism to a token rupee standard, an opportunity for expansion was unconsciously, as it were, provided. Notes were now convertible into rupees,—themselves notes printed on silver. Henceforth, as was to be expected, the paper currency became embroiled with the wider question of the convertibility of the rupees into gold. A branch of the reserve in London was the natural outcome of the development and the maintenance of the exchange came officially to be recognised as one of the objects of the paper currency reserve. In 1861 notes were only payable in silver rupees, the only legal tender money of India. By the end of the century gold was declared legal money. Notes were thenceforward payable in both gold and in silver, according to the choice of the Government. Gold began, therefore, with reason to figure in the reserve in India. But as usually the payments were made in rupees the principle was established of holding the rupee-reserve wholly in India. The new ideas about the reserve were reflected equally in the regulations regarding the Securities portion, some of which began to be held in England and supported exchange. Simultaneously the elasticity doctrine made headway. The fiduciary limit was raised by a series of legislation onward from 1870, and later provision was made for seasonal expansion and contraction of the issue also. To-day the paper currency reserve serves for a multiplicity of objects. It is still primarily meant for the payment of the notes. But it has become an instrument for maintaining exchange whenever circumstances permit. No secret is made of its quasi-currency uses. The Chamberlain Commission,* after

* The Hilton Young Commission openly testify to the double use of the paper currency reserve for maintaining the convertibility of the notes and maintaining exchange. They consider this inevitable and accept the situation as such.

studying developments, concluded that, "while the main object of the reserve was to secure the absolute convertibility of the notes, the location of the reserve and the proportion between the gold and silver in the metallic portion now depended on other considerations as well" (para. 106, Report). The Babington Smith Committee (1919) also seem to have recognised other considerations besides that of purely providing for the convertibility of the notes, in making their recommendations upon the reserve. In the preface to their recommendations, no doubt they assert themselves as convertibility purists,—"the express purpose of justifying the confidence of the Indian public in the note by the provision of an adequate metallic reserve and the grant of ample facilities for converting the note into coin," being what actuated them in forming their suggestions. But the recommendations belie the formula. The "express purpose" of confidence in convertibility requires no portion of the reserve to be held in London at all, yet the members of the Committee do not advise its abolition,—which is proof enough of the fact that besides convertibility they had in view other purposes as well for the currency reserve. The latest official pronouncements are refreshingly explicit on the point. Sir Basil Blackett says—"In spite of the separation between the two reserves, if we are looking at the resources available for maintaining the rate of exchange of the rupee, the sterling securities in the paper currency reserve and the Gold Standard Reserve, all serve the same purpose" (speech, 1st March, 1923). The Currency Reserve, it has already been said, is now used for facilitating the resource operations of the Government. Loans are made from it to mitigate seasonal stringency of money in the market. There are still clinging to it considerations about the general credit of India. A substantial metallic reserve, although it may err on the side of over-security, is believed to help in restoring the credit of the country in outside markets making floatations of loans easier. The reserve has to be organised now with so many different purposes in mind. The task is therefore infinitely more complicated than it was before. But even now Sir Daniel Hamilton is not satisfied. He would make the currency reserve contribute to the development of the country,—build railways, and do similar works—in all possible and impossible ways. (See evidence before the 1914 Commission.)

§ 3. Where the objects in view are themselves so uncertain and changing, it is no wonder that the methods of organising the reserve should occasion controversy. Even with one fixed object it is possible to imagine a diversity of methods. Accepting convertibility as the final aim of the reserve, the question still remains how best that can be secured. The conflict of methods arises independently of a conflict of purpose; when both are present, the confusion is very great indeed. For a space of nearly sixty years the reserve was kept modelled on the issue of the Bank of England. But it has now been discovered that a proportional metallic reserve is as efficient as any other in securing the convertibility of the notes, at the same time conferring other benefits. The exact proportion of metal in the reserve was the next question that arose naturally. Various authorities have prescribed various ratios in which the different components of the reserve should be held, until we have the present division, according to which the security part may not exceed 50 per cent. of the total issue. It must be remembered, however that, strictly speaking, no full reserve is at all kept, as notes not presented within certain specified years are considered to be out of circulation. But if presented afterwards they will be met from the general revenues of the Government. At its widest therefore, the paper currency reserve embraces all the assets of the State. The keeping of the reserve in gold and silver has given rise to difficulties about valuation. A change in the rating of gold, and the rating is entirely made by the Government without any responsibility to maintain it—may diminish or increase the size of the reserve arbitrarily. The paper currency reserve, in spite of all the elaborate precautions taken to make it effective and definite is in large measure an unknown quantity. How far it has any independent existence is doubtful. Its nominal valuation cannot be relied on, as it may be made to represent any figure, even exceeding the value of the notes outstanding, by manipulating the rating of the gold and the sterling holdings. The reserve, as it is, has a most treacherous look.

It will be interesting to trace the development of the quasi-currency uses of the paper currency reserve. Early in its history the reserve was very zealously guarded. its sole purpose being regarded as insuring the payment of the notes. The first attempt to deviate it to side-uses in 1863, met with a storm of protest from many of its guardians. In that year the Government first discovered the possibility of using the reserve for facilitating their resource operations. Seventy-five lakhs of rupees were lying idle, deposited as reserve at Madras against a note circulation of equal amount. Sir Charles Trevelyan took out 35 lakhs of rupees in coins from the reserves and sent them to Bombay where coined money was much wanted "to re-inforce the Government balance there" and repaid the amount to the Head Commissioner of the Currency at Calcutta, to be credited to Madras as part of the existing currency investment. This shuffling of funds between different centres was seriously questioned by Sir Charles's colleagues in the Supreme Council. H. B. Harrington (Minute, 8th Jan., 1864) saw "great evils in this interference with the paper currency reserve, its movement and distribution." He thinks that some time must have elapsed between taking away coin at one centre and putting securities at another and during the interval the notes remained uncovered. Sir Henry Maine, the famous jurist and law-member of the Council, held that there was nothing illegal in coin and bullion being removed from one Presidency to another. Since then the paper currency has been freely used for the resource operations of the Government, and to-day it serves as one of the main instruments for the transfer of funds from one place to another. The principle now is to regard the whole issue as one and undivided, with a reserve distributed according to the convenience of the Government between different places, and not to regard the different circles as having independent and non-transferable reserves. So far as the paper currency reserve is concerned, the whole of India is to be looked upon as a single area where it may be kept, and to judge by the later extension of the domicile of the reserve, even some other portions of the earth may be included. As long as the reserve exists, it does not matter where it is held. The universalising process has considerably helped to bring about this new outlook, but it was more or less inevitable. There is bound to be an intimate connection between the trade and the currency, and economy demands that they be co-related as much as possible so that through the currency money may be transferred easily from one place to another. This connection is very well described in some of the currency reports —notably in that of Mr. Gillan in 1910-11, and some following years. Briefly, the situation is that Government receives money in its Treasuries and sub-Treasuries all over the country in payment of revenue from which it is necessary to provide funds for expenditure at headquarters. Conversely, the trading firms have large remittances to make to the interior in payment for produce. There is thus a coincidence which it is useful for both trade and the Government to dove-tail into each other. Firms requiring money for this purpose constantly apply to the Government for remittance orders from one place to another within the country and the Government meet their requirements as far as they can do

16

so by the issue at a small charge of supply bills or telegraphic transfers through the Currency. The amount of remittance usually effected in this way is very large. The arrangement is economical for all parties concerned, as enabling their transactions to be largely effected without any actual movement of coin. Similarly, the external trade of the country is also utilised for transferring funds through the currency between England and India. Council Bills are sold by the Secretary of State, the proceeds being credited to the Currency Reserve in England ; the equivalent in notes is then issued in India. In all this remittance business, the paper currency practically does the work which more properly belongs to the general Treasury balances of the Government. Along with the Treasury funds therefore it forms an integral part of the machinery by which the resource operations are carried on. The further juxtaposition of currency funds and treasury funds at Treasuries, makes mutual transfers between them very easy. Funds are thus being continually adjusted, not only between different Treasuries in India, but also between England and India. This interchangeability of the currency reserve with the general Treasury balances, does not of course affect the size of any of them, but makes them very mobile as between different places. It brings out the close and almost inseparable connection between the two. Indirectly, as noted before, a second point of affinity between them lies in the fact that notes are issued theoretically not only on the strength of the currency reserve, but also on the general revenue of the

Government of India. Alternately, the reserves are all part of one organic whole, and no sacredness attaches to any one if matters come to a crisis.

Other noteworthy early instances,—like the one given above—of the paper currency going out of its acknowledged purpose of existing only for the credit of the notes, are equally easy to find. The same year, 1863, provides a second instance, although of a slightly different character. Part of the currency reserve was then utilised in exceptional circumstances, in mitigating the stringency in the money market at Bombay. Money was very scarce. The Bank of Bombay charged 11 per cent. on Government bills and as much as 13 per cent. on private bills. A commercial crisis was impending. Although great pressure was put on the Mint, it was not equal to minting and supplying the new coins necessary. In the circumstances, the Government of Bombay permitted a transfer of coined rupees from the paper currency reserve, replacing them by bullion from the Mint. This brought down opprobium on it from the Government of India which wrote thus :—(Government letter, 4th Dec., 1863). "The practice of using the deposit of coin upon which the paper circulation is based as an available fund for supplying the Government Treasury with coin, is entirely inconsistent with the principles upon which the Government note circulation ought to be conducted. Bullion is not of course available for the payment of notes that may be presented." The Government of India therefore urged the readjustment of the funds as soon as possible. We have only to compare this vigilant watch over the currency reserve in former days, with the present attitude when shufflings are the order of the day. We then realise how very elastic the definition of the purpose of that reserve has become.

The earliest lending from the paper currency reserve occurred in 1865. It illustrated once more that the doctrine of the inviolability of the currency reserve was fast being exploded and the reserve was being used for extra-currency purposes. In that year, in order to prevent a commercial crisis at Bombay, Sir Bartle Frere, the Governor of the Presidency, sought and obtained the permission of the Government of India to lend 150 lakhs of rupees from the currency reserve if necessary. No loan was actually made, the assurance being quite sufficient to enable the Bank to tide over the crisis. It is true that when these proceedings were reported to the Secretary of State, he in no uncertain terms expressed his disapproval of them. But the fact remained that the Government was ready to lend from the paper currency in times of monetary crisis. It created a precedent. Readiness to lend for mitigating seasonal stringency of the market was but a natural step to be taken next. To-day the function of the paper currency to serve as a weapon for fighting seasonal scarcity of money is quite well-established.

§ 4. The Government of India possesses three different kinds of reserves. They are (1) the Treasury Reserve which is a fluctuating amount; (2) the currency reserve; and (3) the gold standard reserve.

We have seen the relation that exists between the Treasury reserve and the Currency reserve. It remains now to examine the connection between the currency and the gold standard reserves. The gold standard reserve has a peculiar history of its own. Originally the gold reserve fund, it has grown out of the profits of the rupee coinage, and its declared object has been the maintenance of exchange—as if exchange can be maintained by means of reserves only. It is no wonder therefore that even in the work of maintaining the exchange value of the rupee the gold standard reserve should have been so sparingly used. It is still kept distinct from the paper currency reserve, although their functions overlap in many cases. It is, in fact, difficult to separate them in theory, and in practice they have very seldom been looked upon as distinct funds. The object of the gold standard reserve is ostensibly the maintenance of exchange,—the paper currency reserve is also openly declared to have that aim. Each may be used for this purpose, although it will depend on circumstances which is to be the instrument chosen. The use of the currency reserve for acting as a prop to exchange has been, however, very grudgingly conceded. But now, after its use for that purpose is undisputed, it is difficult to keep the currency reserve strictly apart from the gold standard reserve. In 1900 the Government was still not prepared to accept the new use of the currency reserve as a settled fact. In a Minute, Sir Edward Law wrote 'the sole object for which the currency reserve was originally constituted was to provide the necessary security for the encashment of notes on presentation, and there was certainly no idea of utilising the funds so held for exchange or any other purpose not directly connected with security for the note issue. The connection which has now arisen between the currency reserve and the maintenance of exchange appears to me to have come about in a somewhat fortuitous manner.' In 1904 the Government of India, while still emphatically of opinion that the primary and essential function of the paper currency reserve was to secure the convertibility of the notes into coin, yet, so long as that condition was scrupulously satisfied, they saw no reason why in the management of the reserve, they should not have regard to any incidental advantages which might arise therefrom. Their experience was that the currency reserve in the past formed 'an important, if not an essential part of the machinery by which the par of exchange between the sovereign and the rupee' (letter to Secretary of State, 295 of 1904) was maintained. It may be noted here that one of the motives for opening a gold branch of the reserve in England was the hope of its utilisation in maintaining exchange. In the exchange crisis of 1907, the reserve was freely used as a support for exchange. Gold was released from the paper currency reserve in London and the equivalent was transferred in India from the Treasury balances to paper currency. Later the practice became very well established. In spite of this apparent unity of purpose between the two reserves, the Chamberlain Commission did not think it wise to amalgamate them, but laid it down that the paper currency reserve should be regarded only as a second line of defence for exchange. This seems also to be the view officially held by the Government of India. But in practice the doctrine of a second line of defence has not been shown much respect. In 1919-20 for instance, when the disastrous policy of attempting to maintain a fast-declining exchange by selling reserve councils were being carried on, it was the paper currency reserve rather than the gold standard reserve that was more readily employed. It was impossible then to say which was the first line of defence and which was the second. Sir Malcolm Hailey in the Legislative Council gave three reasons for choosing the paper currency reserve. In the first place he said that the situation was one of high exchange, and that meant that the rupee equivalent of the paper currency sterling reserve stood then at a much smaller value than when the sterling was purchased. Therefore the right policy was to bring back to India portions of that reserve before operating on the gold standard reserve. His second point was based on practical considerations. He was anxious to transfer the paper currency sterling securities to India first, and then the Secretary of State would be able to utilise the gold standard reserve for his requirements if he found himself unable to sell a sufficient number of Council Bills. Thirdly, Hailey pointed out that operating against the paper currency reserve meant 'operating within the paper currency reserve. When you operate against gold standard reserve, it disappears,—it melts away,' and Government is under no obligation to replace it, whereas they were under a statutory obligation to replace the paper currency reserve. Hailey of course, did not explain whether replacing by anything, by creating securities on the spot—in other words replacing by freshly printed notes, was in reality worth much more than not replacing at all. However it is unnecessary to discuss here whether Hailey's arguments were valid or not. The fact remained that the paper currency reserve was preferred to the gold standard reserve, even for the work for which the latter was held to have been constructed.

Apart from this overlapping of objects between these two reserves, there are other common grounds too where they meet. Very often the same causes that affect one will also affect the other. Since one of them converts the paper rupee into the silver rupee and the other is intended to further convert the silver rupee into sovereigns, it follows that the two are linked together. Any change in any one will re-act on the other. The inter-action can be illustrated in many different ways. An excessive issue of paper currency, for instance, will not only put a strain on the paper currency reserve, but supposing it inflates the aggregate amount of currency in the country, will naturally reduce the gold value of the rupee-currency and thus affect the gold standard reserve too. An over-issue thus would create a run on the paper currency reserve as well as on the gold standard reserve. The exchange value of a currency depends on its purchasing power, as compared with the purchasing power of the currency in whose terms it is quoted. Anything that weakens that purchasing power would *prima facie* tend to lower its value and no amount of 'reserves' can stem its downward fall to the level justified by the purchasing power parity. In this respect, the divorce between the paper currency reserve and the gold standard reserve, unhappily, often results in working at cross purposes. On the one hand the government possibly tries to increase the size of the gold standard reserve, with the laudable object of maintaining the exchange. But the means adopted to swell that reserve, are exactly the means that inflate the currency of India and consequently defeat their own purpose by depressing the exchange value of the rupee. The more rupees the government coin, the bigger the gold standard reserve becomes, since it costs less than two shillings to make a rupee, but it is given a stamp of two shillings on it. The gold standard reserve is made out of the difference between the cost value and the created value. The only way to swell the reserve is to coin more rupees, but the only way to give the rupees a higher exchange value is to lessen their quantity in the country—not to speak of coining any more. Hence arises the apparent paradox that the greater the gold standard reserve, the less the chance of its maintaining exchange, as it pre-supposes an excess of rupees in India. If the government then offers to sell rupees at a higher value than what is justified by the purchasing power parity, the government would simply invite the squandering away of their reserves. It is not any reserves, but limitation of quantity that gives any currency a value. A system of reserves that does not bring about this limitation is of no use whatever. The distinction between the paper currency and the gold standard reserve has helped to obliterate these essentially sound principles. It costs very little to back a note by another note. It costs only a little more to back a note by a silver rupee which is also a note under a mask. So that it is quite possible to maintain an adequate reserve of rupees by coining rupees afresh and go on inflating the issue. The coining will add to the gold standard reserve, but the inflation which necessitated the coining will have pulled the value of the rupee downwards. The downward course of the exchange could then be said to be directly due to the altered paper currency policy. It is impossible to disjoin the paper currency from the exchange and hence equally impossible to disjoin the paper-currency reserve from the exchange reserve, which goes by the name of the gold standard reserve. If one more instance was needed to show the complicated relation between the two reserves, the case of the minting of bullion belonging to the paper currency reserve may be cited. Part of the reserve is held in bullion. When it is thus kept notes to the extent of only the purchase price of the bullion may then be issued. The gold standard reserve does not at all come in. But if now the bullion is coined, it will create more rupees than credit was taken (in rupees) for the sterling spent in purchasing the silver bullion. That is to say, if £1 was the amount spent in purchasing silver, then at the rate of Rs. 15 per £, notes to the extent of Rs. 15 could only be issued. But the £1 worth of silver would coin more than 15 actual rupees. This excess goes to the gold standard reserve. Part of the gold standard reserve thus may lie dormant and concealed in the paper currency reserve and may come out any moment when rupees are coined.

There is another consideration that tells against any sort of compartment outlook upon these two reserves. It is that in practice they are quite freely interchanged. Both the paper currency and the gold standard reserves are held in England and in India, and with a little bit of book-keeping mutual transfers and adjustments between the two can be easily carried out to suit the government's convenience. The general cases of such transfers occur mostly in connection with providing funds for the Secretary of State or for the maintaining of exchange. One or two special cases only may be noted here. To meet the depreciation of the capital value of securities in the paper currency reserve for instance, consols from that reserve were transferred in 1920 to the gold standard reserve 'obtaining from that reserve short term securities in their stead.' (Hailey in Legislative Council, 16th September, 1920.) Government also undertook to utilise—and it has been to some extent, actually carried into effect—any excess of the gold standard reserve beyond £40 million, in order to wipe out the created securities in the Indian portion of the paper currency reserves. It amounted to making a gift of part of the gold standard reserve to the paper currency reserve, and provided once more the fictitious nature of the partitioning, between the two.

§ 5. To summarise, there are three points at which the paper currency reserve touches the gold standard reserve. Both have some objects in common. Both are influenced by causes that affect any one of them. And thirdly, there are constant mutual transfers going on between the two. It is perfectly natural therefore that there should have risen a demand for the amalgamation of the two reserves into one. That demand is adequately voiced in the evidence before the Chamberlain Commission. Harrison's plea is worth quoting. If the rupee, he says in effect, is a note printed on silver and a note is a rupee printed on paper, both subordinate and calculated in terms of sterling and redeemable in terms of sterling, there is no reason why the reserves should not be amalgamated. One may add, either give up the pretension of trying to maintain the exchange value of the rupee or connect the convertibility of the rupee with the convertibility of the paper note into a direct link. Most of the witnesses before the Commission, however, spoke against the fusion. Lord Meston, the official spokesman, said that neither the government nor the public would like it. Lionel Abrahams saw the root of all trouble in using the two reserves for the same purpose, and recommended that they be distinctly kept apart and used for different purposes. F. W. Newmarch echoed the same view, but was prepared to allow the paper currency reserve being used as a subsidiary reserve to that of the gold standard reserve for the purposes of maintaining exchange. It should only be drawn upon as a last resource. The Commission's report was 'The overlapping which occurs between the functions of the two reserves makes the suggestion of amalgamation attractive, and it is possible that an amalgamation may be found desirable in the future. But at present the balance of advantage lies in separation' (para. 110, Report). This is still evidently the view of the Government of India, for the reserves still stand separated.*

§ 6. Having so far discussed the connection of the paper currency reserve with the other reserves of the Government of India, we may next come to the reserve proper and deal with the question of location. In 1861 nobody would have ever thought of holding any part of the reserve outside of India, but to-day the reserve may be practically held anywhere under the sun. The extension of the geographical area of the reserve started in 1898, in rather exceptional circumstances. In that year it was found necessary to hold a part of the reserve in gold in England. The reason in Newmarch's words 'was the excessive demand for the Secretary of State's bills which the Government of India was not able to meet from their Treasury balances—at

* The Hilton Young Commission, however, have been more logical. In view of the acknowledged overlapping of the two reserves, they have advocated their amalgamation. Their recommendation in this connection is, however, an inseparable part of a comprehensive plan of currency reform.

any rate, not able to conveniently meet.' Consequently the Act II of 1898 was passed which authorised the government to issue notes in India on the security of gold received in England. The Secretary of State could then set aside gold to the paper currency reserve in London and the Government of India could meet his drawings by issuing an equivalent amount of notes in India. This was done with a view to help the trade of the country which was demanding to buy more rupees in exchange for gold paid in England. It was, as Newmarch suggests, not possibly dictated by the necessities of the Secretary of State, as the Government of India also was quite as insistent in desiring the legislation as the Secretary of State. The Gold Note Act, as it has been called, was, however, a temporary measure valid only for six months. This indicates that the Government still had no mind to permanently shift a part of the currency reserve outside India. But the subsequent advantages of such a system, in helping exchange and transmitting funds between India and England, soon impressed the Government and Act 8 of 1898 extended the duration of the provisions of the previous Act from six months to a period of 2½ years. By 1900, it looked very much as if the provisions had come to stay. Act 8 of 1900 contained elaborate provisions for the holding of gold by the Secretary of State. It laid down that (1) the Secretary of State might hold gold against notes issued in India. (2) If the Secretary transmits the gold, the coin or gold so transmitted 'shall when received by the Government of India form part of the currency reserve.' It is to be noted that the transmitted gold was not to be reckoned as reserve until actually received by the Government of India. The practice of considering bullion on the way as part of the reserve was not yet developed. (3) Thirdly, if the Secretary of State bought silver with the gold and transmitted it, then the silver bullion so purchased would serve as currency reserve until rupees were coined out of it, when an amount of rupees equal to the purchase price of the silver would be credited to the currency reserve (the rest obviously going to the Gold Reserve Fund, later the Gold Standard Reserve). Authority to count silver bullion purchased by the Secretary of State, in the interval of purchase and mintage, as part of the paper currency reserve was taken earlier in 1898 also. This 1900 Act was also to remain in force for two years. Finally in 1902—by Act 9 the arrangement was made permanent by deleting the two years' duration clause. Although thus full power was taken to hold gold in England, the London Branch of the paper currency reserve was not formally opened until 1905 and it was not till 1906 that London gold as well as sterling securities began to figure regularly in the accounts of the reserve. Before 1905 although gold had been once so held, no portion of the security reserve had been held in London. Government has, however, been for some years past contemplating to hold a portion in sterling investments. They had quite good practical reasons for desiring to do so. The position of the rupee paper in the paper currency reserve had, owing to exchange difficulties, become quite precarious. When the system of investing a portion of the reserve was inaugurated, exchange difficulties had not made themselves appreciably felt. But as Sir E. F. G. Law wrote in 1900 (27th July) the situation then was different. He wrote, 'The market value and the ready convertibility of the rupee paper has been prejudicially influenced by exchange difficulties. There is practically no market out of India for rupee paper and in India the market is so small and so easily depressed, that were we suddenly called upon to realise our existing investments we should, I fear, most seriously depress their value and create something like a panic. I may point out that investments in gold securities cannot be prejudicially affected by exchange fluctuations.' It was mainly led by these considerations, that authority was taken to invest some limited part of the paper currency funds in sterling in London. Investment to the extent of 2 crores was first made in 1906, another 2 crores being added in 1911. The 1914 Commission was in favour of holding a limited reserve of gold securities in England. It justified the gold holding and summarised the principal advantages into two. First, gold there was required for purchasing silver with, London being the world's market for the white metal. Otherwise gold for that purpose would have to be shipped from India. By holding gold already in London,—the Government would be saved the not too-negligible costs of remittance. In the second place, gold in London had developed an important use, the maintenance of exchange. The Commission therefore would not remove it from there. Gold in India was not any more wanted, while in London the gold standard reserve was not by itself sufficient to maintain exchange. On much the same grounds as were advocated in 1900, by Sir Edward Law, the holding of English securities was now justified by the Commission. In its opinion 'too large holdings of Indian securities which were likely to be depreciated by the same causes as would possibly entail a run on the paper currency reserve, involving their sale' would be unwise. Therefore some investments in non-Government-of-India securities were a judicious step to take. The securities along with the gold holdings, would further strengthen the support for exchange. In this verdict the Commission was supported by many witnesses, but opposite views were not also wanting. One of the confirmed opponents to this scattering of the reserves between England and India was Sir Montague Webb. He, as well as Sir Dabida Dalal, with a good following, saw in it the sinister motive of benefiting the London financiers 'anxious to unload depreciating sterling security.' The arguments that have been put forward in support of the system, says Sir Montague, have only to be stated in juxtaposition, to stand self-condemned. 'Such a practice of holding a country's paper currency reserve in some other country on the other side of the world, is unprecedented in the history of any nation.' These are very strong words. On the whole, however, Sir Montague has been less convincing than loud in his attacks on the government. His arguments carry plenty of sting but not much of conviction. Most of the Indian witnesses condemned this exile of part of the currency reserve from India. Mr. Sundara Iyer said 'There is absolutely no justification for keeping the reserves in England.' Dalal said 'Gold belonging to the paper currency reserve held in London has no mission to perform there save to underpin the weak gold foundations of the English joint stock banks.' Thackersay and Chunilal Saraiya also could not approve of the London holdings. Sir Daniel Hamilton who wanted the reserve to do some very peculiar services for the development of the country, would hold the reserve partly in London and partly in India. On the other hand, Newmarch and Abrahams, to name only two among a large number, justified the existing arrangements, characterising them as a most expeditious and convenient way of transferring funds and buying silver, as well as maintaining exchange.

§ 7. Thus by 1914, the system of sharing the reserve between England and India was well established. There was just one other development in connection with the location of the reserve before the war. It is worthy of notice here. It was that by Act 3 of 1905 power was taken to regard coin and bullion in transmission between England and

India also as part of the reserve. Then the exigencies of the war further expanded the area of the holding of the reserves and by a series of Acts power was taken to hold them practically anywhere in the world. The great silver famine, as well as the dangerous state of the note issue, almost bordering on inconvertibility, sent the government in anxious search for silver wherever obtainable. In 1917 coin or bullion held on behalf of the Governor-General in Council by or under the control of the government of any part of His Majesty's Dominions for coining or such other temoprary purposes, together with coin or bullion in transit between any such parts and India, was to be considered as part of the reserve. A further widening of the currency reserve map occurred a year later. Act 13 of 1918 authorised silver held in U. S. A. or in transit therefrom, as part of the reserve, and to this provision was added gold also by Act 26 of 1919. The temporary Act of 1920 (Act 21 of 1920) brought together these different provisions, so that gold coin and bullion could be held in any part of His Majesty's Dominions. Gold and silver held in U. S. A. or in transmission therefrom was also deemed to be part of the reserve. In the meantime the Currency Committee of 1919 had gone into the whole question and recommended that the 'silver reserves should, as in the past, be normally held in India, but silver under purchase or in the course of shipment should be treated as part of the reserve pending its arrival in India.' The gold also in the Paper Currency Reserve should normally be held in

India, but some paper currency gold may at times be held in London, either because it has been purchased there and is awaiting shipment, or because it is held in anticipation of its use in payment for purchases of silver. Of the securities held in the Paper Currency Reserve the Government of India's securities would naturally be held in India, while the remainder would be held in the United Kingdom where they would be redeemable or realisable in the event of need (Report, para. 81). It may be noted that the recommendation to hold most of the gold in India was made in response to the strong demand made by Indians in the past—the Commission being of opinion that public satisfaction was a great asset in currency affairs. The spirit of these recommendations has been followed in the permanent constitution of the paper currency drawn out in later legislation. The almost unconscious way in which the Indian domicile of the reserve has, through force of circumstances, been substituted by a more cosmopolitan habitation, is now fairly well accepted as a settled fact. The Act of 1923 provides that coin or bullion, whether it is held in England or in India, or in any part of His Majesty s Dominions, or is in course of transmission to or from any of these parts, may be legitimately regarded as part of the reserve. U. S. A. has been omitted from the list, as it is not anticipated that another silver crisis and another Pittman Act will ever have to be faced again. Securities, forming the other part of the reserve may not, however, be held anywhere else except in India and England.

A question has been raised embracing some legal niceties, which may only be just mentioned in closing this chapter. It has been doubted whether it is safe to keep any part of the reserve with the Secretary of State, seeing that he is not bound by the Indian Paper Currency Act. Whatever its constitutional aspect, practically viewed, the question need not take away any one's sleep and rest. The Government of India is bound by the Currency Acts and wherever it keeps its reserves it has to account for all of them. For paper currency purposes the existence of the Secretary of State may be ignored. I mention this legal tweedledum because it finds a place in the evidence before the 1914 Commission. Now that paper currency funds may be kept in all parts of His Majesty's Dominions, such a question may arise with even greater reason in their case.

CHAPTER VII.

THE COVER OF THE ISSUE (*Continued*).

The Composition of the Reserve.

Sec. 1. The history of the composition of the reserve represents progress from rigidity towards elasticity, p. 142.—Sec. 2. The gold portion of the reserve as it grew up under successive currency Acts, p. 143.—Sec. 3. Criticism of the policy of holding gold in the reserve, p. 147.—Sec. 4. The silver portion of the reserve, p. 154.—Sec. 5. The history of the security portion of the reserve. The process of expansion through successive stages, p. 158.—Sec. 6. A detailed examination of the war and post-war inflation of the paper currency, p. 166. —Sec. 7. The sale of Reverse Councils in 1919-20, consequent on the adoption of the new exchange policy, affects materially the constitution of the security reserve, p. 171.—Sec. 8. The enormous and unsatisfactory fiduciary issue, as it stood in 1920, product of war-inflation and altered exchange policy, p. 176.—Sec. 9. Readjustment of the paper currency as attempted by Act 45 of 1920. Temporary and permanent provisions, p. 178.—Sec. 10. The futility of the permanent provisions. The proposed methods for bringing them into operation, only partially followed, p. 181.—Sec. 11. Limit of fiduciary issue further raised in 1925, p. 189.

§ 1. Like the question of location, the composition of the paper currency reserve has an interesting history behind it. The main consideration, it has been noted, influencing the formation of the reserve has been the convertibility of the note. Hence great emphasis has always been put on the rupee holdings in India. But as the paper currency habit gradually took root in India, and the danger of any crisis of inconvertibility receded more and more into the distance, the metallic reserve was, by degrees, diluted with various kinds of securities. The process was evidently profitable in view of the interest yielded by the securities. Simultaneously, the necessity of introducing elements of elasticity into the note-issue acted as an additional driving force, in speeding up the process. The field of investments was gradually widened. Not only did they form an increasing portion of the whole of the reserve, but greater latitude was being given to the Government in the choice of securities. Here, as in the matter of the location of the reserve, the story has been the story of expansion in all directions. The Act of 1861 provided a rigid note-issue system. The stringent restrictions on the reserve were softened down by a series of Acts, that slowly but steadily increased the amount of security holdings. In 1920 at last, after being cabined for nearly sixty years, the Indian paper currency system broke free from all rigidity. Instead of prescribing a maximum limit of security-issue, a half and half security and metal basis was now laid down. Further an outlet was provided for emergency issue of currency on the foundation of self-retiring trade bills. It is possible to quarrel with the particular ratio in which the reserve has now been divided between metal and securities. As a matter of fact there have been innumerable other suggestions as to the proportion of the component parts. But they can never conceal the fact that the composition of the reserve has been vastly changed from what it was in 1861.

§ 2. In tracing the changes in this composition, it will be convenient to take up the three parts of the reserve, *viz.*, gold, silver and securities, one after another. Gold may be taken up first. It will be recalled that gold was allowed into the paper currency reserve through a permissive clause in the Act of 1861, to a very limited extent. Only one-fourth of the total metallic reserve could be in gold. Gold was not yet legal tender in India and it was more with an eye to its future monetisation rather than on considerations of its efficiency in the reserve, that an humble place was found for it. Gold first came into the reserve actually in 1865, after a notification had been issued on the 23rd November, 1864, saying that notes would be issued in exchange for sovereigns and half-sovereigns at the rate of Rs. 10 per sovereign. From 1865 to 1875, gold figured in progressively dwindling quantities in the paper currency reserve, when in view of the fall in the price of silver, that is, of the rise in the price of gold, gold ceased to come in at that low ratio. The notification was thus made a dead letter. For many years gold was completely out of the reserve. Then, in accordance with the report of the 1893 Commission, which cherished ambitious projects of introducing the gold standard into India, notes were declared issuable for gold at a fixed ratio of 7.53344 grains Troy of fine gold to a rupee, in other words at the rate of 16*d*. to the rupee. This was done by a notification in 1893—the feature of this new notification was that whereas formerly gold holdings could not exceed one-fourth of the total metal reserve no limit was put now. The invitation however had no immediate effect. Gold appears in the reserve in India only as late as in 1898. In that year a new opening was made for it by means of the Gold Note Act. We have already seen how this piece of legislation was passed at first as a temporary measure to meet the urgency of the demand for rupees in India. After being twice re-enacted, the provisions of the Act were made permanent in 1902. Henceforward the Secretary of State could receive gold in England against notes issued in India. In importance this new outlet for gold considerably eclipsed the other part of the gold reserve that was held in India, although from 1906 onwards gold steadily accumulated equally in India as in England. Very soon new purposes were discovered for the currency gold in London. The London gold became the centre of all attention and a great controversy sprang up over the propriety of holding gold in England, in the midst of which people forgot to ask the fundamental question if any gold was at all useful in the reserve, if even the Indian holding of gold in its turn, was of any value. Gold had been declared legal tender in 1899 and that meant equal opportunities for gold coin and bullion and silver rupees (issues against silver bullion having been naturally stopped meanwhile) to be converted into notes. It meant also that notes were payable at the option of the Government in gold coins or in silver rupees legal tender in India. Whatever might have been the ultimate objects of the Government, a kind of bimetallism was thus established. Apart from some mysterious powers ascribed to gold, it was difficult to see why gold was introduced into the currency reserve at all. Government did not want bimetallism. If the reserve was meant as imposing a check on the issue of notes, the service that all reserves unconsciously perform, and thereby give the notes the only condition of value and acceptability, namely, scarcity, the introduction of gold would not certainly serve that in any way. Notes could be now easier to issue against both gold and silver, than they were only against silver. It was easier to inflate the total currency of India now than before, but there was no effective means of contracting the currency. Government did not undertake to return the gold at the rate at which it received it, although up to the time of the difficulties of the War it always tried to supply gold as a general rule of administrative practice. The War developments conclusively proved the difficulties of the "dyarchy" currency of India—composed of gold as well as silver. The gold in the currency reserve is valued at whatever rate the Government chooses to value it, but the people of the country will not always like to receive it at that rate. At certain rates Government will be unwilling to pay it, at other rates the people will be unwilling to receive it, so that the use of the currency gold for the convertibility of the note, is of doubtful efficiency. If in times of panic, the Government forces gold at its own rates, the result would be as good as declaring the inconvertibility of the notes. It is not reserves, but scarcity which reserves imply, that makes notes and all kinds of token currencies acceptable to the people. By adding gold to silver rupees in the reserve, the strength of the reserve is physically hardly more increased than if it be only in silver, while the scarcity of the notes is considerably sacrificed. No convincing arguments, in fact, have ever been given in defence of the gold holdings of the paper currency reserve, or indeed of the general introduction of gold into the currency of India. It has not strengthened the reserve physically, as people want silver rupees, not gold coins. It has failed in its much vaunted task of maintaining exchange at fixed rates. It seems to have only complicated the currency system of India.

§ 3. To turn to the history of the gold reserve. As noted above, the propriety of holding part of it in London, while the holding of any gold reserve at all in India or outside has been left unquestioned—has been very seriously challenged. Our Government has, however, always looked upon it with favour. In 1905 they wrote (quoted from the evidence before the 1914 Commission), " subject to the provision of sufficient rupees, we would allow our gold reserves to grow indefinitely with the expansion of the note circulation, until such time as the invested portion may be raised again. It would strengthen our credit and contribute to the stability of exchange." The holding of a portion of the reserve in England was justified on the ground that " coin held in London was actually nearer the point where it could be useful." The mysterious faith in gold that somehow it would add to the credit of India, was shown by John Morley, the Secretary of State for India, also. " The possession of a large amount of gold by the Secretary of State in Council, or the Government of India " he wrote, " as part of the paper currency reserve, or in the Treasury balances, is of considerable advantage to India as helping to maintain confidence in the permanence of the gold standard and in the stability of the exchange value of the rupee." The evidence before the 1914 Commission showed a variety of opinion. Discussion was however focussed wholly on the portion of the gold reserve held in London. The arguments of the Government in favour of the system summarised by Webb, were first, that gold in London could more economically and quickly buy silver. Secondly the India Office could more easily appropriate and interchange the money with the general Treasury balances and with the gold standard reserve as might be found convenient from time to time. This was obviously a kind of non-currency use for the reserve. Thirdly, the money would be readily available to support exchange in case of a diminished demand for rupee currency. Lastly, gold was not all of it required in India, where already sufficient rupee stores were kept. Sir Montague, it is needless to add, was not convinced by any of these arguments. But they were good enough for many other witnesses. It is useless to reproduce here the individual opinions of all the witnesses—but both for and against the system an equal degree of conviction was displayed. The Indian witnesses generally wanted to bring all the gold back to India. The Commission in its report, justified the gold portion of the reserve held in London, on the double ground of its suitability for the purchase of silver, as London was the principal source of supply, and on its possible usefulness in maintaining exchange. They pointed out that gold accumulated in India would have to be needlessly shipped to London again for buying silver with. Their recommendations dealt with the gold reserve in London, but they never went further to examine the main question of the whole of the gold reserve at all—whether gold, in India or in England, should form any part of the currency reserve. They took that for granted, and were simply concerned about the distribution of the gold. It is quite true as the Commission argued, that the accumulation of an excessive quantity of gold in India is not desirable, but why accumulate at all ? Why not stop issuing notes against gold ?

It must be admitted that the introduction of gold into the reserve made the paper currency of India more elastic. That is perhaps the only claim that can be made on its behalf, but this advantage is rather dearly earned. It works against the other declared objects of the gold reserve. The advantages claimed for the gold holding in London are perhaps quite substantial as far as they go, but in view of the complications that it introduces, they hardly go far enough. No one disputes the fact that gold in London economises the costs of silver purchases, but provided the currency policy is adjusted with an eye upon the price-level of the country, which should be the most important if not the only consideration, guiding that policy, and the ideas of inflation or deflation are banished,—the necessities of silver purchases will, it is presumed, be only few and far between. It is also undisputed that the existence of the currency gold in London helps remittance of funds between India and England, but that it is admittedly not a primary function of the currency reserves. Government may transfer funds just as efficiently as other private corporations do without having to interfere with the currency mechanism. The other claim about maintenance of exchange is as false as it is mischievous. As has been said before, it is comparative price-levels and not the holdings of the reserves, however big they may be, that condition exchange. It is mischievous in the sense that the paper currency reserve should only try to convert the rupee-note into rupees. To expect it to convert the rupees further into sovereigns, at the same time dissociating it from the special gold standard reserve, expressly constructed for that purpose, leads to a confusion in policy. The only real advantage, as said in the beginning of this paragraph, that seems to stand on examination—and this applies to gold in England and India alike—is that it has helped to introduce some amount of elasticity into the note-issue. Whereas formerly only, on the tender of silver rupees mainly, notes were issuable, the permission to issue against gold certainly brought some relief to a rigid paper currency system. But as has already been indicated, it gave an outlet for expansion only. Government was not legally bound to return the gold and cancel the notes even at its own receipt-rates, and hence the circulation could not shrink. The elasticity was thus an one-sided one. In so far as the circulation expanded against gold tendered in London, it was a sort of extra-country elasticity. At least one disadvantage of that is mentioned by the 1914 Commission. It was that the " expansion of currency of India was at the expense of the gold reserves of London, and in some circumstances the resulting stringency in

London was so disadvantageous to India as to make an expansion of currency by this means naturally undesirable." There is not much in this argument, as gold must be had from somewhere if it is to go into the reserve. It is impossible to both have the cake and eat it. If the currency was to be expanded without causing any stringency anywhere, the only way to do so was to print notes right away, without any gold or silver reserves. The Commission's objection is instructive as illustrating the view-point of a class of expansionists who are pure inflationists in disguise. The real objection was that the method founded elasticity wholly on the external trade of India. There was no means of expanding the currency with the growth of the internal commerce of the country. But perhaps on the ground of something being better than nothing, the Commission advocated the retention of the system of issue against gold tendered in London. The developments that have taken place since the Commission reported have however, in a large measure, made that method of elasticity practically unnecessary. Whatever merit it had before, now that elasticity has been secured by establishing a proportional metallic reserve method for the issue, as well as by provision of seasonal issues—the gold issue must be regarded as having outlived its purpose. The question is a very difficult one. Like many points of reform about the paper currency, it cannot possibly be discussed apart from the question of the monetary standard of India. If bi-metallism is what we want and in a sense that is what we at present have, in spite of all the beautiful names we choose to give it, then by all means let the arrangements be as they are. If we want to have an independent rupee standard, which in the opinion of the present writer is the most sensible thing to do, the issue of notes against gold will be found to be incompatible with the ideal.*

It seems right to conclude therefore that the objections against the holding of gold in the paper currency reserve far out-weigh the advantages of the policy. It brings with it many complications mostly noted above, and not the least of which is the problem of the valuation of the gold. For want of a fixed rating, the gold portion of the paper currency reserve is practically an unknown quantity. The reserve may shrink or swell if a change is made in the rating. A recent example is furnished by the 2*s*. valuation of gold in place of the former 1*s*. 4*d*. The first notification in 1864 invited gold at the rate of 2*s*. to the rupee. In 1920 after a long lapse of time paper currency history in this respect repeated itself. The result of the new valuation was the shrinkage of the paper currency reserves by a considerable amount and the void had to be filled up by creating new securities, since otherwise the circulation would have to be greatly contracted. The gold in the currency reserve, after it is received, is earmarked at the Bank of England. The Bank of England makes no charge for the actual " earmark-

* The adoption of a policy of gold standard would correspondingly involve far-reaching changes in the composition of the reserve and in that regard, the comprehensive proposals of the Hilton Young Commission deserve careful consideration. The proposals however cannot be examined here, for they are part and parcel of a scheme of reconstruction and would involve a lengthy digression into the question of general monetary policy.

ing " but a small charge of $\frac{1}{32}d$ per cent. per year is made for holding the gold. When the amount was smaller they charged $\frac{1}{16}d$. This charge is supposed to be for storage and safe custody. It should be taken account of when regarding the gold reserve as offering economies in the purchase of silver. Various suggestions have been made regarding the figure at which the gold reserve of the Paper Currency should stand. The 1914 Commission observed that the total amount of gold " naturally fluctuated inversely with the total stock of rupees in the reserve." But in their opinion " gold (in India) should not accumulate so as to send it back to London later." What was to be a sufficient stock of rupees was to rest on the Government's judgment. It was of course to vary from slack to busy seasons. For normal times, that is, supposing rupees were plentiful in India, they recommended a gold reserve of Rs. 50 million in England, to serve as a second line of defence for exchange ' standing behind the gold standard reserve.' These recommendations were, after the war, still considered sound by the 1919 Committee whose recommendation of holding a partial gold reserve in London, but transferring the main bulk of it to India, on the ground of satisfying Indian public opinion, has already been noticed. Following this recommendation, for the first time in 1920 (Act 45) a limit of Rs. 50 million was put on the gold bullion capable of being held in England. No restrictions were imposed on the size of the gold accumulation in India. The permanent provisions of the 1923 Act (not yet in force) repeat this Rs. 50

million limit, but the temporary provisions do not seem to contain any such restriction of amount.

§ 4. So much about the gold in the reserve. The history of the silver portion of the Paper Currency Reserve has been comparatively simple and uneventful. As notes are convertible into rupees and silver rupees are what the Indian public mostly demands (attempts to force sovereigns into circulation having failed more than once) it was early recognised that silver should form the bulk of the reserve and that practically the whole of it should be held in India. Silver held outside India serves no useful purpose. In actual practice, very seldom, if ever has silver beyond the frontiers of India figured in the currency reserve. If sometimes it had temporarily to be so included in it, the policy has been to bring the silver over to India as speedily as possible. Authority thus to regard silver held by the Secretary of State, as part of the reserve, was taken first by the 1898 Act. Silver is, as a rule, bought in England, and it takes some time before it can be sent to India and coined into rupees. The Act provides that silver bullion in the interval of purchase and mintage could be legally reckoned as part of the reserve. The 1905 Act expressly recognised all coin and bullion in transit to be part of the reserve. These provisions were designed for securing administrative convenience and had no other motives except that. It was only during the war, when the silver reserves in India fell dangerously low that legislation had to be passed empowering the Government to include silver held in all parts of the Empire, as well as in the U. S. A., in the reserve. It was then a question not of administrative facility, merely, but of choosing between convertibility and inconvertibility of the note-issue. The percentage of silver rupees to the whole issue had fallen to near about 30, and but for the temporary legislations expanding the geographical locale of the currency reserve, a critical situation would have arisen. Although once before in 1900, a still lower percentage of silver rupees, perhaps the lowest point on record, namely, 18 per cent. of the whole issue had been reached, still the situation was then not so threatening as in the uncertain after-math of the War. We have already referred to the Pittman Act by which silver was purchased from the U. S. A. in 1918. It is to be hoped that no such emergency will arise again. The latest Currency Act (1923) provides for silver to be held in any part of His Majesty's Dominions or in transit between any such parts and India.

Quite an interesting chapter in the history of the silver reserve is the rise and disappearance of an ' ingot ' silver reserve in the first decade of the century. It arose out of the necessity of having to meet a persistent demand for rupees in India against sterling tendered in London, which was a feature of the times. Consequently, with the permission of the Secretary of State, the Government of India decided since the autumn of 1904, to keep a portion of the paper currency reserve in India, in the shape of silver ingots ' so far prepared for coinage after melting, alligating, assaying, etc., that rupees could be made within five days. Credit for these rupees was taken in the paper currency reserve at their bullion value and the amount of the reserve so held was at first 300 lakhs of rupees, that is, silver purchased at a cost of £2 million (exchange at 15 rupees to the pound). This silver would of course produce much more than 300 lakhs of rupees, but the excess over 300 lakhs would be a credit to the gold standard reserve,' (Newmarch Memorandum, 1914 Commission). It was hoped that this ingot reserve would serve as a hidden stock of bullion from which rupees could be speedily obtained in the event of any unforeseen demand. But the demand for rupees was even greater than the reach of the Ingot reserve. Heavy coinage had to be undertaken in the years 1905-06. The experience of the years proved the inadequacy of the ingot reserve for the purposes for which it was created and ' steps,' says the Currency Report for 1905-06, ' were taken for its replacement by a reserve of greater capabilities and of a different character.' This was nothing other than the merging of the ingot reserve into the gold standard reserve—which was the more natural course to take. Since then, the ingot fund had remained incorporated in that reserve, and has appeared practically as the silver portion of the gold standard reserve held in India.

It may be noted here that originally notes were issuable against silver bullion at fixed rates. After the rupee was made a token coin, commanding a higher nominal than intrinsic value, the practice of issuing against silver bullion had naturally to be put a stop to, on exactly the same ground as the issue of notes on the presentation of printing paper, is disallowed. The valuation of the silver bullion in the reserve follows its purchase price at the rate of exchange accepted by the Government.

The procedure of silver purchase is thus described in the 1920 Manual of Paper Currency—'Purchases of bullion are made from funds in the Treasury in London or India, to recoup which notes and coins from currency are issued to the Reserve Treasury (now displaced by the Imperial Bank of India) on receipt of a transfer order from the Controller of Currency. The shipment of any silver bullion from London or elsewhere to one of the Mints, is advised by the Controller of Currency to the Mint Master who on its arrival credits the *approximate* value as currency silver in process of coinage,' in the Mint Chest Account.........As soon as the exact invoice value is known, the difference is adjusted by payment to Reserve Treasury or *vice versa*. The value of the bullion shown in the account is thus eventually the exact sum expended on its purchase. Some slight change in this rule to value silver bullion according to its purchase price had to be made in 1923 to meet a special situation. At that time a considerable quantity of worn and returned small silver coins had to be melted and kept as bullion. It was no use re-coining them immediately, as there was no demand for them. It would have been wasteful to re-issue them after re-coining. Hence they were put into the paper currency reserve. But according to the Paper Currency Act bullion could only be valued at its purchase price. In this case the purchase price was unknown—as the bullion was not purchased at all. To take credit for it at its existing sale price would have meant loss of some funds. Hence, to patch up the hole that had been discovered in the Paper Currency Act, as a measure of administrative convenience, as A. C. McWatters explained in the Council of State (19th July, 1923), a new silver bullion revaluation clause was added to it. This was done by Act 36 of 1923 (received assent of the Governor-General on the 3rd August, 1923). It provided, among others, that for the purpose of valuation of silver bullion, ' the sum expended in the purchase of silver bullion obtained by melting down silver coin issued under the authority of the Governor-General in Council shall be deemed to be the value of the bullion calculated at the rate of the rupee for 165 grains Troy of fine silver '—in other words the amount of silver contained, for instance, in two-half rupees would, though its actual value be much less than that, be rated as being purchased for one rupee.

§ 5. We now come to the security part of the reserve. It will be recalled that in 1861, a maximum issue of four crores was all that was allowed against securities Beyond that every note had to be backed by specie. Although thereby the issue was made very rigid, yet there was every justification for being on the safe side, even at the cost of elasticity. Both the newness of the experiment of a Government paper currency as well as the peculiar circumstances of India, demanded a comparatively high metallic reserve. But as gradually the people grew more and more used to the new currency and as the circulation increased, the security reserve had to be enlarged by degrees. Since then the security reserve has shown a steady two-dimensional growth. Not only has the total quantity of securities capable of being held in the reserve been increased in different stages, but there has been *pari passu* an enlargement of the area where they could be held. A greater freedom in the choice of securities,—the product of necessity as well as of convenience—has also had to be granted. Briefly speaking, this growth has been caused by three motives : (1) to introduce elements of elasticity into the note-issue, as by degrees the tyrannical hold of the convertibility doctrine gave way, (2) to safeguard against depreciation by holding a multiplicity of securities instead of only those of the Government of India, the solitary class of paper allowed by the 1861 Act, and (3) thirdly, to maintain exchange, as far as exchange was supposed to have been maintained merely by reserves outside India. To these considerations some special emergency reasons were added during the War which was the period that witnessed the most phenomenal increase in the stock of securities in the reserve.

The progress of legislation by which the fiduciary issue was successively raised, may be briefly traced. The four crores limit held good up to 1870, when by Act 15 of the year it was increased to six crores (a crore = 10 million). The next rise came in 1890, from six crores to eight crores. Six years later by Act 21 of 1896 the maximum was still further raised to ten crores. These figures referred to the price paid in the purchase of securities—their value after the purchase might have, of course, stood at quite different sums. But not until late in their history, had the problem of depreciation of their value ever to be seriously faced. In 1905 important changes were made in regard to the security reserve. The maximum limit was raised to 12 crores, but the extra 2 crores was to be held by the Secretary of State in England in securities of the United Kingdom of Great Britain and Ireland. It was the first time that the locale of the security reserve had been extended out of India. The Government had for some years past been contemplating opening up such a security reserve in London. The growing exchange difficulties had made the ready convertibility of the rupee paper too uncertain to rely on. For the sake of security the Government wanted to hold along with the rupee securities, some other more solid class of securities, such as Consols for which there was a world-wide market. A proposal for conversion of rupee-paper into sterling was made by the Government of India to the Secretary of State as early as in September, 1900. But for various reasons, the proposal had fallen through. The 1905 provision was therefore a welcome measure to the Government. It allowed them to hold their eggs in two different baskets. Besides, as the 1914 Commission justified the holding, it was unwise to have 'too large holdings of a security which was likely to be depreciated by the same causes as would possibly entail a run on the paper currency reserve involving their sale.' Once started, the London reserve came in handy for various other purposes, not the least of which was that it was freely used in the cause of exchange. In that capacity it impressed the 1914 Commission, who recommended its retention on that ground among others. From 1905 to 1910 no further interference with the security reserve was made. In 1911 (Act 7) the amount of non-Government-of-India holdings by the Secretary of State was increased from 2 to 4 crores, so that along with the permissible Government of India securities, the total reached 14 crores. There the figure remained until the difficulties of the War tremendously accelerated the process of watering. There was an increase of only 10 crores on the fiduciary issue during over fifty years before the War. Between 1915 and 1919, the permissible total had climbed up from 14 to 120 crores,—an almost incredible pace of expansion. Most of this expansion was effected by means of Ordinances, later given the form of temporary Acts. The first came in 1915 (Act I). While no change was made in the amount of non-Government of India securities, the total amount of securities permitted was increased to 20 crores (which meant 16 Indian and 4 non-Indian securities). By 1916, a still bigger leap had to be taken. In the first place, an alteration in the distribution of the 20 crores reserve was made so that the non-Government of India securities could rise up to 10 crores, and the Indian securities could be 10 crores. Secondly, a step of far-reaching importance was taken by providing for an additional issue of 6 crores (apart from the 20 crores) against British Treasury Bills, notwithstanding anything contained in the Paper Currency Acts. The reasons for this step can be best given in the words of an official publication, *viz.*, the Currency Report for

1915-16. 'The first step,' it says, 'in increasing the fiduciary reserve was taken in connection with the financing of the cotton crop. In order to provide Government with the necessary resources, (*a*) to enable them to place the banks in funds for helping this trade, also any other trade requiring assistance and (*b*) if necessary to meet other liabilities in the event of unexpected emergency, the permissible investments in India were increased.' The explanation for wanting to issue notes against British Treasury Bills was that later there was a brisk demand for Council Bills, but the Treasury Balances in India were unable to meet them 'owing to large disbursements made in India on behalf of the Home Government. (1915-16 Report, *vide* also Financial Statement, 1914-15.) It was of course open to the Government to receive gold in England and issue notes in India. But such earmarking of gold would have put a strain on the gold resources of England. It was a time when nations feverishly began conserving their gold holdings, unmindful of all consequences of their policy and methods—as if the mere presence of gold in the balance sheet of a country would act as a charm against all financial maladies. The fallacy of this blind desire for gold was of course yet to be discovered with the German monetary system going to pieces, in spite of a huge window-dressing of gold holdings. Whatever that may be, there is no doubt that the Indian Government was moved by a genuine desire not to embarrass the Home Government by demanding to earmark gold. The Finance Member Sir William Meyer said (Legislative Council, 21st March, 1916),

'In present circumstances however, it is very undesirable for the Secretary of State to lock up more gold than it is absolutely necessary and it is of course still more out of the question for him to stop Council drawings and let gold come out here as a private import.' It must be remembered that not only was not gold very difficult to safely tranship—but after the outbreak of the war, an embargo was placed on the export of gold from belligerent countries. Sir William Meyer also spoke of such things as 'assisting the Home Government by refraining further from earmarking of gold on account of the paper currency in London.' The result was that rupees were liberated in India in exchange for British Treasury Bills tendered in London, at a rate very favourable to England. It amounted to making very substantial payments by India to His Majesty's Government in an indirect way. It was India's unknown and unrecognised contribution to the cost of the war. If instead of consenting to receive British Treasury Bills at the rate of 1*s*. 4*d*. a rupee, the Indian Government had demanded gold for its earmarking at the Bank, the value of the rupee would have certainly risen higher. Owing to the increase in the price-level in England, the sterling was fast depreciating in terms of the dollar and other currencies. In the absence of gold being sent away as a corrector and leveller of inter-national price-levels, such a depreciation could not be helped in any way. New York in other words, refused to receive sterling at the rate of 4.86 dollars to the pound, and hence the dollar went up in price. In India's case, the exchange was 'pegged' so to say, by artificial means. Government undertook to sell rupees at 1*s*. 4*d*. and thus India's help towards the War could be purchased at far less cost than a higher Indian Exchange would have entailed. The event was, in a sense, of considerable theoretical interest and importance. Normally, it is the price-level that changes first and independently and then drags along exchange after it. Both India and England, in view of the difficulties of transferring funds had become countries with practically, what Gustav Cassel calls 'independent currencies.' The Indian price-level was not changing as fast as the English and hence there was a tendency for the rupee to go up in terms of sterling. But it was kept down by the new facilities offered of issuing rupees at the old rate. Instead of the price-level determining exchange, the price-level of India was changed (for that was what new issues of rupees at the old rate meant), to suit the old exchange rate. It was a case of the tail wagging the dog. Over and over again, throughout the whole history—a rather sad one—of the war manipulations of our currency, the abnormal has taken the place of the normal. This was but one instance among many. Later, when the tragedy of selling reverse Council Bills at impossible rates was being staged, the Government showed the same disregard for the price-level. It began to sell sterling for rupees at rates much higher than what the purchasing power parity would justify. The only way to carry that policy to a success would have, of course, been to make rupees scarcer in India and thus make them command that higher value. While the Government sold away

2*s*. 8*d*. or even 2*s*. 10*d*. for every rupee, the method by which the sales were conducted produced no reduction in the amount of rupees circulating in India. The saner way would have been to dispose of sterling or British Treasury Bills and cancel the equivalent in notes in India so that ultimately rupees might be scarce enough. But nothing like this was done. The sterling resources were dissipated at ruinous rates, but at the same time currency inflation was kept where it was, by substituting *ad hoc* or created securities for the British Treasury Bills lost. Ultimately therefore no appreciable shrinkage was done in the amount of paper currency in India. The Government was the monopolist seller of rupees. Never did a monopolist injure his own interests in a more foolish way. It refused to take off supplies from the market and still wanted to enforce a high price for its goods. The consequence was what was to be expected. The rupee never commanded the 2*s*. gold price. The Government utterly failed in its attempt to take it to that price on the point of almost losing the whole of its reserves. Thus was the penalty paid for forgetting the simple law that the value of anything, currencies not excepted, depends on its scarcity, and not on gold or silver reserves. The exchange value of a currency is intimately linked with its purchasing power. If we arbitrarily fix the exchange value, in order to maintain that, we shall have to alter the price-level to suit it. If we keep the price-level intact, we may have to alter the exchange from time to time. In Indian currency history greater and almost one-sided attention has been paid to the exchange, letting the price-level ' go hang '* rather than keeping prices steady and letting exchange 'go hang.' It is time to turn over a new leaf and start a new currency policy, based on the principle of a stable price-list.

§ 6. To return to the story of the war-inflation. The 1915 and 1916 Acts initiated the new developments. It speaks a great deal about the spirit of currency passivity in India that such an important Act as that of 1916 was introduced into the Legislative Council, business rules suspended, taken immediately into consideration and passed in perhaps five minutes, without a single word of comment from any member. As has been said it authorised for the first time a special issue of six crores against British Treasury Bills. It was the beginning of a mighty Treasury Bill issue. Very little the Government itself knew perhaps that they were taking the lid out of a jar from amidst which the giant was to come out who would over-power them later. The Act contained another significant provision, authorising the inclusion in the reserve of securities created by the Government of India and issued to the High Commissioner of paper currency. This provision also, put almost stealthily into the Act, was destined to play a great part in the later history of the currency.

With the twin Acts of 1915 and 1916 India was thus safely laid on the inclining plane of currency inflation. Henceforward the fiduciary issue went up by leaps and bounds. More currency, thanks to

* As Prof. Cannan would say.

the vicious circle that it breeds, demanded still more money after it. The total permissible security issue in 1916 stood at 26 crores, of which 10 crores Indian plus 4 crore non-Indian, represented the permanent holdings. By increasing the non-Indian part to 10 crores, 6 crores more had been added to the Secretary of State's holdings. Apart from this 20 (14 permanent and 6 temporary) provision was made for six crores of additional issue against British Treasury Bills. By Act II of 1917 the special extra issue against British Treasury Bills was increased to 30 crores, making a total fiduciary issue of 50 crores. Act 19 of 1917 took it to 42 crores (total therefore 20 + 42 = 62 crores), and Act 6 of 1918 to 66 crores (total, 20 + 66 = 86 crores). After the British Treasury Bills had begun to come in so rapidly, various new advantages were naturally discovered for them. They were declared to be the best kind of short-dated securities that the Government of India could think of putting into the reserve. They commanded an instant saleability. But as Sir B. N. Sarma complained later in the Legislative Council, protesting against the sale of reserve councils, many of the virtues of these liquid assets had disappeared by then. When purchased they were considered as good as gold; when disposed of, they were greatly in discount compared to gold. In 1919, although the war had ended, the necessity of inflating currency in India had not yet done so. Expenditure showed no signs of reduction, the budget did not balance. By Act 2 of 1919 the permissible British Treasury issue was taken to 80 crores making a total fiduciary issue of (20 + 80 =) 100 crores. The zenith was reached by the Second Currency Act of that year, Act 26 of 1919, which put the British Treasury Bill issue at the incredible figure of 100 crores,—the total rising up to 120 crores in all. It was a really colossal increase in fiduciary issue. Part of it represented an increase—not insignificant compared with pre-war figures—of the holdings of the Government of India's own securities in the reserve ; but by far the greater portion of it represented a tremendous swelling of the holdings of British Treasury Bills. Whatever way the increase was brought about, it was without doubt a case of thoroughly bad finance. The process really amounted to financing expenditure by means of the printing press. So far as the increase of the Indian securities was concerned, Government confessed that it was done because the revenue of the country did not come fast enough for its expenditure.

If the disbursements side continually exceeds the income side in the accounts of the Government, the balance has to be met from somewhere. In this case, it was met by the issue of notes against its own securities, that is Government issued notes on the strength of its own notes of hand, as Hailey put it once. Nothing could be simpler than this way of manufacturing money. The Government issued its promises to pay and made its Currency Department buy them and thus received the wherewithal to carry on its operations. It was the same method of meeting expenses by printing notes, with all its advantages and evils, that was practised to such perfection by Germany. Only, in India, it was on a far smaller scale and perhaps to a greater extent innocently done. Later, as we shall see on the occasion of the reverse council difficulties, the small scale no longer remained small, nor perhaps was the process of inflation a wholly innocent affair. However, so far as the Indian securities were concerned the increase up to 1919 only showed the way. A far bigger increase came later on.

On the occasion of the second 1919 Act (Act 26), the Finance Member Howard said, ' During the war we were obliged to meet a very large amount of expenditure by issuing short-term debt. That amount of debt has since remained outstanding and has increased.' Then he went on to explain how of the three possible ways of meeting the maturing liabilities, (1) loans from the Presidency Banks were out of the question as they themselves would be demanding back the loans they had made in the busy season. (2) The second way—that of securing bullion to issue notes against, was also equally unthinkable, since the price of silver had gone up very high. (3) Thirdly, there remained the only way which the Finance Member was trying with some success. He expected some relief from selling new Treasury Bills bearing higher interest rates. That meant of course converting one short-term debt into a costlier one of the same class. It was not so much a way out as putting off the evil day. The unhappy Finance Member, Howard complained, was ' like a juggler trying to keep a large number of plates at once in the air, none of which he could afford to let fall to the ground.' It was certainly an unenviable position. The Finance Member assured the Council that Government had no intention of using the powers given by the new law, permanently. They were 'convinced of the undesirability of increasing unduly their fiduciary issues.' It was refreshing to hear the Government speak about the undesirability of undue fiduciary issues, after having magnified them to several times their original size.

Secondly, so far as the increase in the British Treasury Bills was concerned, it was also here ultimately a process of financing expenditure out of note issues. The Government had to meet heavy expenses including what was incurred on behalf of the Home Government, and it printed notes and made payments. True, it received credit in England in the shape of British Treasury Bills, but the fact remained that it kept those funds in London and did not spend them. What it spent was new money that it created on the strength of those funds in London. No wonder the price-level in India would have gone up, as the aggregate amount of money in the country thereby increased. Why did not the Government, it may be asked, bring back those London funds,—the British Treasury Bills—convert them into rupees and meet its expenses with them ?—why did it instead choose to keep them there and issue notes in India on their strength ? The answer is simple. First, because it did not want to embarrass the Home Government by immediately asking for its dues,—it remained generously content with receiving 'Promises to Pay.' Secondly, the funds that are in the shape of Promises to Pay do not bear sea-crossing at any and every time one likes. The Government in the circumstances could not have possibly brought its sterling funds back to India, at anything like a decent and profitable rate of exchange. Consequently it kept the Bills in London and continued to receive more and more of them—while issuing notes in India against them at the rates that it itself chose. The sensible thing of course, would have been that as it received Bills in London so it spent out of its general balances in India—not out of freshly printed notes. But since it had no balance to spend from, at least the balance having fallen short, those being the years of a succession of deficit budgets,—it had to spend new notes. The evil was at bottom due to the fact that the Currency machinery was in the hands of the Government. If the Currency machinery, that is to say, the note-printing press, had been outside its control, the unbridled currency inflation of the period would have been impossible.

§ 7. The second 1919 Act was passed in September, 1919. Meanwhile the time for the official ending of the war drew near and then the validity of all these temporary provisions would expire automatically. The Government looked behind and found itself saddled with a heavy burden of fiduciary issue. Naturally enough, it contemplated with nervousness the setting in order of the paper currency machinery that had been so wantonly used for manufacturing money during the War. It had inflated hurriedly and now the time came for repenting at leisure. The task of renovating the paper currency and placing it on a permanent basis fell to Sir Malcolm Hailey, a very distinguished financier. Act 45 of 1920 by which he sought to remodel our paper currency on an entirely new foundation, neutralising as much as possible the effects of the war-growths upon it—an Act which was later embodied in the consolidating Act of 1923,—ranks in importance with the Act of 1861. Hailey's name should therefore be associated with those of Wilson and others, in whose regime profound changes have been worked in our paper currency system. Before proceeding to deal with the attempts at stabilisation we have to notice another development that came about in 1919-20, which introduced fresh complications and unexpectedly altered the constitution of the fiduciary reserve. That was the sale of reverse councils.

It is beyond the scope of the present enquiry to examine the wisdom or folly of the sale of the reverse bills. To a certain extent it was inevitable. Government had accepted the recommendation of the Currency Committee to fix the rupee at 2*s*. gold. It then made an honest attempt to enforce that rate; there sprang up immediately a strong demand for remittance to England, to take advantage of the favourable rate. Before that demand, the sterling resources of the paper currency reserve flew away like chaff before wind. As currency notes or rupees were tendered in India, Government released portions of the accumulated British Treasury bills in England. The reserve there was getting smaller and smaller. With the shrinkage of the reserve, a reduction in the note issue would have followed in the natural course of events,—but the Government feared a monetary stringency if anything like that happened. It wanted the notes to remain in circulation, and having no more British Treasury bills, it had to create its own securities *ad hoc*, to replace them and serve as reserve. To enable it to carry out this conversion process, for that was what in essence it amounted to, of the British bills into created Indian securities, special powers had to be taken, as the law hitherto in force provided for an issue up to 100 crores out of a total of 120, solely against British Treasury bills. That power was given by Act 21 of 1920. The total permissible fiduciary issue was retained at 120 crores but no proviso was attached, as hitherto, defining the division of the holdings between Government of India and non-Government of India securities. So that Government could now invest indifferently in English or Indian securities, as long as the total did not exceed 120 crores. It was no longer compelled to hold only 20 crores at most in Indian securities and the rest in British Treasury Bills. This act, described as the corollary of the sale of reverse bills, by the Indian Merchants' Chamber and Bureau, whose further qualification of it 'as the inevitable sequence of a misconceived policy' we need not quote, was to be in force only up to 1st October, 1920, when the Government contemplated taking up in hand permanent legislation for the paper currency. In fact, its temporary character was pleaded as its only apology, by its sponsor Sir Malcolm Hailey, who perhaps succeeded in making our legislators believe that when the permanent bill came in, it would be such a marvellous scheme as to set everything right. In his own words, 'If we were proposing this as a permanent or even quasi-permanent feature of the currency reserve, I admit that there might be some ground for apprehension on the part of the public. I should indeed be disappointed if it were not criticised.' (17th March, 1920.) He explained that the Secretary of State had hitherto met reverse Councils from Treasury Balances, but he was now coming to the end of his cash balances and must sell out the sterling securities in the paper currency reserve. 'The result would be in the absence of legislation now proposed, that we should have to cancel currency notes to the full rupee equivalent at 1*s*. 4*d*. of the sterling securities sold out. For example, for every million pound of reverse councils sold by us, we should have to cancel currency notes to the extent of 150 lakhs, although if we are selling at, say 2*s*. 8*d*. we receive in India only 75 lakhs.' (Speech on the same date.) It was overlooked that if they actually, by some happy mistake, did cancel, exchange would probably remain at 2*s*. 8*d*. But by creating *ad hoc* securities they kept the currency as inflated as before, and still sold sterling at 2*s*. 8*d*. per rupee. There was to be no deflation and still exchange was to be high—an instance of trying to make two parallel straight lines meet. The attempt, as was to be expected, had to be given up before reaching infinity. The reason why cancellation was not undertaken was, as said before, that it would have caused dearth of money. Hailey appealed to the business members of the Council, who only too readily agreed with him that 'withdrawing Rs. 3 crores of currency notes a week from the money market would cause serious stringency.' He concluded by saying, as Finance Members always do when in difficulties, "I need hardly say that if the Council agrees to give us these powers (he himself calls them 'considerable') we shall use them to the smallest possible extent. Our first endeavour will be to take notes off the market." It must be said to his credit that some deflation was actually done but mostly the loss of British Treasury bills was made good by the creation of the new Government of India securities.

There was an additional reason for the *ad hoc* securities also connected with exchange. A natural corollary of the acceptance of the 2*s*. gold rupee, was the recasting of the Government's accounts on that basis. The paper currency sterling and gold reserves therefore had to be revalued or rather devalued at that new rate. That would involve a considerable loss. The revaluation had not actually been started yet, but as Hailey said, whenever these accounts were changed, there would appear a deficiency. The total amount of securities and metal, calculated at the new rate, would fall short of the gross circulation. Consequently to balance accounts, some *ad hoc* securities must have to be created or notes to the amount of the deficiency cancelled. But as noted above the Government was not in a position to reduce the issue. Consequently the filling up of the gap by means of Indian Treasury bills, that is Indian securities created *ad hoc*. was inevitable. With that end in view Hailey wanted the maximum fiduciary issue to be kept at 120 crores, although the actual issue had not exceeded 100 crores—but he wanted no restriction on the creation of *ad hoc* securities.

§ 8. This was the situation in which the task of readjusting the paper currency was taken up in the autumn of 1920. Beyond doubt it was a complicated situation. It had arisen out of exceptional circumstances during and after the war. It had totally upset the constitution of our paper currency as laid down by the pre-war Acts. Summarised, the events that caused that upsetting, fall under two heads. First, both during and after the war, a great amount of inflation had been carried on to meet the Government's expenditure. The expenditure may have been avoidable or unavoidable, but the fact remains that it was financed largely by recourse to the printing press. Whether issued against British Treasury Bills or against the Government's own bills, it was expansion of currency all the same. It was expansion along the line of least resistance,—namely, by increasing the fiduciary issue. As Hailey explained later,—'During the war the previous arrangements could not be maintained. We had to make very large issues of notes to finance purchases made on behalf of the Home Government and were unable to obtain the metal necessary to maintain the old ratio.' (22nd March. 1922.) Securities therefore rose to 120 crores. In a previous speech he had equally clearly explained how 'owing to the public revenues having been for several years continually insufficient to meet the expenditure falling on them, the State had been obliged to finance itself to a considerable extent by the issue of currency notes against its own notes of hand.' He fully admitted that the situation was most unsatisfactory. (Speech 1st March, 1922.) The fiduciary issue had climbed to a fabulous figure. Although as Howard maintained, 'our additions to the currency had been on a far smaller scale than the additions made elsewhere' yet the increase had been on a scale sufficient enough to make the task of settlement a difficult one. The fiduciary issue was there like a millstone hanging round our paper currency,—what was to be done with it? It was out of the question to go back to the pre-war provisions, whereby only 14 crores could be held in securities. That meant a cancellation of nearly 100 crores of the issue—an impossible amount to disgorge. Obviously that could not be contemplated.

Secondly, the present unenviable situation was partly the legacy of the new exchange policy of the Government. Originally the increase of the fiduciary issue was done mostly by means of investments in British Treasury bills but the sale of reverse councils practically converted them into created Indian securities. The revaluation of the sterling and gold at the new 2*s*. gold rate, would also mean either cancellation of a part of the circulation or the creation of some more *ad hoc* securities to fill up the gap. As noted above, Government chose the latter course in preference to causing any monetary stringency. All these forebode that not only was the fiduciary issue going to stand at a very high figure, but the division of the securities between Indian and non-Indian was going to be far from what the Government would have liked it to be. According to the pre-war law, the limit of security holdings outside India was put down at 4 crores and that of Indian securities at 10 crores. Neither of these limits could be anywhere near the sufficient, now. On the one hand there was this necessity of creating *ad hoc* securities in India in consequence of the sale of reverse councils and revaluation of gold and sterling. On the other hand was the desirability, now supported by the authority of the Currency Committee, of holding only a limited amount of Indian securities in the reserve, far less create new ones. The task of reconciling necessity with desirability seemed no easy one.

§ 9. Act 45 of 1920 attempted to accomplish that task. It drew out a permanent constitution for the paper currency, but since the provisions of that constitution could not be immediately given effect to, certain temporary provisions were made for the transition period. The scheme was mainly based on the recommendations of the Currency Committee. The features of the permanent constitution were that the fiduciary issue instead of being tied down to a fixed maximum amount, as hitherto, was made 50 per cent. of the whole issue, at its largest. Limitations were imposed upon the amount of the Indian and non-Indian securities admissible. The securities held by the Government of India were not to exceed Rs. 20 crores in all, of which at most 12 crores could be created securities. It was obvious that these provisions could not be at once enforced.

They simply held up the goal towards which Indian paper currency was gradually to move. The temporary clauses provided for a maximum fiduciary issue of 85 crores, instead of 120 crores as hitherto —which proved that some amount of deflation had been in the meantime carried out. But there were to be no restrictions as to the British or Indian character of the securities. They could be indifferently held in Government of India or in non-Government of India securities. There were good grounds for this time-division of the provisions between temporary and permanent. At the time the bill was introduced (August, 1920) the note circulation stood at 162 crores. If the accounts were calculated on a Rs. 15-to-the-pound basis, the reserve of coin and bullion amounted to 93 crores and the balance of 69 crores represented the price of the securities—of which approximately 47 crores were securities held in India, and 22 crores held in England. Calculated on a Rs. 10 parity, these figures would all undergo a change. The metallic reserve would stand at 80 crores and securities held in England would be only 15 crores—making a total of 95. Therefore in order to balance the total issue of 162—either notes to the extent of 20 crores had to be cancelled or new securities had to be created to that extent. As already said, Government preferred creating *ad hoc* securities to contracting the issue. Thus conditions were not suitable, in this direction, for the enforcement of the permanent provisions. The other part of these provisions was not so difficult to fulfil. The metallic reserve, on the

1*s*. 4*d*. basis stood at 57 per cent. of the total issue and even after the revaluation it would not be much lower than the 50 per cent. prescribed in the permanent constitution. Government hoped to carry it to the desired 50 per cent. very soon and in practice was able to do so. But the constitution of the security reserve was sure to take a long time to be fitted into the permanent constitution. The permanent provisions laid down that the created securities of the Government of India were gradually to be brought down to 12 crores. As shown above, after the revaluation, the Indian securities, purchased and created, would together stand at 67 crores. Of these, securities purchased in the open market amounted to only 8 crores. Apart from the permanent investment the rest of the 59 crores were created securities, issued direct to the paper currency department.

It will be observed that the permanent provisions contained no maximum limit to the fiduciary issue—the only important restrictions being that the fiduciary part must not exceed 50 per cent. of the whole issue and must be distributed in a certain manner between Indian and non-Indian securities. It was only for the temporary provisions that a maximum fiduciary limit of 85 crores was set down. It was perhaps put in as a proof of the Government's good faith, its honest desire not to water the issue any more. But in reality the clause did not mean much. After the revaluation the total amount of securities in the reserve would at most stand at 82 crores (47 Indian *plus* 15 non Indian at 2*s*.

parity, *plus* 20 newly created Indian securities). There would, after all the inflation that was done, hardly be any need for further increasing the fiduciary issue and a (85 *minus* 82 equal to) 3 crores margin was more than sufficient. As a matter of fact since there was no necessity for creating Indian securities to the full extent of the gap caused by the revaluation, the margin was more than 3 crores. There would hardly be any occasion for the Government to avail itself of the margin, since it had by the same Act of 1920 a new way open to it for issuing notes against bills of exchange. We shall discuss the details of this new opening later on. Meanwhile the position with an 85 crores maximum fiduciary limit was quite strong. No further permanent increase of the issue was contemplated, which would require a more than 85 crores fiduciary limit. To meet seasonal increases an elastic bill issue was provided. Yet if we may anticipate later developments, this maximum fiduciary limit (Indian and non-Indian) owing to the persistent demand for a permanent expansion of the note issue, had to be increased in 1925 to 100 crores.

§ 10. The realisation of the permanent constitution implied therefore the extinguishing of a huge amount of Indian created securities (59 – 12 or 47 crores). It was not a process that could be undertaken and accomplished with a light heart, save with the assistance of some Alladin's lamp. Meanwhile, the Government would not of course sit idle. It would endeavour in several ways to hasten the conditions that would make the permanent constitution possible. Hailey on behalf of the Government, was full of cheer. 'At the same time,' he assured the members, 'the Council must not suppose that we are nearly taking now a Pisgah sight of the Promised Land and are content to wait on the course of events or an act of providence to enable us to reach the standards given in our permanent constitution. Far from that, we propose to hasten the arrival of the appointed day by setting aside every year for the purposes of our reserve the whole of the interest on our English and Indian securities in the paper currency reserve. Further in order that there will be a full guarantee that we have done so, there will be an annual attestation, by the guardian of our official conscience, the Auditor-General in India. Roughly, this interest will amount to £2 million annually. We shall go further than this, although we have not provided in the bill for this measure, and when our gold standard reserve amounts to £40 million,—it is now £37¼ million, we shall take all the interest from that and place it to the credit of our currency reserve' (Legislative Council, 2nd September, 1920).

It is clear the Government realised that the goal was a distant one. The means proposed to bridge the distance were, as just stated, two in number: the appropriation of the interest of the securities in the Currency reserve, and contribution from the gold standard reserve, when it had reached a certain figure. Both were more or less uncertain. As events proved, however, the second was a little more trustworthy than the first.

It has been to some extent used of late years. At the valuation of the gold standard reserve on the 15th March, 1922, it was found for the first time to have exceeded £40 million. The excess, which amounted to £1,418,690 was then utilised for strengthening the currency reserve in India and 214 lakhs of created securities were cancelled, this being the equivalent for the sterling sum at the current rate of exchange. Next year, in 1922-23, the excess appropriated was £1,400,038 and Rs. 212½ lakhs of created securities in the paper currency reserve in India were cancelled. Since then no further appropriation from the gold standard reserve has taken place. The second method of wiping out, by crediting interest from paper currency securities, had to be postponed year after year, and has not yet been actually used (1926). The temporary provisions have thus remained temporary for ever. The 1923 Act which almost verbatim reproduces the provisions of the 1920 Act (Act 45) except that it is a simpler Act to understand, which is no small virtue for currency Acts, keeps up the distinction between the temporary and the permanent provisions. One fails to see however what the good was of incorporating the permanent clauses into the Acts at all, knowing fully that they could not be realised till after 20 or 30 years*—except that they served to encumber the Acts. The currency system has been

* Prof. Jevons thought that the permanent provisions could be realised in five or six years' time (Money, Banking and Exchange in India, 1922). He could not of course then foresee how later events would belie his expectations.

given the appearance of stabilisation, while in reality, that ideal is still as far off as ever. Those who allow themselves to be deceived by appearances, would perhaps derive some satisfaction by looking at the clauses in the Act. Deflationists will possibly discover in them an honest desire on the part of the Government to deflate. But they may live to be disillusioned, as even a carrying out to the letter of the permanent provisions may not lead to deflation. It will depend on the way in which the Government makes the reserve conform to the permanent provisions. The provisions simply insist on an upward limit of 20 crores of Indian securities. If the excess is wiped out, out of income, cancelling the equivalent note circulation along with the created securities, then that would mean deflation. If, on the other hand, as the created securities go, their place is filled up by new British securities to whose holding, it may be noted, there is absolutely no limit as long as the basic ratio of 50 per cent. metallic reserve is not violated,—the total issue has no likelihood of shrinking. The mere wiping out of Indian securities may not affect the circulation but only alter the constitution of the reserve, replacing the created securities by new British Treasury Bills or silver and gold. Recent evidence seems to show that this is what the re-adjustment process is tending towards. The Government seems to be slowly yielding to the cry of more money which the business community in India is eternally surrounding it with. There are not many signs of contraction of the issue. Although generous provision has been made towards the issue of emergency currency, it seems to have produced a demand for still more money. It is not argued here that deflation would be the suitable currency policy for India. The best currency policy is neither deflation nor inflation, but stabilisation. But it shows the vaccilating nature of currency policy in India. It is doubtful if in recasting the paper currency, the Government had any definite aims of deflation, but that they inclined towards it to some extent, admits of no doubt. The utterances of Government officials give that impression. It is however not known in which way the permanent provisions are going to be given effect to. In 1920 (August) the Finance Member solemnly promised that the interest from the security reserve would be used in wiping out the created securities. He added with grim earnestness on the 16th September, 'Towards extinguishing the rupee securities which during the transitory period we shall need to create, we shall also apply the profits on our rupee coinage when such again arise. Happily for him, no fresh coinage of rupees has since then been undertaken (except recoinage). Hailey even went further. 'I would,' he said, 'add that there is yet a third method which we shall apply for hastening the appointed day. We shall take the interest (or to be more correct, the difference between the discounted and the maturing value) of the commercial bills of exchange which we shall be able to hold as security for the special seasonal and expansional issue which is proposed as a new feature.' This third method was only in reality a part of the first: namely, interest from securities. After all these promises, what did the Finance Member say later? The operation of wiping out of the created securities by means of accrued interest from securities was to commence from April 1st, 1921. On 22nd March, 1922, welcoming a motion by Webb, the erstwhile redoubtable champion of paper currency, to credit the interest rather to revenue than to extinguish created securities, Hailey said that it was clear to them when drawing up the permanent provisions that it would be many years before they could work up to the proportion of securities laid down in them. He appreciated deflation. A deflationist policy would give India credit in Europe. But it would be difficult to carry out in practice. It would produce 'undue stringency in the money market. If the Government had been in the fortunate position with a revenue surplus, there would have been no great difficulty. But working to a deficit they 'were really not appropriating from revenue for cancellation; they were really only borrowing money on Treasury Bills for the purpose and the process therefore was to a certain extent illusory.' A proposal like the one made by Webb was present in the Government's mind when preparing the budget, but it 'rightly felt some scruples in initiating any such itself.' He then spoke with an eye to the British money market, which has had not a little influence on our currency policy. 'We may perhaps hope,' said the Finance Member, 'that financiers in Europe will look rather at the general condition of our paper currency reserve than at the fact that we are temporarily suspending the provisions of the Paper Currency Act—for we have to raise large sterling loans.' After some technicalities Sir Montague Webb withdrew and the 'infant' motion was taken in charge of by Hailey who had no difficulty in carrying it through the House by 56 votes to 41. It is interesting to read in this connection the speech of Mr. M. C. Sahani, one of the few Indian members who spoke, and who evidently thought he understood currency matters as daylight. The wiping out proposal he characterised as an absurd one 'which, however, found acceptance with not a few who did not understand the question of currency and exchange.' The result of the motion was that the employment of interest of the paper currency securities to extinguish created securities was not to commence till 1st April, 1923. That interest was to be credited to revenue as regularly done. In 1923 the time was found still inopportune for devoting the interest to the promised purpose. The need for revenue was more urgent. Hence by the Finance Act of 1923, the wiping out work was put off till 1924, 1st April. In 1924 again the situation was unchanged. The Finance Act of that year, certified by the Governor-General, restored among others the grant of the paper currency interest to revenue purposes till 1925. The wiping out was deferred for another year.* Meanwhile, the prospects of help

* It was the same story in 1925. The Finance Act of 1925 again credited to revenue for a further period of one year up to 31st March, 1926, the interest of the securities of the currency reserve. This was repeated in 1926 and the interest was to go to revenue till March, 1927.

from the gold standard reserve also darkened. It will be recalled that some help from that source came in, in 1921-22 and in 1922-23. But in 1923-24 the Government said, 'When the Act of 1920 was before the Legislature, an undertaking was given to apply to the same purpose (extinguishing created securities) assets of the gold standard reserve in excess of £40 million. But it has been decided to credit them also to revenue in the current year and it is proposed to follow the same procedure for next year.' The statement added that 'there was no cancellation of created securities for the current year and in view of above no sums will be specifically available next year for the reduction of the created securities.' (Budget for 1924-25.)* The resuming of the cancellation process is thus not in sight. The way that the Indian Budget is behaving for the last few years, makes one despair as to when the extinguishing process which is the stepping stone to the permanent provisions is to commence or if it is to commence at all. Yet, in the consolidating Act of 1923 the permanent provisions figure as the goal to which the temporary ones are supposed to be leading. There is only one advantage, if that can be called by that name, of retaining the picture of the permanent constitution in the Act, while neglecting the means to bring it into effect, and that is that it serves as an attractive ideal and allays criticism. But it is after all a hollow

* In his Report for 1925-26, the Controller of the Currency states that the interest yielded by the Gold Standard Reserve amounted to £1,977,674 the whole of which was appropriated to revenue.

pretension, an ideal so distant as liable to be itself changed in the long process of moving towards it and which had therefore much rather been left out, until the time was ripe for taking it into hand.

§ 11. The latest alteration to be made in the amount of the security reserve was recently brought about by the Indian Paper Currency (Amendment) Act 1925. By this enactment the maximum permissible fiduciary issue (Indian and non-Indian securities) was carried to 100 crores from 85 crores, hitherto in force according to the temporary provisions. The reason for the extension is said to be to make the note-issue more elastic. What is wanted is perhaps a permanent extension of the issue and not merely a seasonal increase, as otherwise the provisions of the emergency issue against bills of exchange—a feature of our currency acts since 1920, could be availed of. In view of the steady process of reduction of the total aggregate currency of India during the last few years—a permanent increase of the issue is perhaps desirable. But the powers taken by the Government may prove to be too much. The fiduciary issue, when the Act was passed, had not yet touched 85 crores. To increase the margin suddenly by 15 crores, may be only to tempt the Government to inflate unduly. In that case, the price-level would however soon betray them. Judiciously exercised the new powers ought to create no alarm. The new expansion of the issue will, the Government anticipates, come about against British securities (temporary). But they could have been based upon Indian created securities as well, there being no particular sacredness about British Promises to Pay, as against Indian Promises.

This chapter may now be closed. We have tried here to analyse the composition of the result. We find it to-day to be a heterogeneous miscellany. The complications that arise out of such a reserve, suggest their own moral. It is that the constitution of the reserve should be made simpler. There is no reason why gold and sterling should not be taken out of the reserve. They are not indispensible there. The problem of valuation which they bring with them is a sufficient evil for us to ask them to go. The events of the last few years have proved how much our currency reserve lies at the mercy of 'valuation'—which may be rightly called the reserve-maker. The next few years may intensify the lesson. As these lines are being written the reserve-maker it seems is once more going to make its influence felt. The Hilton Young Commission has recommended a new rate of exchange, *viz.*, 1s. 6d. to a rupee. If his new rate of valuation be adopted, it will mean a change in the size of the paper currency reserve, the gold and sterling portions of which will have to be re-valued on the new basis. The result will be some amount of unsettlement. The Hilton Young Commission, it is only fair to say, proposes a comprehensive recasting of the monetary system and accepting the totality of their recommendations the country may ensure not only a stable and permanent constitution for its paper currency, but may also perhaps solve the whole question of currency and exchange for all time to come. But there is no certainty that the recommendations in their entirety will find acceptance. The Indian monetary system has grown up piecemeal and the currency historian will not be surprised if the recommendations are only partially followed. Whether or not an attempt is now made to overhaul the entire monetary system, it is safe to predict that the 2*s*. rate is doomed. In its place, we shall either have the 1*s*.-6*d*. rate as the Commission advocate or the 1*s*. 4*d*. rate as championed by a powerful section of Indian opinion. The new valuation will materially change the shape of the currency reserve, even if no other interference is made with it. As the valuation pendulum moves, the whole clock of our currency reserve has to be re-adjusted to it. As long as this unsteadying influence remains, so long will the atmosphere of uncertainty reign, and so long will all attempts at stabilisation be a pursuit of the will-o-the-wisp.

CHAPTER VIII.

THE COVER OF THE ISSUE (*Concluded*).

The Question of Elasticity.

§ 1. Elasticity of issue, its different intepretations and its connection, in theory, with the market rate of interest, p. 192.—§ 2. Conscious and unconscious developments in connection with the growth of elascity. Various suggested methods of promoting elascity p. 196.—§ 3. The reason why the currency reserve has been suggested in preference to other sources, p. 202.—§ 4. The recommendations of the Chamberlain Commission and of the Smith Committee with a view to increase the elasticity of the issue, p. 204.—§ 5. The suggestion of the Smith Committee, somewhat modified, incorporated into the paper currency system in 1920. The first regulations in this connection, p. 206.—§ 6. Changes in the procedure of the issue of emergency currency made in 1923, p. 208.—§ 7. The existing double opening for elasticity in the currency system summarised, p. 210.—§ 8. Further changes in the procedure of issue in 1924, p. 212.—§ 9. The question of valuation, depreciation and sundry other points relating to the security reserve, p. 213.

§ 1. In pursuing the history of the security holdings right up to the present time, we had to omit considering the other reforms introduced by the Act of 1920 (Act 45). That Act had also new provisions designed to give elements of elasticity to the paper currency system. We may now conveniently isolate this question of elasticity and trace the developments in its connection, although strictly speaking, the whole question of the reserve must be looked upon as one, no part of it being separable from the others.

The word elasticity, used in connection with paper currency is not very easy to define. When before the 1914 Commission Sir Montagu Webb was asked if he considered the paper currency system as very inelastic, he replied that he was not quite sure he understood the question. Sir Montagu should not have been ashamed of his ignorance. As a matter of fact the word elasticity has been used in many different senses. To different people it had different connotations. It has been used in the first place in the sense of a permanent expansion of the note circulation. It is then practically equivalent to bringing about an increase in the note-issue, by whatever means it may be. Advocates of elasticity in this sense really want facilities for expansion only, not facilities for contracting the issue, if the need arises. They would therefore dilute the issue with as large a proportion of securities, preferably created securities which cost nothing to put into the reserve, as possible. In Indian Paper Currency history, apostles of such one-sided elasticity have not been rare. On the other hand there have been others who have tried to link elasticity to seasonal fluctuations in currency, and wanted the note-issue to correspond to trade demands. They have not been anxious for facilities that would increase the note circulation for good, but wanted to utilise the paper currency for mitigating the seasonal stringency of money in the country. In a country like India, predominantly agricultural, there are bound to be considerable variations in the demand for currency between different seasons. Elasticity in this sense would mean equalising the supply of currency to the demand all through the year. Its advocates want facilities for seasonal expansion as well as seasonal contraction. In actual practice, the confusion

25

between the two schools of elasticity is heightened by the fact that both base their demand for expansion upon the rate of interest. If the rate of interest is high, the market at once puts it down to some defect in the supply of money ; it complains that the Government or the banks are not manufacturing enough money. This is natural, thanks to the 'gross perversion of terms' in J. S. Mill's words, whereby the value of money to the market means simply the rate of interest. The value of money as loanable funds is thus confused with the value of money as purchasing power. When the value of the former rises, when in other words the rate of interest goes up, the market thinks it can lower it by bringing down the value of money as purchasing power, that is its value in the second sense. Now it may succeed in this temporarily and to a certain extent, but such a course provides no ultimate remedy for the ups and downs of the rate of interest. It is impossible to enter into the question of the rate of interest here, a vast and intricate subject upon which full light has perhaps yet to be shed by the science of economics. But the fact is well established that the real rate of interest, founded on the supply and demand of capital, has hardly any connection with the supply of currency, which is merely the symbol for calculation of that supply and demand. It is only the temporary market rate that can be affected by the fluctuations in the amount of currency. To try to correct the long-term interest rate by the issue of more or less money is impossible. Correcting the temporary interest rate by this process has also its dangers. Thanks to the efforts of Prof. Cannan who did so much to introduce the idea into the modern theory of money, we have now to take material account of the elasticity of the demand for money. As is the case with the price of all other things, here also expectation of the supply plays quite an important part. The very assurance that emergency currency will be supplied may considerably affect the demand curve of money and affect the bank rate in an unexpected way. Secondly, it is not known how an announcement that some additional funds are coming to relieve the market would exactly affect the interest rate. We cannot say that a doubling of the available funds will halve the rate of interest, or a halving reduce the rate to half its former figure. That depends on the elasticity of the demand for money Consequently how much money will have to be made over to the market to effect a desirable cut in the rate of interest is always very difficult to say. To try to gauge the exact currency requirements of the community, by the bank rate index, is thus not always a safe way. The mere high interest rate does not prove that more money is needed, as that high interest rate may be substantially the result of the announcement that more money is coming. A continual expectation of more money may take the interest rate high up to anywhere, as the German example only too clearly shows. In Germany the rate of interest had exceeded 100 per cent. and still there was no slackening in the demand for more money at that rate. It was not to be concluded from that that Germany was suffering from a stringency of money-supply. In times of depreciation, the producer's psychology is that if he can buy Rs. 100 worth of goods now, three months hence owing to the rise in prices, he would probably be able to sell them for Rs. 110. Thus, he would not hesitate to pay up to 10 per cent. per three months on the Rs. 100 that he wants to borrow. If the fact that he is ready to pay such a high interest, is construed to mean that there is a stringency of money in the country, and a benevolent Government goes out manufacturing more money, the depreciation of currency would go on at a still greater rate and the temporary loan rate would climb up still higher.

It is not the intention here to go into any lengthy theoretical discussion on the rate of interest. All that has been said is just to show that the meaning of elasticity, as linked to the rate of interest and as a remedy for long-term or seasonal stringency, has to be accepted with care. Granting that this elasticity is a desirable thing, the exact method by which the paper currency system has been suggested to promote it, has also given rise to a difference of opinion. As said above, the mere-expansion school would be satisfied with watering the reserve, that is increasing the amount of securities therein. The seasonal expansionists propose various schemes. Some propose lending from the paper currency reserve in times of need, others prefer an additional issue, not in lieu of the existing reserve but in excess of it, for which the reserve may be in the shape of temporary securities.

§ 2. Having thus put ourselves on guard about the different meanings of elasticity and about the difference in methods by which it has been sought to be achieved, we may go on to trace the developments in its connection. The idea is really an old one. Whenever the question of the reform of the paper currency has arisen, the idea of introducing elements of elasticity has always accompanied it. It has been already seen how later enactments after 1861 all put up steadily the amount of the fiduciary issue. The business community consistently complained of the lack of elasticity. In 1899 for example in a letter to the Government, the Bank of Bengal suggested more elasticity in the shape of loans from the Treasury or failing that from the paper currency reserve. 'My directors,' the letter said, 'would also submit that the paper currency reserve is the most suitable fund to devote to this purpose, not only because it is large and steady......but because it is to the paper currency that other nations look for assistance. If effect is given to the proposal, the elasticity of the central banking resources of which the Indian Money Markets were deprived by the transfer of the paper currency to Government, will be restored.' (Letter to Government Dec., 1899.) The proposal of the Bank of Bengal was also supported by the Bank of Madras. But the Government opposed it. It was still the time when the currency reserve was looked upon as a sacred trust solely maintained for the convertibility of the notes, which might not be encroached upon by any means. Writing in 1900 to the Secretary of State the Government said 'this is a suggestion which is open to fatal objections' (Abraham's memorandum, 1914 Commission). But though averse to any particular method of bringing it about, the Government was not averse to the idea of elasticity. In fact they had a plan of their own in connection with the transfer of the issue to a central bank which would have given considerable powers of seasonal expansion to the note-issue. Writing to the Secretary of State in 1900 (18th Jan.) the Government suggested that the proposed bank should be allowed to issue additional uncovered notes on payment of a tax at 10 per cent. This was evidently borrowed from the German Reichsbank system of elastic note-issue. But Government did not consider it safe to 'graft' the German tax system on the issue as long as it was in its own hands. As however the project of a central bank did not then materialise, nothing more was heard about elasticity. It must be remembered that already in half-hearted or indirect ways some elasticity had been introduced into the paper currency. The growth of events saw a great deal of the rigidity that marked the system in 1861, removed by the end of the century. Extended facilities, for one thing, had been granted for the issue of notes against gold since 1893. Notes up to any amount could be issued for gold now. Secondly, as the Fowler Commission recorded, the effect of the Gold Note Act of 1898, by which notes could be issued against gold tendered in England, brought further elasticity to the system. The Act was made among other reasons 'in order to afford a measure of relief to the severe stringency' then prevailing in the Indian money market. In 1902 it will be recalled, the provisions of that act were made permanent. From 1905 onwards, the opening of the London Sterling reserve further helped elasticity. Notes could be now issued against sterling resources or Council Bills in England. For various reasons however, not least of which was that such a process of expansion at the expense of the gold reserves of London caused undesirable stringency there, the arrangement was not considered a very satisfactory method of promoting elasticity. Apart from all this, the metamorphosis of the rupee, from a free to a token coin meant indirectly substantial elasticity to the note circulation. The development had affected the character of the paper currency system in an almost imperceptible but deep way. Up to that time it could be correctly said that the note system of India was similar to that of England, both equally rigid, the excess notes in both countries being practically bullion certificates (speaking of pre-war England of course). But whereas in England the coin remained equivalent to bullion, in India it itself became a note, and thus the costs of an increase of the note-issue on the backing of a token coin, fell considerably below what they otherwise would have been, had the rupee retained its free coinage. Whatever facilitates the expansion of an issue introduces elasticity. England has escaped from rigidity by developing remarkably her cheque system, India tried a way out by appreciating her coins artificially. Hence for the same real cost, she could issue more notes now. However, although the net result of all this developments was evident in a steady increase in the gross circulation, still there remained considerable room for more elasticity. The demand for some form of tangible elasticity was voiced by nearly all the witnesses before the 1914 Commission. It will be impossible to reproduce here all the suggestions made before the Commission. Mention might be made however of a few typical opinions. Sir Dabida Dalal wanted the notes to be based mainly on metal, with a portion of the issue against discounts as in the American Federal Reserve System. Sir Daniel Hamilton would lend freely from the paper currency reserve in order to mitigate the stringency of money and finance various internal development projects. His views are as interesting as they are impracticable. Hunter suggested a fiduciary issue of 40 per cent. of the total. But he realised the theoretical difficulty of laying down a fixed percentage, as, if at any time the security reserve stood exactly at that figure, then the encashment of one single note would reduce the metallic portion to less than sixty per cent. and take the fiduciary portion to just over forty per cent., by however small a fraction it might be, and the legal line would have been crossed. (For a discussion of the theory of the different kinds of reserve, no better book can be perhaps referred to than Kinley's Money.) Hence, as an after-thought, Hunter would make the fiduciary proportion variable between fifty and sixty per cent. Lionel Abrahams whose suggestion conforms most to what the Paper Currency Acts now provide for, said, ' It would be an improvement if arrangements were made by which *additional* notes could be issued at suitable terms specially in the busy season either uncovered altogether or against first class bills which became due to be paid off three or four months hence. Then by putting such securities in the paper currency reserve and issuing notes against them, there would be a possibility of elasticity, humanly speaking, without any risk at all.' For an opposite view Sir Clinton Dawkins, an ex-Finance Member may be quoted. He said that if any lending was to be made at all from the paper currency reserve then, for the interest of the tax-payer, that is of the Government, it should not be lent for a few months in the busy season and left idle throughout the rest of the year, when opportunities were available for lending it for the whole year. He put himself against all seasonal lending. His view, based upon the philosophy of profit and loss embodying a narrow and departmental outlook, was also the view of many others. Lord Inchcape and Sir B. N. Mitra (then Mr.) suggested an one-third fiduciary issue, the former 'with diffidence,' and the latter adding that a part of the fiduciary issue instead of being put into securities might be utilised for assisting trade. F. C. le Marchant thought a proportion of the minimum circulation would be a safe practical basis. He would take a series of years and find out the average minimum circulation. Lord Meston had an elaborate scale according to which the issue should be graded, namely forty per cent. of the reserve for prompt conversion, 20 per cent. in gold for prompt purchase of silver in the case of a run, 30 per cent. in permanent securities and 10 per cent. temporary investments in assistance of the market. Sir Felix Schuster also had a scheme of his own. Howard advocated loans from the paper currency to the banks in the busy season. As a suitable rate of interest would be charged, he saw no danger to the interests of the tax-payer. Sir Montagu Webb also supported the idea of loans from the fiduciary portion. C. D. Saraiya, late Managing Director of the Indian Specie Bank was opposed to lending as he thought that any meddling with the reserve would shake Indian faith in and stop the expansion of the paper currency. Mr. H. M. Ross suggests lending 10 crores for easing the market. The loan would be in lieu of part of the fiduciary issue, not in excess of it. M. L. Currie favoured lending. He pointed out that by lending to the banks for half the year the interests of the tax-payer would not suffer in the least, as the permanent loans fetched interest usually at a rate of 3½ per cent. while the temporary loans would be able to earn about 7 per cent. in half a year.

§ 3. It may be noted here that Government possesses two possible sources from which temporary loans in aid of the market may be given. Of these the general Treasury Balances although they locked up a great amount of funds, were in the opinion of the Government not a suitable source to tap. The balances, as Hunter has explained, often come as fast as they go. If the market got into the habit of expecting assistance from them, a crash would come if suddenly that was withdrawn in any bad year. On the other hand the Government has no choice but to collect its revenue just at the time when the market most demands money, that is to say at the time of the harvests in the busy season, as otherwise the taxes could not be perhaps collected at all. The time when the crops come in is the most suitable time for collecting the revenue. The abolition of the Reserve Treasuries has now in a large measure liberated the general treasury funds for the relief of the market. But at that time the Government could not contemplate lending from the treasury balances. The other fund, the paper currency reserve, was also equally out of their reach. They considered it as a 'Trust Fund' (Meston's words) which must not be encroached upon. It would be useless to accumulate more opinions on the question. It was a peculiar thing in India that just at the time when the paper currency reserve was at its strongest, there existed in the market a strong demand for loans. It came about thus that the ability to lend from that reserve stood at its maximum when the necessity for loans was most urgent. It was natural therefore that owing to this coincidence, the paper currency reserve should be so often suggested as the source wherefrom to advance the loans. In the busy season the people take out notes, and in the slack season they generally buy back coins for the notes. In the busy season, as Mr. Keynes showed by facts and figures, the 'active circulation' (that is the circulation among the public) stands at its largest, and that means that the call on the reserve is at that time the least, and consequently, the power to lend the greatest. In all recent years on his showing, the maximum circulation has been in January, February and March, the busy season in India, when usually the bank rate stands at 8 per cent., and the minimum has been in June, July and August, when the bank rate goes down to about 3 per cent. The time when trade most requires assistance, is the time when the currency reserve can best afford to give it. Lord Meston agreed that this was so, but did not still think the currency reserve was the most suitable fund to lend from.

§ 4. In view of all this evidence it was natural that the 1914 Commission would suggest some means of increasing elasticity in the note-issue. They recommended the fiduciary issue to be forthwith increased from the then existing 14 crores to 20 crores. But instead of merely fixing this figure as a maximum they proposed that the maximum of the fiduciary portion should thereafter be fixed 'at the amount of the notes held by the Government in Reserve Treasuries plus one-third of the net (meaning gross minus notes held in the Reserve Treasuries) circulation for the time being.' Secondly a substantial portion of the securities in the reserve were to be short-dated ones. They further recommended temporary loans from the reserve both in India and in England. In India, this would enable the Government to 'earn interest on sums which would be otherwise idle needlessly.' At the same time the market would be relieved. Temporary loans in England were justified on similar grounds of profit to the Government. Before any of these recommendations could be fully considered or carried out, the War had intervened and the fiduciary issue had to be increased perforce—to a huge extent. The question was reconsidered in the light of War experiences by the 1919 Committee. It was their recommendations which, slightly modified, were incorporated in the 1920 Act (Act 45), and now figure as the permanent features of the Indian paper currency constitution. The suggestion of the Smith Committee was that the statutory minimum for the metallic portion of the reserve should be 40 per cent. of the gross circulation. Although this would ensure, by itself, very great expansive powers in the note-issue, for meeting special seasonal demands, they suggested a plan of issuing a limited amount of notes against temporary bills of exchange. In this respect their recommendation was based upon an examination of the proposals submitted by Mr. Howard. The Committee says, ' The proposals formulated by Mr. Howard contemplate that the note-issue should be based in part upon commercial Bills of exchange. We have given careful consideration to this plan, with special reference to its application on the largest scale as the basis of the Federal Reserve Note system in the United States of America, and we recommend that it should be tried experimentally in India on a small scale, as the basis for the special power of expansion which we find to be advisable. The requirements of the case would, we think, be met by authorising in the first instance the issue of notes up to 5 crores on the security of commercial Bills of exchange in addition to the normal issue. The issue would take the form of loans to the Presidency Banks on the collateral security of Bills endorsed by the Presidency Banks and having a maturity not exceeding 90 days. The interest charged to the Banks for such advances should be not less than 8 per cent. per annum. The advances should be outside any loans made from Government Treasury balances. The Bills tendered as collateral should be *bona fide* commercial Bills against goods under export, not only because such Bills would lead to the automatic retirement of the emergency note-issue on their maturity, but also because such Bills are more easily identifiable as representing a definite commercial transaction than internal Bills, which may be created for purpose of finance or against goods held for speculative transactions. If the difficulty of connecting internal Bills with definite transactions in commodities can be overcome, we should see no objection hereafter to authorising the tender of such Bills as collateral in addition to export Bills, but we think that at the inception of a scheme which is admittedly experimental it would be wiser to authorise the tender of export bills only ' (para. 80, Report).

§ 5. Following this recommendation a clause was inserted in the Act of 1920 (Act 45) authorising an issue of 5 crores against Bills of exchange. Thus the long projected step was taken of introducing an element of seasonal elasticity into the paper currency. The new method came in the way not of a direct loan from the reserve, but of an additional bill-covered issue. The first rules and conditions, prescribed for the new issue show that in certain respects, a departure was made from the recommendations of the Currency Committee. The regulations laid down the following conditions for the issue of seasonal currency :

1. In the first place, the Bills of exchange were to be internal Bills or ' hundis ' drawn for trade purposes.

2. If the documents themselves did not bear any evidence of being drawn for such purposes, the

Imperial Bank of India was to certify that, to the best of its knowledge, the accommodation provided for was for the furtherance of trade.

3. The Bills would remain in the custody of the Imperial Bank of India, as securities held on behalf of the Currency Department and should, if the Controller of the Currency so requires, be endorsed by the Bank to the Controller.

4. The rate of interest was to be fixed by the Controller of the Currency, and was not to be less than 8 per cent. per annum.

It will be recalled that the Currency Committee had suggested export, not internal Bills. The Government of India, however, after 'consulting commercial opinion in the country rejected the idea of basing the new procedure on export Bills.' But it is difficult to see how by merely examining documents or insisting on a certificate from the Imperial Bank of India, they were going to safeguard against speculating transactions finding their way into the issue. The manufacturers of Finance Bills, it is presumed, take a good care to give their bills every appearance of genuine commercial paper and it is very difficult to distinguish the chaff from the grain. The task would be no less easy for the Imperial Bank than for the Government of India. No information is at all available on the point as to how the Government satisfies itself thoroughly that the Bills are genuine. An enquiry that the present writer made at the Currency Department elicited the usual courteous reply of regret at not being able to furnish any new light. There is reason to suspect therefore that the emergency issue is not fully speculation-proof.

§ 6. The first loan made under the new system bore interest at the rate of 8 per cent. per annum. It was made to the Imperial Bank on the 10th March, 1921, and was repaid on 27th April. Act 10 of 1923 consolidating the law on paper currency retained the provisions of the 1920 Act almost word for word. But whether because 5 crores was really an insufficient amount or a taste of the new emergency currency had created a desire for more money in the business community,—a keen demand grew up for more generous provisions. Further, the conditions under which the additional notes were issued were offensive to the people eager to have money at cheap rates. As just noted, the loans could only be made when the bank rate had touched 8 per cent. This was considered too high an interest rate. Consequently as a result of the pressure from business quarters, the provisions were revised in 1923 (August). By Act 36 of that year the maximum permissible bill-issue was raised to 12 crores, from 5. Government also announced its intention of introducing a sort of sliding scale in dispensing this amount, corresponding to the rise in the rate of interest. Sir Basil Blackett announcing the new changes gave a review of the problem of seasonal currency in India which is well worth quoting. 'The seasonal currency problem,' Sir Basil said, 'arises from the fact that when the crops have been harvested payment has to be made for them by dealers whose balances have to be kept in the form of credit, to growers whose balances are kept in the form of cash, so that during that period the dealers have to draw out the rupees required and if they have not sufficient balances at the bank have to borrow. The cash resources of the banks are diminished and the loans required from the banks have been increased. If the banks have no other means of obtaining fresh currency they are bound to defend their cash resources by raising the rate of interest and discount.' It is at this juncture that the Government steps in and lends to the Imperial Bank which acts as a medium in broad casting the loan. Sir Basil explained that there was no special virtue in a limit of 5 or 12 crores, but 5 was perhaps too small and 12 might be too much. The plan of sliding scale which he then outlined provided for an issue not exceeding 4 crores, if the bank rate did not exceed 6 per cent., a maximum issue of 8 crores so long as the rate remained at or below 7 per cent., and for a further instalment of 4 crores if the bank-rate exceeded 7 per cent. This scale was an experimental one. What was wanted was elasticity which could not be had by too rigid rules. Therefore the Government reserved powers to change the rules whenever they considered that necessary. Apart from the provision of this seasonal currency, the Act of 1923, also reproduced the stipulation of a 50 per cent. fiduciary issue at utmost, which was a new feature in the Act of 1920. In this connection, the Government had showed a greater concern for ' safety first ' than the 1919 Committee had done. The recommendation of the Committee was for a maximum fiduciary issue of 60 per cent. The reason for choosing a lower fiduciary proportion is not far to seek. It is that a far bigger quantity of metal in reserve is still necessary in the case of India, than in the case of any other country.

§ 7. Thus was launched the double-edged elasticity into the Indian Paper Currency system. First, the fiduciary issue was made proportional to the whole, and secondly, liberal provision was made for temporary emergency currency. The former made the issue elastic over long periods, while the latter introduced seasonal elasticity. If we choose to designate them by new names, we may say that both vertical and horizontal elasticity were provided for under the new Acts. It is obvious, the Government has been able to overcome the difficulty in connection with internal 'hundies,' apprehended by the Currency Committee, as loans are at present made on their security in preference to export bills. On the whole, the experiment of emergency currency has been a success, though doubts have been expressed in some quarters, including high circles of officialdom, as to its efficiency as a complete remedy for high bank rate and seasonal stringency. All depends on whether the business community expects a continual increase in the amount of currency yielded from this sources or not. If the Government shows signs of complying with their demand for more money, if in other words, the business people are led to hope that the Government would every time yield to their request, and increase the available emergency currency then the bank rate, as explained above, would in spite of the new currency, show a tendency of rising up. Every time wore currency is created, the currency is depreciated (*Caeteris paribus*, of course). An expectation of a continually depreciating currency is the surest precursor of a high bank-rate in the short loan market. Hence, the Government would be well advised not to hurriedly increase the amount of such currency, loanable to banks. But one fears it may again yield. Already the Bengal Chamber of Commerce in a letter to the Government considers it a defect of the existing currency system that there is no means of a 'permanent or quasi-permanent expansion of the currency to meet the requirements of the country' (*Statesman*, Weekly Mail edition, 24th July, 1924). A more unsophisticated person than the august body of Bengal Commerce would have considered it a merit rather than a defect, as in his opinion the price-level of the country would have been the most important test of the 'requirements of the country' as regards currency. To the Bengal Chamber of Commerce and other bodies who think similarly, the requirements of the country perhaps signify their own requirements or on the most liberal interpretation, the necessity of bringing about a state of things when money could be borrowed at very cheap rates. The lessons of Germany in exposing the treacherous bank-rate as anything but a too sure index of currency requirements, seems to be entirely lost upon them. Sir Basil Blackett, who, in his speeches has shown an enlightened conception of the monetary problems of India, has already grown suspicious of the advantages of the emergency issues. The Finance Member suggests, and quite rightly, that the very knowledge that the emergency currency would be available accentuates the stringency, because in the summer when money is plentiful banks lock up funds which they would have kept liquid for use in winter, had they had to depend on their unaided sources. ' If this be so,' he concludes, ' we are as well off without the emergency provisions which contribute nothing towards a solution of the problem ' (Speech in opening Central Bank Offices in Calcutta, July, 1924).

§ 8. In 1924 further changes were made in the procedure of issuing emergency currency. The effect of the new alterations is to slacken the screw still further in favour of a speedy issue of seasonal currency. In the autumn of 1924 the Government, as a result of urgent representations made to it by various public bodies, thought it desirable to modify the conditions governing the issue of emergency currency. It was proposed in future, while retaining the limit of 4 crores when the bank rate was at 6 per cent., to permit the issue of the remaining 8 crores when the bank rate was at 7 per cent. or over, without any specified limit at 7 per cent. The new regulations mean practically the end of the scale system. While however the sliding scale has disappeared, the existing maximum limit to the Bill issue remains as before, at 12 crores. It would, in the opinion of the present writer, be unwise to further increase this limit without some years of experience.

Another change made in 1924 also has the effect of increasing the elasticity, in a limited and special sense, of the issue. By the Paper Currency (Amendment) Act of 1925, as noted in the previous chapter, the maximum permissible fiduciary issue was raised to 100 from 85 crores. Taking all these measures together, it may be said that the Indian Paper Currency System now enjoys as fair an amount of elasticity as could be wished for for the present.

§ 9. We have now been long upon the subject of the reserves. It can now be finished with a few remarks upon certain points regarding the security reserve. It will be recalled that the 1920 Act (Act 45) provided for a 20 crores limit of securities held in India as a permanent policy. Not more than 12 crores of this amount could be created securities. Conditions were also put down as regards the period of maturity of the securities. The reason why 20 crores was considered a safe limit for Indian securities was because that represented practically the portion of the note circulation which was in the hands of the Government, lying in its own treasuries or at its credit at the Imperial Bank. They could be thus suitably regarded as a permanent lock-up. These provisions strictly followed the recommendations of the 1919 Committee. The Committee had also advised that, of the rest of the securities held in England, ' not more than 10 crores should be invested in securities with more than one year's maturity and any securities so held should be redeemable at a fixed date. The balance of the invested portion of the reserve over and above the 30 crores already provided for (20 crores Indian plus 10 crores long term English) should be held in short-dated securities with not more than one year's maturity issued by Governments within the British Empire other than the Government of India.' The recommendation of the 1914 Commission had been on much the same lines. These recommendations, more or less, find expression in the new Currency Acts (permanent provisions). The method of valuation of all securities is the calculation of their purchase price. In the case of created *ad hoc* securities, or securities issued direct to the Currency Department, the market price of same or similar securities, on the day of issue, would be taken as their price. The problem of depreciation of the permanent securities appeared in acute form during the War. Government had therefore to do something to keep up the value of the reserves. On this point Haily's speech in the Legislative Council on September 16, 1920, gives a resumé of the Government's policy. 'Regarding consols,' Haily said, like all prudent persons, we realised some time ago that it was necessary to write down their value. Accordingly in 1916 and '17 we placed a sum of £850,000 for that purpose. More recently we have transferred our holding of Consols to the gold standard reserve, obtaining from that reserve short term securities in their stead. Therefore there is no further question of loss in capital value in regard to our consols. Regarding sterling investments in England, the Bill (also the 1923 Act) provides that in future they should be short term securities. We are therefore fully protected against a fall in value in that respect. Regarding Indian permanent securities we now hold 8 crores, 2 crores being 1896-97 3 per cent., and 6 crores being 3½ per cent. issue (*cf.* the figures for 1924 in next Chapter). The Bill, (also 1923 Act) provides for 20 crores holding of rupee securities. Both these securities have depreciated. Speaking for myself, I cannot of course bind my successors, I may say that it will be fully recognised by the Government of India that when we have written off the depreciation in our gold securities which is caused by the recent change in the rating of the sovereign, we shall do our best, we shall indeed make it an obligation to proceed to apply, preferably from the interests of paper currency investments the sums necessary to bring these securities up to the value at which our 3 and 3½ per cents. will stand at that time in the market. That disposes of the 8 crores long term securities (in 1923, 10 crores). Regarding 12 crores which we shall be now allowed to create under the (permanent) provisions of our Bill, it is our intention to create them in short-term securities preferably in our own Treasury Bills.' The extraordinary demands upon the revenue of the Government that have delayed the utilisation of the interest from securities in extinguishing the created securities, have also delayed its employment for the rehabilitation of the depreciating securities in the reserve. When the task of starting a depreciation fund to compensate the falling off in the capital value of the securities, will again be taken up, it is impossible to foretell.

Our paper currency system, it will appear from the foregoing survey, rests on the Act of 1920 (Act 45), reproduced in the Act of 1923. Act 45 of 1920 is a landmark in the history of the paper currency. The next landmark will be reached when the time comes for declaring the 'appointed day' when the permanent provisions, now only in the Act serving as a picture of the distant goal, will have been realised. For all our optimism, the day is still far off. In view of the recommendations of the Hilton-Young Commission, that day, for all we know, may not arrive at all. The Commissioners have proposed a thorough scheme of monetary reconstruction and if their ideas are accepted, which is not unlikely, the whole of the permanent and temporary provisions will have to be scrapped and an entirely new set of provisions put in.

A Note on the Federal Reserve Note-Issue System of U.S.A. in Comparison with the Indian System.

The note-issue system of the federal reserve board of U.S.A., from which the principle of the Indian seasonal issue against bills of exchange has been borrowed, (see report of Smith Committee, 1919), offers a number of features which have not all been copied in the Indian system. It is well-worth studying these features. They serve to show how in most respects the American provisions are far more liberal than the Indian in ensuring an easy elasticity in the note-issue, and how in certain respects they seem to be comparatively conservative. In both countries there is a periodicity in the demand for currency, although the high industrialisation of U.S.A. makes the seasonal variations of the rate of interest there far less marked than it is in India. It must also be borne in mind that the cheque habit is prevalent to a far greater degree in U.S.A. than in India. The federal reserve Act has introduced a considerable amount of elasticity not only in the note-issue but also in the deposit currency system. Even as regards notes, it may be noted that the federal reserve notes although forming a substantial part of the total issue, still do not form the whole of it. In India on the contrary the Government notes are the only paper money in circulation and consequently it is far more important that it should have adequate elasticity than would be the case if we had a number of other sources to fall back upon.

The elasticity in the American System operates in the following way :

Member Banks if they need notes rediscount eligible paper with their federal reserve bank and take the proceeds of the rediscount in federal reserve notes which pass readily as hand to hand money. In contrast to India these notes are not legal tender money but they are always readily accepted. They are obligations of the U.S.A. Government and are ' a first and permanent lien on all the assets ' of the issuing federal reserve banks, including double liability of member banks on their subscription to federal reserve bank stock. The notes are issued against certain high grade collateral. The value of the collateral must fully cover the value of the notes. The collateral may consist of

(1) Paper endorsed by member banks and drawn for strictly commercial industrial or agricultural purposes or for the purposes of carrying or trading in securities of the U. S. A. Government, in other words paper of the type which is eligible for rediscount at a federal reserve bank. Limitations regarding both time and purpose characterise these eligible papers. As to time, notes rediscounted must have a maturity at the time of the rediscount of not more than 90 days (exclusive of days of grace), except that a limited amount of bills drawn for agricultural purposes or based on live-stock may be rediscounted, provided they have a maturity not exceeding six months (exclusive of days of grace). As to purpose, only two classes of paper are admissible :

they are (*a*) notes, drafts or bills of exchange bearing the endorsement of a member bank and 'arising out of actual commercial transactions' that is, issued or drawn 'for agricultural, industrial or commercial purposes, or the proceeds of which have been used or are to be used for such purposes'; (*b*) notes, drafts and Bills of exchange bearing the endorsement of a member bank and issued or drawn for the purposes of carrying or trading in bonds and notes of the Government of the U.S.A. It is to be noted that only U.S.A. Government securities are mentioned, the law expressly prohibiting the rediscount of paper issued or drawn for the purposes of carrying or trading in stocks, bonds, and other investment securities.

(2) Bills of exchange endorsed by member bank and bankers' acceptances bought by the federal reserve bank in the open market.

(3) Gold and gold certificates.

The federal reserve bank secures these notes on application to the federal reserve agent after depositing with the agent tne rediscounted paper or other eligible papers in its portfolio. This process may continue as long as (*a*) the federal reserve bank gets eligible papers and (*b*) as long as its gold reserve does not fall below the normal legal minimum of 40 per cent. It will be observed that in India no such minimum metallic reserve is compulsory. The notes are issued here simply on the strength of the Bills, without any further backing of metal.

The eligible papers in U.S.A. thus offer a far greater freedom of choice to the banks wanting notes, than is thc case in India. In India neither external Bills of exchange nor Government paper is allowed to serve as the basis, and the conditions regarding the maturity of the paper seem to be stricter. In America further, extraordinary powers are given to the board to meet emergency situation. In such critical times the Federal reserve board may permit a reduction of the note reserve below 40 per cent., provided it imposes a graduated tax upon the amount of the deficiency (of the *reserve*, not of the issue)—a tax which will consequently be added to the rate of interest and discount fixed by the Federal reserve board. In extreme emergencies the Federal reserve board may suspend for a period not exceeding 30 days and from time to time renew such suspension for periods not exceeding 15 days, any reserve requirements specified by the Act.

The Federal reserve notes naturally retire themselves. Any reserve bank, the Act says, may retire notes by depositing them with the Federal reserve agent or with the U. S. A. treasury, and then the bank receives back the paper (collateral) it had deposited with the agent. To make this process of retirement still quicker, certain additional provisions have also been made. In the first place the national banks are not permitted to count the notes in their vault as legal money in forming their legal cash reserves. So that as soon as convenient they always return the notes and take back gold or some other kind of notes that may serve as part of the legal reserve. Transportation charges to further facilitate their speedy return are paid by the Federal reserve bank. When such packets of notes contain notes of other

Federal reserve banks these must be sent to the respective banks. A second device to ensure the eventual contraction of the issue, although this has not been up to now (1922),* made use of, is that the Federal reserve board is empowered to charge such a rate of interest as it may choose on Federal reserve notes (uncovered) issued to Federal reserve banks. Evidently this feature has been borrowed by India. It will be noted however that in U.S.A. no interest is charged on all the notes, but only on those notes which are not covered by a 40 per cent. gold reserve or gold certificates. There is no place for any scale of interest rates as we find in India, in the American system.

---

* The A.B.C. of the Federal reserve system by E. W. Kemmerer, 1922.

A NOTE ON THE RATES OF INTEREST CHARGED FOR THE ISSUE OF SEASONAL EMERGENCY CURRENCY.

The terms of the issue of additional paper currency in times of monetary stringency, against self-retiring bills of exchange, have varied much since the system was introduced. Not only has the maximum amount been increased but the scale of interest charges has also been altered. How the government has proceeded in preparing its new scale of charges, it is not known. The Smith Committee in making the first proposal for the new bill issue, also suggested a certain rate, but the Committee does not say what considerations governed its choice of that particular rate. The only basis on which such a scale of charges can be prepared is obviously the money rates in the market, and it may be presumed that both the government and the committee satisfied themselves by an exhaustive study of the rates ruling month by month for a number of years, before they selected their scales of rates. The study of the seasonal periodicity of the bank rate, which I am appending here, does not pretend to be a very exhaustive one. The quantitative measurement of seasonal fluctuations is as interesting as it is an important subject. It is curious however that in none of the text books on Indian Currency and Banking (including even Mr. Shirras' otherwise useful work and Mr. Rao's recent study of Indian Banking), except in Mr. Keynes' book, do we find any thorough attempt at dealing with the question of this periodicity. Still Mr. Keynes does not give us any general averages so as to indicate the trend. In the tables that I am giving here I have taken up the rate of interest of the Presidency Bank of Bengal and later of the Imperial Bank of India (demand loan on government paper) ruling at the end of each month and I have averaged them. I have thought on the advice of Prof. Bowley, that a period of 20 years, 1903—1922, is quite sufficient for the purpose in hand. I have thought it proper to stop with 1922, because after that year the seasonal issues of paper currency substantially affected the rates in the busy seasons. Since my object has been to study the monthly fluctuations of the rate *before* there was any emergency currency to relieve the market, it would have been unwise to go beyond 1922. Further the fact that the war period of 1914-18 has been included need cause no appreciable error, as whatever abnormality they may have contained, has very likely been swamped in the result. To notice if the war period really made any difference, I had made separate calculations, leaving out the war years altogether. But the result has been substantially the same. It will be seen from the figures that money conditions have been abnormally easy in certain years. During 1914-15 and 1917-18, the bank rate never exceeded 6 per cent., the rate now selected for the release of seasonal currency. This again happened during 1925-26, the year having been remarkable for the abundance of the supply of floating credit. Consequently there was no occasion for issuing any additional currency during the year.

MONTHLY RATES OF INTEREST.

Years.	Jan.	Feb.	Mar.	Apl.	May.	Jun.	Jul.	Aug.	Sep.	Oct.	Nov.	Dec.
1903	7	8	7	5	6	5	4	3	3	3	3	6
1904	7	7	6	5	4	3	3	3	3	5	6	6
1905	6	7	7	4	4	4	3	4	5	5	6	7
1906	8	9	7	5	6	4	3	5	6	7	8	9
1907	9	9	9	7	5	5	3	3	5	5	6	6
1908	9	9	7	7	6	5	3	3	4	4	6	6
1909	8	8	7	6	5	4	3	3	4	4	5	6
1910	6	6	7	7	6	4	3	3	4	5	6	7
1911	7	8	7	7	6	4	4	3	5	5	5	5
1912	8	6	8	6	5	4	3	3	4	5	7	7
1913	8	7	7	7	6	4	3	5	6	6	7	7
1914	7	7	6	6	5	4	3	5	5	5	6	6
1915	6	6	6	6	6	5	5	5	6	6	6	6
1916	8	8	8	8	7	6	5	5	6	7	8	8
1917	8	7	6	6	6	6	6	6	6	5	5	5
1918	6	6	6	6	5	5	5	5	5	5	6	6
1919	7	7	6	6	6	5	5	5	5	5	5	5
1920	6	7	7	7	7	6	5	5	5	5	7	7
1921	7	7	6	6	6	5	5	5	5	5	5	7
1922	7	8	8	7	7	5	4	4	4	5	5	7
Average for all years.	7.25	7.34	6.9	6.2	5.7	4.65	3.9	4.15	4.8	5.1	5.9	6.45

These figures are interesting and useful. They provide a fairly reliable index of the rates of interest month by month which is invaluable to the paper currency administrator in fixing a scale of interest at wnich seasonal loans are to be made.

By adding these monthly averages together and dividing the sum by twelve we can next find out a general average for all months for all years. This comes out to be 5.69. By comparing now the monthly averages with this general average for all months, a picture of the seasonal trend in interest rates may be easily drawn. The excess and the defects will provide a quantitative measurement of the expected ups and downs of the rate of interest, from the general rate for all months. Thus provided conditions are normal, we may expect January to add 1.56 to the average yearly rate, February to add 1.65 to it and so on. The complete list of monthly deviations are as follows (some plus, some minus) :—

Jan.	Feb.	Mar.	Apl.	May.	Jun.	Jul.	Aug.	Sep.	Oct.	Nov.	Dec.
1.56	1.65	1.21	.51	.01	1.04	1.79	1.54	.89	.59	.21	.76

Taking the yearly average (5.69) as the zero line these deviations can be if necessary shown in the form of a very convenient graph. It will serve as a chart of the seasonal trend of money rates.

The table and the figures ought to throw some considerable light on the preparations of a scale of charges for the seasonal issue. It clearly points out that most of the money ought to be available when the rate of interest stands at 6 per cent. and the rest ought to be liberated when it reaches 7 per cent. On this basis for five months of the year, namely, from December to April, we can profitably have the additional funds placed in the market, no sum as a general rule being lent in the remaining seven months.

The results for the years 1898 to 1922 leaving out the 4 War years of 1914—1918 were much the same. The 20 yearly monthly averages were as follows :—

Jan.	Feb.	Mar.	Apl.	May.	Jun.	Jul.	Aug.	Sep.	Oct.	Nov.	Dec.
7.5	7.8	7.25	6.45	5.9	4.75	3.75	3.8	4.6	4.9	5.5	6.4

The general average, all months and all years, came out as 5.71. The deviations of the monthly averages from this general average were as follows (plus and minus) :—

Jan.	Feb.	Mar.	Apl.	May.	Jun.	Jul.	Aug.	Sep.	Oct.	Nov.	Dec.
1.79	2.09	1.54	.74	.19	.96	1.96	1.91	1.11	.81	.21	.69

CHAPTER IX

The Growth of the Issue.

§ 1. Summary statistics of the growth of the paper circulation p. 227.—§ 2. Explanation of the growing popularity of the notes despite several unfavourable factors, p. 229.—§ 3. The division into gross and active circulation, with figures of such circulation, p. 232.—§ 4. Comparison of circulation and the price-leval. A typical currency return, p. 235.—§ 5. Seasonal demand for currency and its bearing on the gross and active circulation, p. 237.—§ 6. The distribution of the issue by circles and denominations, p. 239.—§ 7. Sources of information, p. 242.—§ 8. Currency profits and currency forgeries, p. 243.—§ 9. A chronological survey of currency legislation, p. 244.—§ 10. A biographical notice of Lushington, p. 250.—§ 11. Of James Wilson, p. 251.—§ 12. Of Sir Charles Wood, p. 253.—§ 13. Of Samuel Laing, p. 254.—§ 14. Of Sir Malcolm Haily, and Sir Basil Blackett, p. 255.

This chapter shall deal with three things. First, it shall try to interpret some of the statistics concerning the issue, secondly, a running survey will be made of the progress of paper currency legislation, and thirdly, a number of short biographical notices will conclude it. For considerations of space I had to condense the statistical tables as much as possible.

Statistical.

§ 1. The history of the paper currency as revealed in the figures of circulation is briefly a history of growth. Ever since the foundation of the issue, the circulation had been steadily increasing. Barring the War period, the rate of this increase has been a remarkably steady one. From 1862 to 1914 the issue presents generally a slowly rising curve through the years. There have been one or two sudden jumps, as in the year 1891 when the circulation nearly doubled from that of the previous year. Some years again disclose rather sudden contractions in the issue. But taking the rise with the fall, in a bird's eye view over the whole period, it is a story of the progressive increase in the gross circulation. According to Newmarch, the extension of the issue has been up to 1914 almost in geometric ratio. In 1864 there were Rs. 5 crores worth of notes in circulation. In 1914 the circulation stood at 66 crores. In 50 years the note issue had multiplied to 13 times its original size, a not inconsiderable rate of increase. But all this progress was thrown into insignificance by the tremendous growth during the War. In the last 50 years before the War, the aggregate additions to the note currency amounted to a little over 60 crores, but between 1915 and 1920 the additions amounted to the colossal figure of 113 crores. India thus in 5 years practically travelled a track that normally she would have perhaps taken one hundred years to cover. It is true that the War inflation carried on in India was many times smaller in scale than what was undertaken in many belligerent countries. But although relatively to other countries, the increase may not have been very striking, yet as compared with the traditions of the country the increase must be regarded as an enormous one. At the end of 1918 the gross circualtion increased 10 per cent. as compared with the pre-war level. The following index numbers, taken from Shirras, of the relative growth in circulation, present the facts in a readily comprehensible fashion.

Quinquennial averages

	1900-4	1905-9	1910-14	1915-19
Circulation (gross)	100	136	185	285
,, (net)	100	141	186	310
,, (active)	100	137	183	317

It must be observed that after 1919 the circulation had still further increased. Between 1864 and 1924 the growth of the circulation can be conveniently studied by means of the following decennial figures :—

Increase in Average Ciroulation. (Gross).

Financtial years ending in 31st March.	Lakhs of rupees.	years.	Lakhs of rupees.
1864	5,19	1904	36,41
1874	11,15	1914	65,55
1884	13,17	1924	179,01
1894	28,29		

§ 2. What is the explanation of this huge increase ? The notes are by no means an ideal form of currency, considering the special circumstances of India. To the average Indian, bereft of any proper house wherein to shelter himself and his notes they are very often more an encumbrance than a help. Paper is destroyed by fire which is unhappily a familiar visitor to his thatched cottage. The floods and white ants are equally dangerous enemies. Above all, the age-long tradition of using metal money makes it very difficult for the paper habit to make any headway with him. He is naturally suspicious about the sincerity of the promise written on the face of the note and very often he cannot read it himself. The risks of forgeries further dissuade him from using the notes. His dress almost always and his occupation sometimes, are also obstacles in the way of a ready acceptance of the notes. In the face of all these difficulties it is no small wonder that the note currency in India has been able to make such long strides, in less than three-quarters of a century. It is a testimony alike of the wisdom with which the government has managed the paper currency and of the disappearance of currency prejudices in the unchanging East. The spread of education and the increase in the means of communication helped in this work considerably. The provision of adequate conversion facilities, the breaking down of the circle barriers and throwing the whole country open to universal notes, have been also important factors in bringing about the increase. Further the absence of any appreciable use of cheques, the rival form of paper money, made the note in India do the work practically of both. With the rise in the prestige of the government, the confidence in the note issue also increased. The issue of small notes took the new cheap currency to the doors of the poor people also and the increasing popularity was reflected in the increasing circulation. How strong the foundation of faith in the note issue had become was proved by the shock of the War. In spite of untold difficulties the convertibility of the notes was maintained. Not only that, the issue was increased manifold. No doubt, the want of other forms of currency then contributed to a great extent to the increase in the circulation. Notes were pressed into circulation by every means possible. But this element of forced circulation cannot by itself account for the very conspicuous growth of the issue. The growing confidence in the issue, begotten of the judicious administration of the previous fifty years, together with the decline of sentimental objections against the notes, primarily accounts for it. The issue was almost taken to the breaking point, but it showed wonderful properties of elasticity. How much in recent years the note habit had permeated into the ignorant farmer classes would appear from the fact that in 1918, for the first time the bulk of the jute crop in Bengal was financed by notes. In that year the Bank of Bengal remitted to Dacca, Narayanganj and Chandpur Rs. 567 lakhs in notes and fifty two lakhs in rupees during the busy season for jute, from August to October. For moving the same crops in the corresponding period of 1913, a sum of 678 lakhs in rupees and only 2 lakhs in notes was necessary (Shirras). Similarly the cotton crop was almost entirely financed by notes. A further illustration of the extended use of notes, according to Shirras, was found in Calcutta 'where one of the largest exchange banks in March, 1914, received 86.7 per cent. of its total receipts in notes, in March 1919 this had risen to 96.27 per cent. leaving only a paltry 3.73 per cent. in rupees.' All this goes to show that the note in India has been now very well established. If there was any doubt as to its popularity even 10 years ago, that doubt has now entirely disappeared. The notes are now as acceptable a form of currency as the coins.

§ 3. A distinction used to be made in the former statistics of the note issue between gross, active, and net circulation. The gross circulation comprises all the notes that have been issued and not yet paid off. Net means the gross circulation minus notes held by the government in its treasuries. Active is narrower by one more degree. It is the net circulation less notes held by the presidency banks at their head offices. Whatever value this three-fold classification had before, with the handing over of the reserve treasuries to the Imperial Bank of India in 1920, the line between the gross and the net circulation automatically disappeared. Onwards from 1920 therefore only the dual classification into gross and active has been used. The latter means the total amount of notes outstanding, less those held in (1) Government treasuries and (2) in the local head offices of the Imperial Bank of India. It gives therefore a fairly accurate idea of the amount actually in circulation among the people at any given time. Notes held by the Imperial Bank at its local head offices consist usually of high value notes forming part of the Bank's cash reserve which might be regarded as a permanent lock-up. They should therefore be omitted from an estimate of the net circulation among the people. The point in not omitting also the notes held at the branches of the bank is that usually they ' consist of such an amount of notes as is sufficient to provide for the ordinary current transactions of the banks and the tendency will be for these balances to be reduced to lower figures in view of the facilities which the bank enjoys for obtaining transfers through currency. The notes held at branches are therfore legitimately treated as in circulation and are included in the figures of active circulation. This procedure has the additional advantage of maintaining continuity in the previous statistics.' (Controller's report 1920-21). But it involves an anomaly. It is that as the Imperial Bank will be opening new branches or taking over more and more the work of the treasuries, the same amount of notes formerly excluded from the active circulation (since being in the treasuries) will now have to be included in that (since being at the branch banks). Although by this means the figures of a few years hence will not be strictly comparable with the present figures, yet the difference would have represented a real change of affairs. It will indicate that notes that formerly used to be held by the government, have now been transferred to the branch banks where they form part of the active circulation being used in current transactions. This method of dividing the issue into active and gross is certainly less open to criticism than that of trisecting it into gross, active and net. But objections are not wanting against this system of treating the government as a separate entity with regard to paper currency. In 1914 before the Chamberlain Commission, Lord Meston, a high authority on Indian finance, seriously questioned the wisdom of the procedure. He saw no reason why a difference should be made between the note circulation held by the public, and the other part held by the government. 'Government,' he said, 'in all matters connected with what I may call their currency trusts or standard trusts, should put themselves out of court, rather that they should treat themselves as being private creditors. From that point of view, I should like to see the notes held by the government treated in exactly the same way as the notes held by the public.' The utility of a classification depends on the object with which the classification is made. If the object of the statistics supplied under the two heads is to indicate the relative impact of the circulation upon the convertibility of the note, the distinction between gross and active is certainly worth while, as it shows the part of the circulation in the hands of the government, which is not likely to be presented for payment. It is a rough and ready index of the popularity of the note. But if we want our statistics to interpret for us the total purchasing power in the country, no useful purpose is served by separating the amount of notes in the hands of the public from the amount held by the government. Both represent so much purchasing power. The effect of each upon the price-level is the same. As it is, there is a balance of advantage in maintaining the classification into gross and active.

The statistics of the gross and active circulation as well as the total investments of the paper currency reserve, are summarised below.

CIRCULATION OF NOTES AND CURRENCY INVESTMENT.

IN LAKHS OF RUPEES.

Year 31st March.		Circulation Gross.	Circulation Active.	Currency Investment.
1864	...	5,35	4,95	2,49
1870	...	10,47	9,66	3,60
1880	...	12,36	11,03	6,00
1890	...	15,77	13,31	6,00
1900	...	28,74	22,09	10,00
1910	...	54,41	39,98	12,00
1920	...	174,52	153,78	86,86
1924	...	185,85	169,06	71,53

It is to be noted that the figures of active circulation up to 1890 are not quite correct, as they included notes held at the Presidency Bank's Head offices. It is only after 1892 that the notes held at the head offices began tc be separated, and correct figures of active circulation were available.

§ 4. The rather close correspondence between the increase in note issue and the rise in the index numbers of general prices, will be apparent from the following table (1903-22). This correspondence will have been equally apparent if figures for average circulation instead of gross circulation had been taken. It is not contended that paper currency was the sole cause of the changes in the price level. Many factors had been at work of which paper currency inflation had been a most important one.

General Index Numbers of Prices in India. 39 Articles, 1873 being taken as 100.

Years		Gross Circulation 31st March. Lakhs of Rs.	Price-Level.	Years	Gross Circulation 31st March. Lakhs of Rs.	Price-Level.
1903	...	35,72	99	1913	68,98	143
1904	...	38,21	101	1914	66,12	147
1905	...	39,18	110	1915	61,63	152
1906	...	44,66	129	1916	67,73	184
1907	...	46,95	137	1917	86,37	196
1908	...	46,89	138	1918	99,79	225
1909	...	45,49	124	1919	153,46	276
1910	...	54,41	122	1920	174,72	281
1911	...	54,99	129	1921	166,16	236
1912	...	61,36	137	1922	174,76	232

This parallelism between the price-level and the note circulation will be strikingly apparent if the figures are shown in the form of two historical graphs plotted on the same base line of years.

The gross circulation of paper money and the composition of the currency reserve* were as follows on 31st March, 1924. Returns for later years are easily available in the Currency Reports.

---

* In the Currency Report for 1923-24 (p. 30) the reserve of internal bills of exchange held against the issue is not included; it is difficult to say why. One awkward result is that the total reserve there shown, does not tally with the total issue, leaving for want of any explanation, an impression of incorrectness about the figures.

LAKHS OF RUPEES.

Gross Circulation	Silver coin	Gold coin and bullion	Silver bullion under coinage.	Securities	Internal bills of exchange.
185,85	74,18	22,32	5,82	71,53	12,00

The security reserve (other than the 12 crores of bills of exchange) was made up of the following classes of paper :—

Rupee securities.	Cost price.
3½ p. c. of 1842-43	... 8,00,00,000
3 p. c. of 1896-97	... 1,99,99,945
Indian Treasury bills	... 47,52,75,000
Sterling securities—	
British Treasury bills	... 13,99,94,800

Throughout the above figures, gold and sterling securities have been valued at the rupees 10 parity, that is, 2 shillings for every rupee. On an 1s. 4d. basis, the rate that many people would like to see adopted, the total gold and sterling holdings would stand at Rs. 54,47,82,220 instead of at Rs. 36,31,88,147 as at present (on 2s. basis). The currency reserve consequently will be swollen by Rs. 18,15,94,073. This excess will have to be either appropriated for revenue or credited to the gold standard reserve or go to inflate the note circulation.

§ 5. The seasonal variations in the size of the circulation is another interesting point about the figures of Indian paper currency. It has been said before that the currency requirements of an agricultural country are bound to be jerky in nature, spread unevenly over the whole year. In India normally, the the cold weather is the time when the need for money is the greatest. One harvest comes after another and the cycle, briefly is as follows :—During the rains from July to October, enormous amounts of currency are required to finance the jute crop in Bengal. With the close of the jute season begins, in the cold weather, November to March, the season for cotton, seeds, and wheat in Northern and Southern India, and this is followed at the end of December by the rice trade in Burma. The ebb and flow of the paper circulation which result from the uneven distribution of the harvests, would have been quite striking by themselves. But the situation is further complicated by the revenue collections of the government. While public expenditure continues fairly regularly throughout the whole year, the greater part of the revenue is collected during January, February and March. A large part of the government balances, when at this period they are at their highest, is converted for convenience into notes, and the gross circulation is thus increased. The balances of the Presidency Banks also used to vary considerably, as they also in slack times turned into notes so much of their cash as was not wanted for use at once. After the recent handing over of the main part of the Treasury work to the Imperial Bank, the effect of the revenue collections as well as of the slack and busy seasons, may be regarded as being focussed on the same agency. The key to the situation lies in the conversion of the idle coins into notes by the banks in the slack season, thereby increasing the gross circulation as well as the metallic reserve. The active circulation, however, decreases. In the busy season, the operation is reversed. Banks obtain coins by the tender of notes, so that the metallic reserves as well as the gross circulation decline. The active circulation, however, increases. It must be observed that there are no two well-marked busy and slack seasons. A busy season in one province often overlaps a slack one in another and may either be delayed or arrive early. No strict uniformity of trade cycles should therefore be looked for.

The statistics of the note circulation given in official reports mostly refer to the circulation as on the 31st March in each year. This is the time when the official year ends. It is the time when the busy season is declining and the figures of circulation would be then different from the average circulation throughout the year. For a comparative basis, the figures for 31st March, are, however, quite satisfactory. How the note habit has increased is testified by the per capita active circulation on the last day of March, since 1915. In 1915 it was 1.4, in 1917 2.1, in 1919 4.2, in 1921 4.6, finally in 1923 it stood at 5.0.

§ 6. About the distribution of the note-issue by circles, tables used to be given in the yearly-published currency reports showing the relative circulation in the different provinces. The competition, in this respect, for the first place used to be between Calcutta and Bombay, while the other circles followed at a respectable distance. In 1921-22 the lead was taken by Calcutta, but in 1922-23 the Western Presidency showed an increase of circulation over Calcutta. The distribution into circles is no longer shown, a departure having been made since the last issue of the Controller's report. The reason for ceasing to publish these figures is that they are not of much value. With the universalisation of all notes up to 100 rupees, the circles no longer possess any real significance. Still, as some few high value notes yet remain outside the scope of universalisation, the distribution of circulation by circles would have been interesting to compare.

Most interesting is the question of the distribution of the issue by different denominations of the notes. The following table taken from Shirras shows the percentage distribution of the circulation between notes of different denominations from 1910-14 to 1919.

	Percentage to Total.									
Denominations	1	2.8	5	1^	20	50	100	500	1,000	10,000
Pre-War average 1910-14			2.2	24.5	.4	3.2	26.3	4.6	14.7	24.1
1915 (31st March)			2.6	24.3	.1	2.8	26.0	3.8	15.0	25.4
1916 ,,			3.3	27.8	.1	3.3	30.1	3.4	13.3	18.7
1917 ,,			3.8	26.2	.1	2.9	29.3	2.8	13.0	21.9
1918 ,,	.3	.2	5.5	27.4	0.4	3.5	32.6	2.5	13.8	14.2
1919 ,,	.68	1.2	6.0	30.6	.02	3.2	28.6	1.6	9.8	12.2

It will appear from the above table that the Rs. 10 and the Rs. 100 notes have consistently taken the lead. In later years too, they have been undoubtedly the most popular. Except that the Re. 1 and Rs. 2-8 notes formed a greater portion of the circulation, the character of the issue in recent years, has remained practically unchanged. In 1920-21 the percentage of the Rs. 10 and Rs. 100 notes were 35.5 and 31.9. respectively (of the total issue excluding the Rs. 10,000 notes). The Rs. 5 note increased to 9.5. The Re. 1 note declined from 8.7 to 6.4 but this was no evidence of the lack of popularity of India's tiniest note. Owing to restrictions upon the issue of metal, Re. 1 notes had to be issued formerly in very large quantities, but in 1920-21 payment was renewed in coins or notes freely, as the payees wanted. The circulation of the Re. 1 note in former years was to some extent forced. But in 1920-21 the circulation for the first time represented acceptance by pure choice. By 1922-23 a slight increase was noticeable in the percentage of the Re. 1 note. It was then 6.7 of the total issue (excluding Rs. 10,000 notes). The share of the other important notes will be seen from the table below (the Rs. 2-8 note being omitted as negligible) :—

Year		Re. 1	Rs. 5	Rs. 10	Rs. 50	Rs. 100	Rs. 500	Rs. 1,000	Total
1921-22	...	6.2	10.0	36.3	2.5	34.2	1.3	9.3	100
1922-23	...	6.7	10.0	34.7	2.3	36.4	1.0	8.8	100
1923-24	...	6.6	9.3	33.4	1.8	40.5	.9	7.5	100
1924-25	...	2.5	9.3	40.5	1.5	37.7	.8	7.7	100
1925-26	...	.4	9.2	45.2	1.3	35.4	.7	7.8	100

The Rs. 2-8 note has now finally disappeared from circulation. Never since it was introduced has that note really been a popular form of value. In 1921-22 it formed only .2 per cent. of the circulation and was no longer being issued. In 1922-23 its share had still further declined, falling down to .1 per cent. of the whole. In popularity the Rs. 10 and the Rs. 100 note, still lead. The new forgery-proof design of the Rs. 10 note has perhaps highly

31

contributed to forcing its share to such a high percentage of the total.

§ 7. A word about the sources of information. By far the best source of paper currency statistics is of course, the 'Currency Report' issued annually by the Controller of the Currency. Independent Currency reports had been published for a very long time, although some of the earlier copies are hardly available now. Since 1910-11, however, the two separate reports which formerly dealt with (1) the movement of funds and the resource operations of the government and (2) the operations of the currency department respectively, have been combined into one report. The reason was the re-organisation of the currency department and the discovery that the management of the government balances was closely bound up with trade and currency. After this amalgamation, the Currency Report has suffered in some respects. There is space now for fewer currency tables than were possible to give in former reports. The Currency Report is a general review of the monetary conditions throughout India and deals with exchange, foreign trade, banking, and several allied matters, incidentally. The share of attention falling upon paper currency has, no wonder, declined. Besides these yearly reports, abstracts of accounts of the department are published in the Gazette weekly. Up to 1891 they were published once every month, but the more frequent publication once every week, was decided upon in that year (*vide* 1897-98 report). Selected paper currency tables also appear in the Statistics of British

India, new series (1923), although in more contracted form than in the older series (of several volumes).

§ 8. The paper currency department is a revenue-yielding department of the State. The profits of the paper circulation, though not very considerable in former years, have grown up to quite respectable figures in recent years. The growing profits are illustrated in the table below :—

Years ending 31st March	Profits in lakhs of rupees	Years ending 31st March	Profits in lakhs of rupees.
1870	14	1910	27
1880	25	1920	349
1890	21	1924	212
1900	29	1925	249
		1926	284*

Before passing on to a review of legislation, mention might be made of the great increase in forgeries, along with the increase in circulation. A portion of the Currency Report is every year concerned with the forgeries, which are sometimes quite cleverly done. Sir G. Fleetwood Wilson said once that the most perfect forgery he ever saw was on a Japanese pocket handkerchief. In the centre of it was an absolute facsimile of the Rs. 10 note. Every Currency Report will speak of forged notes equally cleverly done. Some figures are given below which will serve to illustrate the great increase in the number of forgeries. They disclose a situation which calls for prompt and vigorous action. The forgeries recorded in the Currency reports refer, however, to

* The figure for 1926 is only approximately true.

detected cases. How many remain undetected can only be left to conjecture.

Number of Forged Notes Received at Currency Offices.

Years.	Number of Notes.	Years.	Number of Notes.
1892-93	19	1919	1,174
1900	155	1020	1,896
1905	100	1921	4,597
1910	129	1922	6,042
1915	170	1923	7,237
1916	97	1924	11,638
1917	96	1925	14,160
1918	396	1926	11,445

Progress of Legislation.

§ 9. The following are the successive enactments that have been made in relation to paper currency in India.

(1) Act 19 of 1861. It founded the government paper currency in India. Reproduced in full in appendix A.

(2) Act 24 of 1861. An act to enable the Presidency Banks to enter into arrangements with the government for managing the issue, payment and exchange of government currency notes, and certain business hitherto transacted by the government treasuries.

(3) Act 1 of 1866. An amending act. Lays down revised procedure for receiving notes for bullion.

(4) Act 30 of 1867. To be read and taken as part of Act 19 of 1861. Empowers the Governor-General in Council to transfer for purposes of the Currency Act, any town from any Presidency to another. Currency circles may thus cross provincial frontiers.

(5) Act 15 of 1870. An amending Act. (*a*) Constitutes a separate and independent Head Commissioner of the currency other than the Mint Master. (*b*) The maximum fiduciary issue raised to 6 crores from 4.

(6) Act 3 of 1871. Consolidating and amending the law. The minimum denomination of notes brought down to 5 rupees. The Government takes power to make and alter rules and regulations.

(7) Act 20 of 1882. Called the Indian Paper Currency Act 1882. Act 3 of 1871 is repealed. New features are (*a*) Paper currency extended to Burma. (*b*) Currency Agencies introduced. Certain supplementary powers taken.

(8) Act 15 of 1890. An amending Act. Increases the invested portion of the reserve from 6 to 8 crores.

(9) Act 8 of 1893. An amending Act. (*a*) Stops and discontinues the issue of notes in exchange for silver bullion. (*b*) Removes the limit of the amount to which notes will be issued for gold.

(10) Act 21 of 1896. An amending Act. The invested portion of the reserve further raised from 8 to 14 crores.

(11) Act 2 of 1898. Provides for the issue of currency notes on the security of gold received in England. The Act to be in force for only six months.

(12) Act 8 of 1898. Amends the preceding act and lengthens its duration from six months to two years and a half.

(13) Act 12 of 1899. Amends the law relating to forgery of currency notes. Additions of new sections to the Indian Penal Code imposing heavy penalties for forgeries.

(14) Act 22 of 1899. An amending Act. Gold coins made legal tender at Rs. 15 to a sovereign. Notes to be issued in exchange for not only rupees but also for gold coins legal tender in India.

(15) Act 8 of 1900. An amending Act. To remain in force for two years. Makes elaborate provisions for the issue of notes against gold received by the Secretary of State in England.

(16) Act 9 of 1902. An amending Act. The provisions for the issue against gold tendered in England are made permanent.

(17) Act 6 of 1903. An amending Act. Universalises the Rs. 5 note except in Burma.

(18) Act 3 of 1905. Consolidating and amending the law relating to paper currency. Called the Indian Paper Currency Act 1905. New provisions are (*a*) notes beyond certain years to be reckoned as out of circulation. All notes deemed to have been issued on the credits of the government and if presented afterwards, will be redeemed from the general revenues. (*b*) Coin and bullion to remain part of the reserve during transit between England and

India. (*c*) Limitations as to the character and amount of securities in the reserve. Total investments put down at 12 crores of which non-government of India securities could be, at their maximum, 2 crores. (*d*) Transfers of office of issue from Allahabad to Cawnpore.

(19) Act 2 of 1909. An amending Act. The exception as to Burma regarding the five rupee universal note withdrawn.

(20) Act 2 of 1910. Consolidating and amending. New features are (*a*) Notes up to Rs. 50 universalised and power taken by the Governor-General in Council to declare any other note a universal currency note by notification in the Gazette. (*b*) Whereas in the 1905 Act the currency circles were Calcutta, Madras, Bombay and Rangoon, to the list are now added Lahore, Cawnpore and Karachi. All previous currency Acts affected by the new act are repealed.

(21) Act 7 of 1911. An amending Act. Total amount of investments increased to 14 crores. Non-government of India securities not to exceed 4 crores.

(22) Act 5 of 1915. A temporary measure amending Act 2 of 1910. ' During the continuance of the present war and for a period of six months thereafter,' the total fiduciary issue to stand at 20 crores instead of 14 crores.

(23) Act 9 of 1916. Next temporary war measure. (*a*) Of the total fiduciary issue of 20 crores, the Secretary of State's holding of non-government of India securities, raised to 10 crores. (*b*) Special

power to issue 'notwithstanding anything in the Act' notes up to 6 crores of rupees against British treasury bills of equivalent value held by the Secretary of State. (*c*) Power to include created securities in the reserve, 'any securities created by the government and issued to the Head Commissioner of paper currency, shall be deemed to be securities purchased by the Governor-General in Council and the market price on the day such securities are issued, of similar securities shall be deemed to be the price at which the securities so created were purchased.'

(24) Act 11 of 1917. Consolidating the temporary amendments made in the act of 1910. To be in force during the war and six months afterwards. New addition—the British Treasury Bills issue carried to 30 crores from 6.

(25) Act 19 of 1917. Amending and a war measure. (*a*) Geographical area of the coin and bullion reserve widened, including now coin and bullion in any part of His Majesty's Dominions and in transit thereto or therefrom. (*b*) Issue of the one rupee and the two-and-a-half rupee universal notes. (*c*) The special British Treasury Bills issue increased to 42 crores.

(26) Act 6 of 1918. An amending Act. Also a war measure. The issue against British Treasury Bills further increased to 66 crores.

(27) Act 13 of 1918. A war measure. Provides that silver held in the United States of America or in course of transmission therefrom to be deemed part of the reserve.

(28) Act 2 of 1919. Next war measure. An amending Act. The special issue against British Treasury Bills raised to 80 crores.

(29) Act 26 of 1919. A temporary and amending Act. (*a*) The British Treasury Bill issue carried to 100 crores. (*b*) To silver holdings in the U.S.A. or in transmission therefrom, gold now added as part of the permissible reserve.

(30) Act 21 of 1920. Consolidating and amending the enactments amending temporarily the Indian Paper Currency Act, 1910. Received the assent of the Viceroy on 23rd March, 1920. To be in force up to 1st October, 1920. Total permissible securities in the reserve put down at 120 crores but no prescribed division between England and India.

(31) Act 36 of 1920. Amends the Indian Coinage Act. Sovereigns are valued at Rs. 10 per sovereign.

(32) Act 45 of 1920. Amends Indian Paper Currency Act, 1920. New features are: (*a*) It provides for issue of currency notes according to the new valuation of gold at Rs. 10 per sovereign and Rs. 5 per half-sovereign; (*b*) lays down the permanent constitution of the paper currency reserve. The metallic reserve not to fall below 50 per cent. of the whole issue. Gold coin and bullion held by the Secretary of State not to exceed Rs. 5 crores in value. The securities held by the Secretary of State not to be of longer maturity than one year from the date of purchase. Securities held by the Governor-General in Council to be securities of the Government of India and their amount not to exceed Rs. 20 crores of which not more than 12 crores may be securities

created by the Government of India and issued to the Controller of the Currency. (*c*) The statutory constitution to be brought into force on a day appointed by the Governor-General in Council as soon as conveniently may be after the relation of the amount of currency notes to the amount of the Reserve has been brought into conformity with the provisions outlined in the permanent constitution. Pending that, during the intermediate period certain temporary provisions are to be in force. According to them total securities held in the reserve to be limited to 85 crores. So long as the created securities forming part of this 85 crores exceed 12 crores, interest from all securities to be applied towards extinguishing the excess. (*d*) Special seasonal issue up to 5 crores against approved bills of exchange.

Act 47 of 1920. The Imperial Bank of India Act.

(33) Finance Act of 1922. The employment of accrued interest from securities to wipe away created securities until they stand at 12 crores, a process which began from 1921, 1st April, put off till 1923, 1st April.

(34) Act 10 of 1923. Consolidates the law regarding paper currency but ' makes no change in the existing law ' (Blackett), only simplifies it. Sir Basil Blackett thus explained the necessity for a simplified act. ' It is ' the Finance Member said, ' almost impossible to understand the existing Acts in the form in which they are printed. One of the first things that happened to me when I found myself in the Finance Department, was that I asked

for a copy of the Paper Currency Act in its present form, and after a hard day's labour I gave it up.' A copy of the Act is attached to the work as Appendix B.

(35) Indian Finance Act, 1923. The employment of interest to wipe out created securities postponed till 1st April, 1924.

(36) Act 36 of 1923. Amending the Indian Paper Currency Act of 1923. It introduces certain minor changes in the method of valuation of silver bullion in the currency reserve.

(37) Indian Finance Act, 1924. Among other things it amends the Paper Currency Act. The employment of interest of the securities to extinguish created securities further postponed till 1st April, 1925.

(38) The Indian Paper Currency (Amendment) Act of 1925. The maximum amount of investments permissible under the temporary provisions, raised to 100 crores from 85 crores.

(39) The Indian Finance Act, 1925. The employment of interest of the securities in the reserve for extinguishing created securities postponed again till 31st March, 1926.

BIOGRAPHIES.

Short biographical notes of persons who have mainly shaped the growth of paper currency legislation in India are given below.

§ 10. *1.* C. Hugh Lushington. Very few particulars are available about his life and activities.

Lushington, it appears, is a most usual name to come across in the list of Indian Officers before the Mutiny. Not less than 5 or 6 are met with in the Bengal Establishment. One of them E. H. Lushington actually came to occupy later the same post of Financial Secretary to the Government of India as Chas. Hugh did. There is thus some fear of confusion between the two. This particular Lushington (C.H.) joined the Indian Civil Service in 1830 and after serving his probation as an Assistant to the Magistrate and Collector of Sarun up to 1838 he was, in that year made special Deputy Collector for Shahabad and Sarun. From that position he rose to be the special Deputy Collector of Behar in 1841. In 1845 we find him to be the Resident at Malacca (See East India Registers 1830-61), then in 1896 Additional Collector of Chittagong, a rather curious transfer. In 1851 he worked as the 'Commissioner for the purchase of lands for railway purposes.' Having thus seen through a diversity of official work Lushington was made in 1852 Secretary to the Board of Revenue, Lower Provinces (Bengal) from where three years later he rose to be the Secretary to the Government of India, Financial Department and ex-officio Deputy Accountant-General to the Government of India. He remained at that post up to 1861 when he retired from service. This is about all that is known about him. What he did in his later life or when he died, it is difficult to say.

In 1863, his namesake E. H. Lushington became the Financial Secretary to the Government of India.

§ 11. 2. James Wilson (1805-60). A distinguished politician and political economist. At sixteen, he was apprenticed to a hat manufacturer at Hawick, his native place, but he had a passion for study. He is said to have still 'pursued far into the night the practice of reading and study.' After going through some turns of fortune, in 1844 he retired from business. Even before retiring he had made a name for himself by writing three works :—

(*a*) 'Influence of the corn laws as affecting all classes of the community,' 1839. In this he argued against the Corn Laws. His book is known to have made considerable influence on the mind of Cobden.

(*b*) 'Fluctuations of the Currency, Commerce and Manufacture,' 1840.

(*c*) 'The Revenue, or What shall the Chancellor do ? ' 1841. In this he urged the increase of direct taxation and reduction of tariff.

A great event in Wilson's life was his founding of the 'Economist.' This he started as a weekly paper in 1843, after consultation with Cobden and Villiers. It at once became a power in the business world and it has maintained its position ever since. Through the medium of this paper, Wilson went on holding up the principles of free trade and urging the repeal of the Corn Laws. It is said in the early stages of its existence, he used to write nearly the whole of the paper. In 1847 he brought out another work—'Capital Currency and Banking,' containing mostly his articles in the 'Economist.' He stood as a strenuous advocate of the sure convertibility of the bank note.

Wilson joined Parliament in 1847 and between 1853 and 1858 he was Financial Secretary to the Treasury, a post which has supplied India with not a few Finance Members. In 1859 he was offered the post of Finance Member in the Governor-General's Council. ' He hesitated about accepting it, for he appreciated his influence in the House of Commons, recognised the gigantic difficulties which awaited him in India and was not tempted by the high salary, as through the success of his paper aided by some prudent investments he was possessed of affluence.' On public grounds however he determined to go and on 20th October, 1859, he left England. In India he was face to face with a deficiency in revenue and an enormous increase in public debt. He proposed, among others, an income tax on all incomes above Rs. 200 a year, but with a reduction for those not exceeding Rs. 500 a year. His proposals met with considerable opposition through the action of Sir Charles Trevelyan, but that official was promptly recalled. Wilson's budget and Trevelyan's recall excited much criticism in England. Besides starting the Government's Paper Currency, he introduced great reforms in the public accounts. ' He, it was who first evoked order out of the chaos of Indian finance.'

On August 11th, 1860, Wilson died at Calcutta of dysentery and was buried in the Circular Road Cemetary. There is a full-sized marble statue in the Dalhousie Institute at Calcutta, with a brief but impressive inscription. Wilson was of active temperament and fertile in ideas. ' His memory was marvellous and an iron constitution enabled him to accomplish a vast amount of work.' (The Dictionary of National Biography.)

§ 12. 3. Sir Charles Wood, first Viscount Halifax (1800-85). Liberal M.P. in 1826, in 1832 Joint-Secretary to the Treasury. In 1846 he was Chancellor of the Exchequer. He is said to have been exceedingly well informed upon the Indian questions and as the President of the Board of Control had been responsible for passing the India Act of 1853. After some intermediate official experience he became the Secretary of State for India, on 18th June, 1859. By means of a series of measures, he reformed the finances, adapting them to the new state of things arising out of the extinction of the East India Company. For railway growths and other purposes he was obliged to borrow largely. That resulted in an increase of the Indian Debt. For this and 'for the dispute which led to the resignation of Samuel Laing in 1862, he was severely but unfairly blamed.' The budgets of 1863, 1864 and 1865, were prosperous and he was able to reduce expenditure and extinguish debt. In 1865, he met with a serious accident in the hunting field which obliged him to give up all arduous official work. He therefore resigned the Secretaryship for India on 16th February, 1866. He was raised to the peerage as Viscount Halifax of Monk Britton. His only return to official life was as Lord Priby Seal in 1870-74. He died in 1885. He was 'sound in counsel, exceedingly and widely informed and industrious, punctual and admirable man of business.' (Dictionary of National Biography.)

§ 13. *4.* Samuel Laing (1812-97). Politician, author, and man of business. He finished his education at Cambridge, where he was wrangler and Smith's Prizeman and was later called to the Bar. He joined the office of the Board of Trade and distinguished himself under successive Presidents as an authority upon railways. In 1844 he published a report on the British and Foreign Railways, a valuable work embodying the results of his experience. In 1845 he was a member of the Railway Commission. Then he resigned office at the Board of Trade and returned to his practice at the Bar. In 1848 he became Chairman and Managing Director of the London, Brighton and South Coast Railway, and under his administration the passenger traffic showed very rapid growth. Laing was elected to Parliament in 1852. In 1859 he was Financial Secretary to the Treasury. He was not long in this post when he was appointed to be the Finance Member of the Governor-General's Council in India. (October, 1860.) When first asked to go to India, Laing said to Palmerston, ' You want me to go to India to doctor a sick budget with a deficit of six millions ; this is a question of military reduction and the possibility of military reduction depends on peace. Tell me candidly what you think of the prospects of peace that I may regulate my financial policy accordingly.' Parmerston replied ' I do not trust the man at the Tuilleries an inch further than I can see him, but for the next two or three years, which is enough for your purpose, I think you are fairly safe of peace ; therefore go in for reduction.' Having effected the object of his mission, Laing returned to England and again joined Parliament. From 1873 to 1885, he sat in the House of Commons without any interruption.

Laing came prominently before the public only at the age of 70 and after he had retired from Parliament. He was a versatile man. His works, although they do not possess in themselves any great scientific value, showed his readings, especially in anthropology to be very wide, and were remarkable as the relaxation of a man who had spent over half a century almost exclusively immersed in worldly affairs. The more important of the works are :—

(*a*) England's Foreign Policy. (*b*) Modern Zoroastrian, 1887. (*c*) Problems of the Future and other essays, 1889. (*d*) The Antiquity of Man, 1892. (*e*) Human Origins, 1892. (*f*) India and China: England's mission in the East, 1863.

In 1867, Laing had once more become Chairman of the London, Brighton and South Coast Railway Company—a post which he held up to 1894. He died at 86.

§ 14.5 Sir Malcolmn Hailey (1872—). Educated at Corpus Christi College, Oxford. He joined the Indian Civil Service in 1895 and successively became Financial Commissioner, 1898, Colonisation Officer, Jhelum Canal Colony, 1902, Secretary, Punjab Government 1907, Deputy Secretary to the Government of India, 1908, Chief Commissioner, Delhi, 1912-18, Member of the Executive Council of the Governor-General, 1919. In 1922 he was made a K.C.S.I. He is now the Governor of the Punjab. 'The part played by the Honourable Mr.

Hailey,' said Rai Saheb Seth Nathmal, in the Legislative Council of India, in September, 1920, 'in the financial history of India, specially at this turning point, will be a record,—a notable and glorious record of one who has done ample justice to this important Department of Finance.'

6. To this distinguished list, the name of Sir Basil Blackett, the present Finance Member of the Supreme Executive Council will have now to be added. Sir Basil has already introduced certain wholesome reforms in our financial administration. But his most memorable contribution, which is yet to come, will be in the domain of currency and banking. To him belongs the credit of instituting the most exhaustive enquiry ever made in the Indian currency system and his regime bids fair to witness the most momentous changes, wrought in that system. If his expectations come true, the new currency order will replace the old in the course of the year 1927. In the general reconstruction, the paper currency will take a new character and a new appearance.

Born January, 1882, Sir Basil was educated at Marlborough and University College, Oxford, where he obtained a first class in Litt. Hum. in 1904. He has had considerable experience of financial affairs at Home having been connected with the Treasury which department has supplied not a few Finance members to India. Sir Basil's special acquaintance with Indian financial problems began perhaps in 1913 when he was called upon to act as the Secretary to the Chamberlain Commission on Indian Currency and Finance. Later he went on special mission to the U.S.A. Government in 1914, in connection with the exchange problems arising out of the War and was a member of the Anglo-French Financial Mission to U.S.A. which raised the Anglo-French Loan of 500 m. dollars in 1915.

He is genial in conversation, incisive and acute in debates and capable of doing any amount of hard work. His term of office as Finance Member is to end in 1927.

CHAPTER X.

THE FUTURE OF THE ISSUE.

§ 1. Programmes of reform, long called for, have now taken definite shape and direction in connection with coming vital changes in the monetary framework, p. 260.—§2. Two basic principles to be recognised, p 263.—§3. First, regarding the relation of paper currency to the entire monetary system, which is a relationship of the part to the whole, p. 264.—§4. Secondly, regarding the aim of sound monetary policy, which is price-stability, p. 267.—§5. Of false considerations, the consideration of profit leads to a baneful subordination of paper currency to general finances, p. 268.—§6. In the altered monetary outlook, transference of the issue to a central bank, logical and inevitable, p. 271.—§7. Facilities of convertibility, legal and extra-legal, p. 273.—§8. The importance of convertibility exaggerated, p. 275.—§9. A combined reserve for rupees and notes, p. 277.—§10. The composition of the reserve, p. 279.—§11. The location of the reserve, p. 282.—§12. The paper currency and the gold standard reserves amalgamated, p. 283.—§13. Provision for elasticity, p. 284.—§14. Sundry suggestions regarding the technique of the issue, p. 285.

The survey of the paper currency system is now over. It only remains to indicate in the light of the past working of the system, the possible lines of reform. In the treatment of the various subjects in the foregoing chapters, very often suggestions for reform have been interstitched between the discussions. An attempt will be made here to restate and develop further some of the more important of them. There have been mistakes and omissions in the past; but, for all that, the Government may perhaps claim more credit than discredit for their management of the charge which they took over in 1861. The lessons of the past may serve to show the way to a glorious future. What is that future to be?

NEED AND POSSIBLE LINES OF REFORM.

§ 1. The subject bristles with difficulties. What is proposed is to isolate the Paper Currency as far as it bears isolation from the rest of the monetary structure and present a few thoughts on its reform. I am fully aware of the organic unity of the different parts of the currency system and of the risks involved in treating Paper Currency in isolation as in treating a limb by the method of amputation. Paper Currency reform is bound up with the question of general monetary reform. They do not lend themselves to complete separation. Yet perhaps, there is some advantage in treating Paper Currency apart, if only because of the unwieldy complexity of the task of recasting the whole of the currency machine. Overhauling the entire currency system is, perhaps, a more attractive pastime than overhauling one of its parts; still the problem of our Paper Currency reform, to judge by the number and variety of puzzles that it presents, should amply repay single-minded attention. Reform is, besides, more urgent in this field than elsewhere. We cannot afford to defer reform of the Paper Currency, even if we agree to shelve the question of general monetary reconstruction. Happily, now that the whole monetary system of India is on the eve of being thoroughly recast and renovated, the hour seems peculiarly auspicious for Paper Currency to claim its individual share of attention. Its reform comes in as an integral part of the general scheme of reform and being so linked, the subject can now be discussed with an amount of ease and definiteness which would have been otherwise unattainable. It is a relief to know where we stand and whither we are moving in currency matters. But even if the larger task of remodelling the entire currency structure had not been at present undertaken, Paper Currency reform could not have been any longer neglected. Reform in this field, as a detailed study of its different aspects has disclosed, is overdue. The Paper Currency constitution to-day is a temporary constitution, based upon temporary provisions of the Act of 1923. A certain goal has been taken for granted and the purpose of the temporary provisions, is understood to be to bring about that desired state of affairs. Then, when all the conditions necessary for that final constitution are fulfilled, the 'appointed day' will be declared. The situation is as unreal as it is mistaken. It is a mistake to accept the permanent constitution for which we are supposed to be preparing as the last word in sound Paper Currency organisation. It is unreal because we are not moving towards that goal at all, or if we are, we are progressing so slowly as to put the realisation of the desired constitution beyond the boundaries of the visible future. The permanent constitution was drawn up in 1920. In 1927, it is as far off from realisation as ever. We have been permanently living under the temporary provisions. The steps necessary for bridging the distance are being mostly neglected. One example is the continued appropriation to revenue of the interest of the securities in the paper currency reserve in preference to utilising it for wiping out created securities. Again, since the goal is too far off and the period of march long and weary it is producing the expected effect on our morale. The faith in the selected goal has shaken. On the advice of the Hilton-Young Commission we are preparing to change our direction in the middle of our march. The whole of the permanent provisions, hitherto regarded as the goal, is to be scrapped and a new set of transitional and permanent provisions substituted. Whatever new constitution is adopted, the old constitution figuring in the permanent provisions' is doomed. The way, a well-thought out Paper Currency system came thus to be rejected within six years of its adoption, would be remembered as a tragedy in our currency history. It should serve as a warning against planning too far ahead. A scheme of reform, overloaded with too many transitional provisions, designed to extend over a number of years, sometimes breaks down under its own weight. It is well to remember this point, in estimating the worth of reform proposals.

Not least of the defects of the present law is its unintelligibility, except perhaps to University people who are ominiscient for the sake of their pupils. I have mentioned elsewhere how Sir Basil Blackett has confessed that when he first took up our Paper Currency Acts, he had to give up the task as hopeless after a hard day's labour with them. That was said about the Act of 1920. The present law is in many ways a replica of the 1920 Act and is hardly an improvement so far as simplicity and perspicuity are concerned.

The Principles of Reform.

§ 2. Let me begin by calling attention to two basic propositions touching Paper Currency reform. In the past, Paper Currency has been rather lightheartedly handled, reformers not having been over-mindful of principles. Indian Paper Currency has been rich in reforms and richer still in suggestions of reform. We started with a bank issue, changed it for a State issue after a while, and have experimented by altering the conditions of issue from time to time. Altogether some forty Acts have been passed regarding Paper Currency since 1861, nearly, every Finance Member playing a part, big or small, in its evolution. But we have more often followed expediency than proceeded logically. We never started by defining the relation between Paper Currency and the rest of our monetary structure. We never realised in a comprehensive manner the ideal currency policy to be pursued, nor what part the Paper Currency has to play in carrying out that policy. Consequently, Paper Currency worked independently and often conflictingly with the totality of the currency organisation. There was not much of consistency and coherency. The Hilton-Young Commission in this respect have shown an enlightened conception of currency reform in so far as they have broad-based their recommendations on (1) a study of the relations of the many parts of the currency to each other and to the whole, and (2) also attempted to lay down a common policy for the whole. Touching these two points two categorical propositions can be laid down.

§ 3. First, that all reform should build upon the recognition of the fact that Paper Currency is not the whole of the currency. Paper forms an important part of the money of the country, but it forms only a part. The currency triangle requires the two other arms of metallic currency and credit currency as well. Only the three together can enclose a workable policy. It follows that the management of the Paper Currency is closely bound up with the management of the other media of circulation. No effective control of the one is possible without, at the same time, controlling the other two. Yet it was this separation that we have long maintained. The Paper Currency authority has been divorced from the credit-controlling authority, if ever we had a truly controlling authority for credit. Consequently, we have, on not a few occasions, worked at cross purposes. The question is more important than that of a mere economy of reserves. Separation of reserves is wasteful but separation of policies is disastrous. Paper is part of a whole. Its character changes with the character of the whole. Its future depends on the future of the whole. Any uncertainty of outlook regarding the whole is reflected in vascillation and weakness in the Paper Currency policy. Fortunately much of the uncertainty has now cleared up, and the currency horizon is less befogged than ever before. The country is on the eve of definitely adopting the gold standard. We can now expect and plan for a definite Paper Currency policy and organisation.

The situation would have been altogether different if the unstability of monetary outlook had continued, or if some other course of action had been taken. For long, we have been hesitating about the proper standard we should adopt. We started with silver monometallism but before long started flirting with gold also. At times we have been so divided in our minds between the attractions of the yellow and the silver metals that we went very near to adopting bimetallism. The spectre of bimetallism has not yet entirely disappeared, to judge by some recent proposals for reviving it. Our monetary policy, managed from London and Simla, have been periodically reviewed by commissions of experts, but have been characterised, if anything, by a lack of policy. After an eventful history, we came, to all intents and purposes, to settle down, after the war, to, what Gustav Cassel would call, an 'independent' rupee standard. We had an inconvertible rupee printed on silver which served as our standard money. The system had its difficulties. But I am not prepared to admit that with proper safeguards, it could not be worked successfully and give us as good a system of currency as the gold bullion standard now advocated. It would have preserved continuity and ensured cheapness, no small points in favour of a currency system. This is, however, not the place for entering into a discussion of the relative merits of rival monetary standards. That the uncertainty has been cleared up and that we have definitely selected a standard, is, beyond question, a big step forward. A project of paper currency reform to suit and supplement a rupee standard, silver monometallism or bimetallism, would of necessity be different in nature, from a project fitting in a gold standard. If instead of gold, we had enshrined the rupee, a strong case could have been made for banishing gold and gold securities from the Paper Currency reserve. It has been seen, in the chapter on reserves, how the gold assets are more of an encumbrance than of assistance in the reserve, so long as we go by the rupee as an independent standard of value unconnected with gold. But in the new order of currency implied by a gold standard, the situation is radically different.

§ 4. The second categorical proposition is this. The aim of all sound monetary policy including that of Paper Currency is primarily to maintain a stability of prices. Without such a declaration of policy, no project of reform can be constructed or criticised. The Currency Commission, be it said to their credit, recognise price-stability as the final principle. They will even have external as well as internal stability, to which length I, for one, would not be prepared to go, having my doubts about the practicability of maintaining both simultaneously. I shall be content with the less ambitious aim of internal stability and let 'exchange go hand' (in Prof. Cannan's words) if that is its implication. I shall not, for the sake of stability, shrink from marrying Miss Gold who happens to be an American, although I continue to be an impenitent subscriber to Mr. Keynes's arguments against the gold standard. A gold standard through the safety-valve of the exchange, equalises price-levels through the world, but the world-level itself may go up or down. A gold standard *corrects* changes in price levels after they have taken place, it does not absolutely prevent those changes from taking place. In theory, a gold standard is only the next best, the best being a standard based on index numbers of prices, although perhaps it is more practicable and fool-proof.

PAPER CURRENCY AND PUBLIC FINANCE.

§ 5. The recognition of these two propositions furnishes the foundation. When we have found the right foundation, half the building is already done. Paper forms part of the circulation of the country. The administration of the Paper Currency, in so far as it expands or contracts the total amount of money in circulation, must be carried out in strict subordination to the principle of price-stability. No other considerations should be of importance. Unfortunately, in our Paper Currency history, price stability has had but scant respect. The Paper Currency has been often in the clutches of the general finances of the Government and used as an instrument for filling up the gap between revenue and expenditure. As noticed in an earlier chapter, this has been particularly the painful experience of India for a number of years during and after the War. The budgets did not balance and the Paper Currency came in handy for supplying revenue for the time being. Nothing can be more vicious and suicidal than to use the Paper Currency for manufacturing revenue, as most European countries have learned to their cost. Not to speak of creating fresh revenue, I would even go to the length of renouncing the idea of any normal or usual profits derived from the administration of Paper Currency. The Paper Currency department is to-day a revenue-yielding department. Even if, in carrying out its mission, it did not yield any profit there would be nothing uneconomical about it. We should be satisfied if it just pays its way. Just as improved communications promoting the mobility of people and of goods throughout the country, repay themselves in a thousand indirect ways, so also the provision of a sound currency helps in the fluidity of funds, itself its own reward. Both should be raised from the short-sighted profit and loss philosophy.

The Indian Government, it must be said to their credit, did not make as unscrupulous an use of the printing press as some of the belligerent nations. But that quite considerable advantage was taken of it. is apparent from the procession of deficit budgets beginning with 1918-19. In 1918-19, there was a deficit of 6 crores, in 1919-20, it stood at 24 crores. Next year it was 26 crores, in 1921-22, a further one of 28 crores, making the prodigious grand total of 84 crores in all the 4 years. Where did the money come from, to finance these deficits? Chiefly, the printing press of course. Hailey, in his budget speech (1922) reviewing the situation, said, 'We have been living on credit. About 27 crores have been obtained by the issue of fiduciary currency notes, namely, notes the only backing on which are our own I. O. U's'. In 1922-23, there was once again a deficit of 15.02 crores. It was left for the new Finance Member to repeat much the same story of covering the deficit by means of various makeshifts, including the printing press, as his predecessor did. It was only in 1923-24, that an improvement in the situation was noticeable. The realised surplus for that year amounted to 2.39 crores. In 1924-25 again, happily, the budget was balanced and there was an estimated surplus of 4 crores. Since then happily, we are having a series of surplus budgets. The Finance Member, Sir Basil Blackett deserves well of the country for his services to the public finances and indirectly to the Paper Currency. Whether this will continue, heralding a return to the days of sound finance, remains however to be seen. 'Currency stability,' as the Dawes Report admirably puts it, 'can only be maintained if the budget is normally balanced; the budget can only be balanced if a stable and reliable currency exists.' In India, as elsewhere, the truth of the proposition is likely to be often forgotten. Meanwhile, the harm that was done in taking recourse to the printing press in the last few years has borne unmistakable fruit. The price-level has been steadily increasing, raising the costs of administration higher up in every direction. From 147 in 1914, the base being 1873, the price thermometer went steadily rising until in 1920 it stood at 281, about which figure it is still swinging. Inflation demanded a further inflation and the vicious circle was complete. The lessons of the past few years have shown clearly, if anything, the impolicy of putting the currency machinery at the disposal of the Government. Short of taking it substantially out of the reach of the Government, no means can be discovered of preventing its spoliation.

Apart from profit, there have been various other false considerations influencing the administration of Indian Paper Currency—as we have previously seen. Expediency, for instance, has very often shaped Paper Currency legislation without any definite principle in view. 'Convertibility' has been a fetish nearly throughout its whole history. The idea has been that so long as convertibility is maintained, the notes will take care of themselves. The ultimate and more important convertibility of coin and paper into commodities at fixed rates, was lost sight of. Various more or less irrelevent considerations also occasionally intruded. Our Paper Currency has consciously contributed little towards maintaining a stable price level, very often it has made for positive unstability.

Let me next from the cloud-land of principles come down to concrete suggestions of reform. The currency of India is going to be thoroughly rebuilt on the basis of the gold standard. For good or ill we are committed to the change. The Paper Currency must take its proper position in the reconstructed edifice and fulfil its part, loyal to the policy laid down for the whole. What exact constitution are we to give to it?

The Agency of Issue.

§ 6. Let me first take up the question of the agency of issue. Obviously, the existing divorce between the Paper Currency and the rest of the currency must cease. The unity of currency policy demands co-ordination between the parts. and failing any alternative method of bringing about that co-ordination, the management and control of these different parts should be unified. This is the postulate of the gold standard and a uniform currency policy. The agency entrusted with the supervision of the Paper Currency must also supervise credit. The

Currency Commission suggest a Central Bank. It is more or less inevitable that they should. The task cannot be left to the Government without the risk of political considerations finding their way into the currency administration, nor is the Government a suitable agency to control credit. If I had been pro-American, I would have perhaps advocated an Indian Federal Reserve Board, a quasi-public authority to be entrusted with the joint responsibility. But the Indian soil is hardly likely to be promising for the experiment, and the new developments brought about by the adoption of the gold standard have made such a commission substantially unnecessary. The idea would have been worth considering in a system of managed currency implied by an 'independent' rupee standard and the task of regulating currency so as to preserve a stability of prices might have been entrusted to the commission. In a gold standard which is a gold standard in theory and in practice, the price-level is automatically kept steady, if not absolutely at least relatively to other countries, and a commission is not much wanted for that purpose. With the proposed Reserve Bank materialising, credit will be already sufficiently centralised. The new conditions do not thus call for a Federal Reserve Board for India. Yet perhaps the idea remains full of possibilities for the future. In the altered circumstances, the Central Bank thus seems to be the best suggestion. Yet the transference of the note issue to a bank, whatever pompous name we call it by, is frought with certain risks. The credit of the note in India stands on a delicate poise, likely to be upset if the connection of the almighty

Government is severed or loosened. The Commission realise this and propose a Government guarantee of the notes. The necessary implication of such a guarantee, if real, is mixing up Government with the issue in an indirect way, if unreal, no addition to the security of the notes. A bank-Government partnership, in the peculiar circumsstances of India, is more or less inevitable. It is doubtful if the terms of this partnership, outlined by the Commission, whereby the Government guarantees, but is supposed to have no voice, is the ideal partnership. It is an open question if a Central State Bank, rather than a private one, would not have answered better.

The transference of the monopoly of note issue to a central bank will close the long but interesting chapter of Government issue. As we know, the Government took over the issue in 1861, not without misgivings and not until a great duel had been fought between Samuel Laing and Sir Charles Wood. Laing advocated and Sir Charles resisted bank connection with the issue. Laing's cause is at last triumphant, though in a manner hardly conceivable by him. Currency history is repeating itself. Starting with a bank issue, we are completing the cycle by reverting to it. The Controller of the Currency will have to be on the list of the unemployed very soon.

The Conditions of Issue.

The Question of Convertibility.

§ 7. Not only the issuing agency is to be changed, but consistent with the new currency policy adopted, the conditions of issue also must be thoroughly revised. The notes hitherto have been convertible into rupees. They were also convertible into gold at rates which made that convertibility very often a dead-letter. All this, obviously, must be changed. Since we have decided to drop 'dyarchy' in currency and adopt gold and bid good-bye to the rupee, the fellowship of the rupee and the note is automatically dissolved. Let the new notes be convertible only into gold as of right, say the Currency Commission, and facilities only be provided for their conversion into rupees on demand. It will be incumbent on the bank to provide rupees for notes tendered, but no one will have a legal right thus to claim rupee coin. The arrangement is likely to produce serious friction at the outset. The rupee is preponderatingly the money of daily use and the withdrawal of the legal right of buying rupees with notes might produce a discount of notes in terms of rupees. The fear is strengthened when we consider that there will be no gold circulation. Convertibility into gold will be a peculiar and limited convertibility. Only notes exceeding a specified value can be converted, this again at specified places. With the bars of gold thus obtained payments could not be effected (gold being obviously not legal tender), nor rupees obtained for them as of right. There is much to be said therefore for improving this conditional convertibility and make the notes legally exchangeable into rupees. Yet the Commission are justified in not having done that. The aim being the dethronement of the rupee and its eventual withdrawal from circulation, they could not obviously provide for anything which might have led to fresh coinage of rupees. With such a possibility, the realisation of the complete gold standard would have been inevitably delayed and with that the stabilisation of the price-level. I would therefore accept the Commission's suggestion. I would only suggest that all notes, new and old, be subject to the same provisions and none be convertible into rupees as of right. Discrimination will be very confusing. The Government of India's promise to redeem their notes in silver rupees cannot be regarded as too sacred and unalterable. Currency promises have in the past frequently been ignored and honoured in the breach. It is the unwritten promise to convert the note into fixed quantities of goods that counts, and for its sake written face promises may be changed without much biting of conscience.

§ 8. We will accept the conditional and limited convertibility and we need have no misgivings. The value of notes, like the value of every thing else, depends upon the limitation of supply, not on solemn promises of convertibility. As long as there is no over-issue so long will they have value and convertibility, and a lessening of facilities of conversion would not matter. Too much can easily be made of facilities for convertibility, as if it was the all-important thing. It has, however, been explained elsewhere how it is not convertibility, but limitation of supply that gives value to any currency. Convertibility comes after value, not before it. We must be careful about the proper positions of the cart and the horse. While in regard to the market value of all other commodities, this sound rule is most readily recognised, some mysterious superstition seems to stand against its acceptance in the domain of money. Yet, the law of the value of money is exactly the same as the law of the value of any other thing. Money must be first scarce in order to command a value and then, it will be convertible into other kinds of money and things. The silver rupee in India is a note printed on silver. It has got all the characteristics of a note. Except at the choice of the Government, it is not convertible into gold at any fixed rate. Although thus, practically it is an inconvertible note, yet it commands purchasing power. It is curious even after the experiences with the rupee, the convertibility fallacy, applied to the issue of notes, should have still persisted in India. When the notes were first introduced, the possibilities of their presentation for coin were much greater than they are now. Consequently, a far larger proportion of metallic reserve was necessary then, than it is now. A time may come when the paper-note, like the silver rupee-note will be equally freely accepted without insisting on convertibility, and then no reserve may at all be necessary to be kept for guaranteeing the convertibility. Does it follow that notes should then be allowed to be issued *ad infinitum*, as fears of their presentation would have entirely disappeared? The answer is certainly no. Convertibility has kept up the value of the notes, not because there is any special virtue in convertibility, but because convertibility means limited issue. Convertibility has indirectly provided a salutary check to the indiscriminate and excessive issue of notes. If the paper circulation was curtailed to a very small fraction of its existing amount, no facilities for conversion would perhaps at all be required to keep up the value of the notes. Their inconvertibility will be no obstacle to their acceptance. The real significance of conversion facilities is to limit the issue which ensures the value of notes, and as long as that is achieved, it is immaterial what exact facilities for conversion are provided. whether into gold or into silver, backed or unbacked by legally fixed requirements of reserves.

THE PAPER CURRENCY RESERVE.

§ 9. This brings us to the question of the reserves, the function of which as just indicated, is really to limit the issue and only ostensively to provide for convertibility. The new ideas must considerably affect the reserve regulations. In this respect the recommendations of the Commission are as ingenious as they are complicated. They propose a joint reserve for the note issue as well as for the rupee issue, if I may use the expression. The note issue is to be backed cent. per cent. and only a reserve amounting approximately to one-eighth of the total estimated rupee circulation and one-fifth of that part likely to return from circulation, is to be held against the rupee issue. If the rupee circulation increases or decreases, the liability of the bank will increase or decrease by one-fifth of such increase or decrease, while the remaining four-fifths will fall to the Government for having thoughtlessly printed token rupees in the past and accumulated handsome funds out of the profits. These ratios are selected after a due consideration of the contractibility of the rupee circulation, the existing and probable difference between the face value and the intrinsic value of the silver coins, the volume and nature of the assets made over to the new bank by the Government, and several other factors some of which are, admittedly, highly conjectural. They are challengeable. But any other figures would have been equally conjectural and open to challenge. Perhaps the Commission are right, perhaps they are wrong. The particular figures chosen do not however constitute the most important feature of the proposals. The really important thing is the unity of reserves for a duality of issues. The idea of the combined reserve is novel, stimulating, very bold and certainly economical, since both the rupee and the note are notes at bottom. But it imparts an uncertainty to the reserve, the rupee liability being quite an uncertain amount. It will produce anomalies in many ways. A portion of the reserve for rupees is bodily contained in the coins, while the notes are intrinsically valueless. The total reserve may thus fluctuate in size according to changes in the price of silver. Again, part of the reserve will consist of rupee coins. So far as the note liability is concerned nothing can be said against holding rupees. But to keep rupees in reserve for a totality of issue, a good part of which consists of rupees, seems to be a little awkward and self-deceiving. I wish, therefore, the Commission had examined whether a separate 'account of issue' for the rupee notes (as distinguished from the paper notes) was not a practicable suggestion. If the banking account is to stand separated from the issue account why not also the issue account of rupees from the issue account of notes? It would have made for simplicity and intelligibility.

§ 10. Detailed proposals regarding the location and composition of the reserve can hardly be fully discussed here. Only a few brief remarks can be made on some points. The Commission have given their blessing on the proportional reserve system and suggested a minimum of forty per cent. gold and gold securities in the reserve. The Smith Committee, it will be remembered, recommended a forty per cent. metallic reserve. The law in force demands a fifty per cent. Since, however, the suggested forty per cent. embraces both gold and gold paper it is a far more liberal provision than it seems and leaves a freeer hand to the bank than if the whole of it had referred to gold. Still, the laying down of a fixed percentage is, in my opinion, essentially unsound in principle. As long as mutual conversion of gold and paper is insisted on and maintained, internal prices can not exceed world gold prices, and for the rest, complete freedom can be safely given to the bank. After safely tying down the issue to the chariot wheel of gold and by that means to a stability of prices in practice, we can afford to give the bank the greatest possible latitude in its work. There is no more justification in interfering for maintaining the convertibility of the notes than for maintaining the convertibility of bank cheques. If we have confidence enough in the bank regarding the one we ought to have also for the other. The bank is entrusted with the issue on condition of maintaining convertibility.

To encumber it with further provisos regarding how to ensure that convertibility, bespeaks a hesitating attitude of mind. So far as price-stability is concerned, such further interference is not called for. The Commission suggest the percentage " in the light of experience of other banks." In the light of theory it seems to be superfluous.

I have also my petty quarrels about the Commission's specifications regarding the other assets in the reserve. The reserve is to be a heterogeneous collection consisting of rupee coins, gold securities, rupee securities (in the new dispensation, wherein however will lie the distinction between rupee securities and gold securities, since the rupee will become a fraction of gold), gold and domestic bills of exchange. Bullion silver naturally has no place in the new order. Gold is to be eventually at least twenty-five per cent. but never to fall below thirty crores. The percentage will be reached by a gradual march extending over a period of years. What sacredness there is in a twenty-five per cent. ratio, it is difficult to see. One may enquire why a lower percentage should not do and if it does, whether that would not be more economical. Rupee coin is not to exceed ultimately twenty-five crores or ten per cent of the whole, whichever is greater. Here again, the Commission lay down certain arbitrary stages for the final attainment of the ratio which are likely to needlessly fetter the work of the bank, and may also cause undue pressure on the finances of the Government of India. For, it can be presumed that the excess rupees will go from the bank to the Government. The withdrawal of every single rupee in this manner will be financed by the Government and the bank in the proportion of one-fifth (by the bank) and four-fifths (by the Government). Exception can thus be taken to the rigid stages outlined by the Commission for the reduction of the rupee reserves. What is wanted is their diminution as rapidly and as smoothly as possible, and this could have perhaps been ensured without the laying down of definite stages. The cost of the currency reform, on which we have embarked, will be none too small for the country. Steps calculated to arrange for the payment of the bill by easier instalments, so as to bear the lightest on the Government's finances, should naturally commend themselves. The rupee securities are to be limited to twenty-five per cent. or fifty crores whichever is less. One wonders if this is really safety or prejudice. It is easier to expand the circulation permanently with rupee securities, for the Government I. O. U.'s have little cost of manufacture. But is that a disadvantage if and when permanent expansion is desirable? Let it be remembered that if expansion in this manner is undesirable, it will be painfully brought home to the bank by a drain on its gold resources and cause it to give up such expansion. Why lay down rigid rules? Equally unreasonable is the Commission's treatment of the "created" securities. The fault of these securities is that they are created, they are low-born and pariah securities. The Government is ordered to take them forthwith out of sight and replace them by marketable securities. I suggest that the created securities deserve life as much as any other kind of securities. The function of the reserve is primarily to limit the circulation and only secondarily to provide for convertibility, and that part of the reserve which is not likely to be used for converting notes may be in the form of I. O. U.'s of the Government of India or of the Government of Honolulu, for all one cares, so long as they are the least costly. The Commission in their anxiety to remove the "createds" go to the length of suggesting their replacement by newly created sterling securities. One fails to see what distinction there is, except a distinction of colour, between *ad hoc* sterling securities and *ad hoc* rupee securities created by the Government of India. In a regime of bank issue there would be no further risk of new created securities finding their way into the reserve and the Commission might have been kindly to the "createds" already there. I suggest this part of the Commission's recommendations, a wilderness of percentages, and a too elaborate laying down of stages of evolution, will bear simplification.

§ 11. On the question of the location of the reserve again the Commission have not failed to express their opinions. Their suggestions in this field however go somewhat ill with their over-solicitation for the maintenance of convertibility which their refined percentages for gold and other holdings seem to indicate. They would not shrink from keeping half the gold outside India in foreign banks and would also allow gold held in any Mint or in transit to count as reserve, although this privilege is not extended to gold securities. Since the primary function of reserves is to limit the issue, so long as convertibility is not really threatened, there can be no objection to widen the area of their holding and the Commission might have even gone further in this direction. It may be noted that the present regulations permitting the scattering of the reserves practically throughout the world originated mainly during the War.

§ 12. *Paper Currency Reserve and the Gold Standard Reserve.* On one point there will be universal agreement with the Commission, *viz.*, the proposed fusion of the gold standard and the paper currency reserves. The purpose of the one was ostensively to maintain the external value of the rupee and of the other, the rupee value of the note. In practice, the purposes of both were rather mixed up and uncertain. In the new order brought about by the gold standard the external and internal value of the currency can not deviate from each other and consequently, the forces recruited for keeping them steady may be conveniently collected together. The amalgamation of the two reserves, long advocated, is the logical accompaniment of the adoption of the gold standard. The one great impediment in the way of their fusion so long, was the uncertainty about the future of the rupee. Now that the rupee is formally and finally going to be relegated to the position of a token, the reserves held primarily for the conversion of rupees into gold may be merged in the reserves held for the conversion into gold of notes. The issue, although it may be described as a double-barrelled issue, consisting of rupees and notes, need only have a unified reserve for its effective regulation so as to keep prices equivalent to the value of gold. If the bank was not called upon to shoulder the liability for the rupee circulation, obviously the gold standard reserve could not have been transferred to it. The anomaly of two separate reserves, with more or less overlapping functions, would now be finally removed.

§ 13. *Paper Currency and Elasticity.* I can but barely touch on the question of elasticity of the currency. Earlier in a special chapter, the question has already been discussed in some detail. Elasticity is a desirable thing, particularly in a country like India with a marked periodicity in the demand for currency. But elasticity is a treacherous word and there is also such a thing as over-elasticity. Again, the bank rate may not be the surest index of judging the necessity for money, the anticipation of fresh funds may take up the bank rate to over hundred per cent., as in Germany, and still the market might want more money. The Commission have provided doors on all sides for elasticity. I wish their scheme all success, but consider that a little conservatism in this respect would have been more cautious. The proportional reserve system itself means elasticity. There is to be also a self-liquidating bill issue, the amount of which is only limited by the limits imposed on the other parts of the reserve, and which may be anything up to sixty crores at the outset. This seems to be an extraordinarily liberal provision of elasticity, considering that at present a maximum of twelve crores only can be so issued and that no stipulations regarding rates of interest, as we have to-day, encumber this provision. A jump to sixty crores from twelve crores, which again is admittedly in the experimental stage, is indeed a bold jump. It is bolder still when we consider that in the gold securities the bank may include foreign bills of exchange maturing into gold money. What with the Indian and what with the foreign bills, a substantial part of the issue will thus contribute towards elasticity. Lastly, as if not satisfied with such extraordinary facilities, the Commission provide for the temporary suspension of normal reserve requirements during exceptional times and a graduated tax on the issue (with a minimum of six per cent.). The aggregate effect of all these provisions will be to ensure for the Indian Paper Currency system a remarkable degree of elasticity.

§ 14. *The Technique of the Issue.* Only the barest mention can be made of other suggestions for reform. The re-introduction of the one-rupee note is a legitimate corollary of the dethronement of the rupee and its gradual withdrawal from circulation. How far the rupee-note can be the correct substitute for the rupee coin is, in the circumstances of India, very doubtful. If I had my own way, I would have voted for a nickel rupee, but that would have been perhaps too radical. I would also, if I am to make a last suggestion, do away with the "circle" system and throw open the whole country to notes of all denominations. The universalisation process has come to a stop with the hundred-rupee note. There is no reason why it should not be carried further.

The circle system has become an anachronism and I wish the Commission had not omitted to pronounce its death verdict in their comprehensive report. Perhaps the suggestion is implied in the transformation of the issue into a bank issue. Sir Daniel Hamilton does not like the proposed design of the new bank note. He would have room for a little display of imagination in it and include a portrait of His Majesty the King. The suggestion is interesting. A royal figure would undoubtedly add to the dignity and the popularity of the notes. If there be no risk of interpreting it as too close an association of the state with the issue, the suggestion ought to be carried by acclamation.

Evolving on sound lines, the Paper Currency that is to be promises to be much better than the paper currency that is. Never before has Paper Currency been called upon to play such an important role as in the reconstructed currency theatre of India with its gold bullion standard. For we must note that gold will be the standard but not currency, the sole currency being paper. Never before was need for reform greater, never proposals of reform made on a more comprehensive scale. The scheme of reform outlined by the Hilton-Young Commission bespeaks thought and carries weight. The Commission deserve unstinted praise and warm gratitude for their monumental report, their labours and troubles. I have ventured to make certain observations regarding that part of their recommendations which concerns Paper Currency. But I realise the essential soundness of the frame-work which they have planned. I congratulate the Commission on the scheme they have outlined. I shall congratulate the Currency when the suggestions are translated into facts.

BIBLIOGRAPHY

There is an extensive, though rather scattered literature dealing with the Indian Paper Currency onward from 1862. A short bibliography is appended below:—

A.—General Works and Pamphlets.

1864.—The Indian Paper Currency System by Indopclite (India Office Tract No. 339).

1868.—Remarks on the State Paper Currency in India by G. W. Cline, LL.D., Assistant Commissioner of Currency (India Office).

1869.—Aliquis—A simple plan for circulating throughout India a State Paper Currency and some remarks on the report of the Commission to enquire into the operations of Act 19 of 1861 (Goldsmith's Library of Economic Literature).

1866.—Ottomar Haupt—L'histoire monetaire de notre temps (British Museum Library).

1890.—R. Chalmers—Colonial Currency.

1894.—Carl Ellstaetter—Indiens Silberwährung (B. M.) Translation by Laughlin, 1895,—the Indian Silver Currency.

1897.—L. C. Probyn—Indian Coinage and Currency.

1898.—H. D. Macleod—Indian Currency.
Sir James Brunyate—An Account of the Presidency Banks (not published).

1903.—O. Heyn—Die indische Währungs-Reform.

1904.—M. Bothe—Die indische Währungs-Reform seit 1893.

Of recent works mention might be made of

J. M. KEYNES, C. B.—Indian Currency and Finance, 1913.

F. SHIRRAS.—Indian Finance and Banking, 1920.

These two books are the most outstanding of recent works on Indian Currency.

DORAISWAMI.—Indian Finance, Currency and Banking 1915.

E. W. KEMMERER.—Modern Currency Reforms, 1916.

S. K. SARMA.—Indian Monetary Problems.

H. F. DODD.—History of Money in the British Empire and in the United States, 1911.

M. WEBB.—Advance India.

K. SINGER.—Die Motive der indischen Geldreform. An examination of Indian Currency on the basis of Knapp's State Theory of Money. The author is a disciple of Knapp.

A. ARNOLD.—Das indische Geldwesen Unter besonderer Berücksichtigung seiner Reforemen seit, 1893. 1906.

ALAKH DHARI.—The Growth of Currency Organisations in India, 1915.

V. G. KALE.—Currency Reform in India, 1919.

K. T. SHAH.—60 Years of Indian Finance, 1921.
Indian Currency and Banking Problems.

H. F. HOWARD.—India and the Gold Standard, 1911.

H. S. JEVANS.—Money, Banking and Exchauge in India, 1922.

WADIA AND JOSHI.—Money and the Money Market in India, 1926.

H. L. CHABLANI.—Indian Currency and Exchange, 1925.

B. R. AMBEDKAR.—The Problem of the Rupee, 1923.

B. R. RAU.—Present Day Banking in India, 1922.

B.—Official Reports, Accounts and Papers.

Dispatches to and from Government as to the Issue of Paper Money in 1862. Parliamentary Accounts and Papers, 1862, XXXVIII. (Newspaper room in the British Museum Library).

Papers and correspondence as to the issue of paper money. Parliamentary Accounts and Papers, 1864, XLIII.

Further papers and correspondence, 1864, XLIII.

Resolutions on Government Currency, etc., 1865, XXXIX.

Report on Finance and Financial Administration in India, 1871, VIII.

Annual reports of the Paper Currency Department, issued by the Head Commissioner and later by the Controller of the Currency up to 1926. Some of the earlier reports are not, however, available.

India Gazette, 1861-62.

Proceedings of the Legislative Council of India, 1861-62 and also 1914-1924. Formerly part of the *India Gazette*, now issued separately.

Statement of the Moral and Material Progress of India, up to 1923.

Imperial Gazetteer of India. Volume dealing with Finance.

Manual of Indian Paper Currency Notes, 1887, by W. T. Piercy (see Campbell's Catalogue of Indian Government Publications in the British Museum).

Indian Paper Currency Manual, 1920 (India Office Record Department).

General Statutory Rules and Orders, 1915 Edition (India Office).

Budget Speeches of the Finance Member, 1915-1924.

Financial Statistics, older series volume 2 of the Statistics of British India. Last issued in 1921.

Statutes of British India (Acts and Ordinances), 1861-1924 (India Office).

C.—Currency Commissions.

These provide the most important source books on Indian Currency History.

1867.—Report of the Commission to enquire into the working of Act 19 of 1861. President—General Sir W. R. Mansfield (India Office).

1893-94.—Indian Currency Committee (the Herschell Committee) Report and Volumes containing evidences.

1899.—Indian Currency Committee (the Fowler Committee) Report and Evidences.

1914.—Indian Currency Commission (the Chamberlain Commission) Report and Evidences.

1919.—Indian Currency Committee (the Babington Smith Committee) Report and Evidences.

1926.—Royal Commission on Indian Currency (The Hilton-Young Commission) Report and Evidences.

APPENDIX A

ACT No. XIX OF 1861

(Received assent of the Governor-General on 16th July, 1861.)

AN ACT TO PROVIDE FOR A GOVERNMENT PAPER CURRENCY.

WHEREAS it is expedient to provide for the issue by the Government of India, of Promissory notes payable to bearer on demand, and to regulate the mode of issuing and securing payment of the same; and whereas due notice has been given by the Governor-General of India in Council to the Banks of Bengal, Bombay and Madras respectively, as required by Acts VI of 1839, III of 1840 and IX of 1843, that the said Banks are to be modified by the power of the said banks to issue Promissory notes payable on demand, ceasing from and after the day hereinafter provided, it is enacted as follows:—

I. Section 31 of the said Act 6 of 1839, Section 31 of the said Act 3 of 1840, and Section 33 of the said Act 9 of 1843, so far as the said sections authorise the banks of Bengal, Bombay and Madras respectively to issue promissory notes payable on demand, are repealed from and after the 1st day of March, 1862.

II. After the passing of this Act no body corporate person or persons whatsoever, in British India (except Banks of Bengal, Madras and Bombay, up to the said 1st day of March, 1862 and except as hereinafter provided) shall draw, accept, make, or issue any bill of exchange or promissory note, or agreement for the payment of money payable to bearer on demand, or borrow, owe, or take up any sum or sums of money on the bills or notes payable

to bearer on demand of any such body corporate or any such person or persons. Provided that cheques or drafts payable to bearer on demand or otherwise, may be drawn on bankers, shroffs or agents by the customers or constituents of such bankers, shroffs or agents, in respect of deposits of money in the hands of such bankers, shroffs or agents, and held by them at the credit and disposal of the persons drawing such cheques or drafts.

III. There shall be established, by the Governor-General of India in Council, a department of the public service to be called The Department of Issue, either in connection with the Mints or otherwise, and from and after the passing of this Act, there may be issued from the said department as hereinafter provided, Promissory notes of the Government of India payable to bearer on demand for such sums not being less than 10 rupees as the Governor-General of India in Council shall from time to time direct.

IV. The Governor-General in Council, after the passing of this Act, shall appoint some person who may be the Master of the Mint at Calcutta, to be called the Head Commissioner of the Department of Issue, and two other persons who may be the Master of the Mint at Madras and the Master of the Mint at Bombay, who shall be called respectively, the Commissioners of the Department of Issue at Madras and Bombay, and it shall be lawful for the Governor-General of India in Council from time to time, by rules to be published in the *Gazettes* of Calcutta, Madras and Bombay, to make such arrangements through any officers of Government, or with any persons. banks or bodies corporate, either at Calcutta, Madras and Bombay or elsewhere as may be required to regulate and facilitate the issue and payment under the provisions of this Act of promissory notes of the Government of India of such denominations as shall be prescribed under the last foregoing Section, not being for less sum than 10 Rupees.

V. It shall be lawful for the Governor-General of India in Council from time to time by order to be published in the *Gazettes* of Calcutta, Madras and Bombay to establish in British India districts to be called "Circles of Issue" three of which circles shall include the towns of Calcutta, Madras and Bombay respectively, and in each circle to appoint some one city or town to be the place of issue of notes, as hereinafter provided. It shall be lawful for the Governor-General of India in Council by an order to be published as aforesaid from time to time to alter or extend the limits of the said circles, or any of them. Promissory notes of the Government of India may be issued in the several circles of issue as hereinafter provided.

VI. For each circle of issue other than those which include the towns of Calcutta, Madras and Bombay, there shall be appointed by the Governor-General in Council, an officer of the Government or other person to be called the Deputy Commissioner of Issue. In any circle of issue there may be also established an agency or agencies of issue in connection with a bank or otherwise.

VII. For the purposes of this Act, the Commissioners at Madras and Bombay shall be subordinate to the Head Commissioner. The Deputy Commissioners and Agents in the Presidency of Fort William in Bengal shall be subordinate to the Head Commissioner; and the Deputy Commissioners and Agents in the Presidencies of Fort St. George and Bombay shall be subordinate to the Commissioners of Madras and Bombay respectively.

VIII. The Head Commissioner of Issue for the time being shall provide, on paper to be specially manufactured for the purpose, Promissory notes of the Government of India payable to bearer on demand, of the denominations which shall from time to time be prescribed under Section 3 of this Act and shall supply or cause to be supplied to the Commissioners at Madras and Bombay and to the several Deputy Commissioners and Agents, such notes as they shall require for the purposes of this Act, and all notes shall bear upon them the name of the city or town from which they are severally issued, and shall be payable only at the office or offices or agencies of issue of such city or town, and at the Presidency town of the Presidency within which such city or town is situated.

IX. The Head Commissioner, the Commissioners and the Deputy Commissioners and Agents shall, in their respective "Circles of Issue" on the demand of any person, issue from such offices or agencies of issue as shall be established in the appointed city or town in their respective circles, Promissory notes of such denominations as shall be prescribed under Section 3, not being for any less sum than 10 Rupees, on the terms following:—

First, in exchange for the amount thereof, in current silver coins of the Government of India.

Or secondly, in exchange for the amount thereof in standard silver bullion or foreign silver coin computed according to such standard at the rate of 979 Rupees per 1,000 tolahs of standard silver fit for coinage.

Provided that the said Head Commissioner, Commissioners, Deputy Commissioners and Agents, shall, in all cases, be entitled to require such silver bullion and foreign coin to be melted and assayed at the expense of the person tendering the same; and provided also that in all places where there is no Mint of the Government of India, it shall be optional for any such Head Commissioner, Commissioners, Deputy Commissioners and Agents to issue notes in exchange for silver or foreign coin under this section.

Or thirdly, in exchange for other notes of the Government of India, payable to bearer on demand, of other amounts issued within the same circle. Provided also that it shall be lawful for the Governor-General in Council from time to time to direct, by order to be published in the *Gazettes* of Calcutta, Madras and Bombay, that notes to an extent to be specified in the order, not exceeding one-fourth of the total amount of issues represented by coin and bullion as herein provided shall be issued at such offices or Agencies of issue, as may be named in the order, in exchange for gold coin of full weight of the Government of India or for foreign gold coin or gold bullion computed at such rates, and according to such rules and conditions as shall be fixed by such order and which rates, rules, and conditions shall not be altered without six months' previous notice. Whenever such order shall be issued, the Head Commissioner, Commissioners, Deputy Commissioners and Agents at the offices or agencies specified in the order shall be bound to issue notes on demand in conformity with such order.

X. The whole amount of the bullion and coin so received for notes shall be retained and secured as a reserve to pay such notes, with the exception of such an amount not exceeding four crores of rupees as the Governor-General in Council, with the consent of the Secretary of State for India, shall from time to time fix. The amount so fixed shall be published in the *Gazettes* of Calcutta, Madras and Bombay and shall be invested in Government securities, and the said coin, bullion and securities shall be appropriated and set apart to provide for the satisfaction and discharge of the said notes; and the said notes shall be deemed to have been issued on the security of the coin, bullion and securities so appropriated and set apart, as well as on the general credit of the Government. Provided that any gold coin or bullion which may be received under this Act, may be sold or exchanged for silver coin or bullion to be appropriated and set apart, instead of the gold coin or bullion.

XI. The Government Securities purchased under this Act in the Presidency of Fort William in Bengal shall stand in the name of the Head Commissioner and the Master of the Mint at Calcutta, the Government securities purchased under this Act in the Presidency of Fort St. George shall stand in the name of the Commissioner at Madras and the Master of the Mint at Madras, and the Government Securities purchased under this Act in the Presidency of Bombay shall stand in the name of the Commissioner at Bombay and the Master of the Mint at Bombay. Provided that if the Head Commissioner or Commissioner in any case be the Master of the Mint, the

Governor-General in Council shall appoint another trustee or trustees in addition to the Master of the Mint.

XII. The Head Commissioner from time to time shall frame rules to be approved by the Governor-General of India in Council, for keeping the accounts of the said Department of Issue, and for the auditing of such accounts and for otherwise regulating the business of the department; provided that such rules shall be in no wise inconsistent with the provisions of this act.

XIII. An abstract of the accounts of the department showing the whole amount of notes in circulation, the amount of coin and bullion reserved, distinguishing gold from silver and the amount of the Government Securities held by the said department shall be made up monthly in Calcutta, Madras and Bombay.

XIV It shall be lawful for the Head Commissioner in respect of the Presidency of Fort William in Bengal and for the Commissioners at Madras and Bombay in respect of the Presidencies of Madras and Bombay respectively, at any time when they shall be ordered so to do by the Governor-General of India in Council, to sell and dispose of any portion of the above mentioned limited amount of Government Securities standing in their names respectively and in the names of the Masters of the Mint or trustees as aforesaid; and for the purpose of effecting such sales, the said Masters of the Mint or trustees respectively shall, on a request in writing from the said Head Commissioner or Commissioners in their respective presidencies at all times sign and endorse such Government Securities as shall stand in their names respectively, and it shall be lawful for the said Head Commissioner or Commissioners if directed by the Governor-General of India in Council to purchase Government securities to replace their sales.

XV. The interest accruing due on the Government Securities purchased and held under this Act shall be entered in a separate account to be annually rendered by the Head Commissioner to the Governor-General of India in Council; and the amount of such interest shall from time to time as it becomes due be paid by the Accountants-General in the several Presidencies of India into the Revenues of the Government of India, under the head of "Profits of Note Circulation," and an account showing the amount of profits of the note circulation and of the charges and expenses incidental thereto, shall be made up and published annually in the *Gazettes* of Calcutta, Madras and Bombay.

XVI. Within any of the circles of the issue as hereinafter provided, a tender of a note or notes issued under this Act from any office or agency of issue of such circle of issue, shall be a legal tender to the amount expressed in such note or notes and shall be taken to be valid as a tender to such amount in payment of any revenue or other claim to the amount of Rs. 10 and upwards due to the Government of India and in payment of any sum of 10 rupees and upwards due by the Government of India or any body corporate or by any person or persons in British India on all occasions whatsoever on which any tender of money can be legally made. Provided that no such note or notes shall be deemed to be a legal tender of payment by the Government of India at any office of issue or at the issue department of any agency of issue.

XVII. The name of the Head Commissioner, of either of the Commissioners, of any Deputy Commissioner, or of any other person authorised by the said Head Commissioner or by either of the said Commissioners, to sign notes issued under this Act may be impressed or affixed by machinery provided for that purpose by the Government of India and such printed names shall be taken to be good and valid signatures to all intents and purposes, as if such notes had been subscribed in the proper handwriting of any one of the persons aforesaid, whose signatures the said printing purports to represent.

XVIII. All notes issued under this Act shall be deemed and taken to be promissory notes of the Government of India and may and shall be described as Promissory notes of the Government of India in all indictments and in criminal and civil proceedings, any law or usage to the contrary notwithstanding.

XIX. If any body corporate or person after the passing of this Act shall, contrary to the provisions of this Act, draw, accept, make or issue any Bill of Exchange Promissory note or engagement for the payment of money payable to bearer on demand, or borrow, owe, or take up any sum or sums of money on the bills or notes or engagements for the payment of money payable to bearer on demand of any such body corporate or person, such body corporate or person shall be liable to a penalty to the amount of every such Bill of Exchange, Promissory note or engagement for the payment of money, to be recovered on the prosecution of the Head Commissioner, Commissioners or Deputy Commissioners as the case may be of the circle of issue in which such Bill of Exchange, Promissory note or engagement for the payment of money is issued, before any Police Magistrate or Magistrate within such circles of issue and in case of conviction and default of payment of such penalties, the Police Magistrate or Magistrate who shall try the case shall issue his warrant to levy the amount thereof together with the reasonable costs of the prosecution, by distress and sale of the goods and chattels of the body corporate or person so convicted.

XX. The words " British India " in this Act shall denote the territories that are or may be vested in Her Majesty by the Statute 21 and 22 Vic. C 106 entitled " An Act for the Better Government of India," except the Settlement of Prince of Wales' Island, Singapore and Malacca.

APPENDIX B

ACT No. XX OF 1923

As Amended by the two Indian Paper Currency (Amendment) Acts of 1923 and 1925.

An Act to consolidate the law relating to the Government Paper Currency.

WHEREAS it is expedient to consolidate the law relating to the Government Paper Currency; it is hereby enacted as follows:—

PRELIMINARY.

1. (1) This Act may be called the Indian Paper Currency Act, 1923.

(2) It extends to the whole of British India, inclusive of British Baluchistan and the Santhal Parganas.

2. In this Act, "universal currency note" means—

(*a*) a note of the denominational value of one rupee, two and a half rupees, five rupees, ten rupees, fifty rupees, or one hundred rupees, or

(*b*) a note of any other denominational value which the Governor-General in Council may, by notification in the *Gazette of India*, specify in this behalf.

THE CURRENCY DEPARTMENT.

3. There shall continue to be a Department of the public service, to be called the Currency Department, whose function shall be the issue of promissory notes of the Government of India, to be called Currency notes, payable

to bearer on demand, and of such denominational values as the Governor-General in Council may direct.

4. At the head of the Department there shall be an officer to be called the Controller of the Currency (hereinafter referred to as the Controller).

5. The Governor-General in Council may by notification in the *Gazette of India*—

(*a*) establish districts to be called circles of issue, seven of which circles shall include the towns of Calcutta, Madras, Bombay, Rangoon, Lahore, Cawnpore and Karachi, respectively;

(*b*) appoint in each circle some one town to be the place of issue of currency notes, as hereinafter provided;

(*c*) establish in each such town an office or offices of issue; and

(*d*) establish in any town situate in any circle an office, to be called a currency agency.

6. For each circle of issue there shall be an officer in charge to be called the Deputy Controller of the Currency, and for each Currency Agency an officer to be called the Currency Agent.

7. For the purposes of this Act—

(*a*) Deputy Controllers of the Currency shall be subordinate to the Controller and (*b*) the Currency Agent at any town shall be subordinate to the Deputy Controller of the Currency for the circle of issue in which that town is situate.

8. All officers under this Act shall be appointed by the Governor-General in Council.

Supply and Issue of Currency Notes.

9. (1) The Controller shall provide currency notes of the denominational values prescribed under this Act, and

shall supply the Deputy Controllers with such notes as they need for the purposes of this Act.

(2) The Deputy Controllers shall supply the Currency Agents subordinate to them, respectively, with such notes as those Agents need for the purposes of this Act.

(3) Every such note, other than a universal currency note, shall bear upon it the name of the town from which it is issued.

10. The name of the Controller or one of the Deputy Controllers, or of some other person authorised by the Controller or by one of the Deputy Controllers, to sign currency notes, shall be subscribed to every such note, and may be impressed thereon by machinery, and, when so impressed, shall be deemed to be a valid signature.

11. The officers in charge of circles of issue shall, in their respective circles, on the demand of any person, issue, from the office or offices of issue established in their respective circles, currency notes of the denominational values prescribed under this Act, in exchange for the amount thereof

(*a*) in rupees or silver half-rupees or in gold coin which is legal tender under the Indian Coinage Act, 1906, or

(*b*) in rupees made and declared to be a legal tender under the provisions of the Native Coinage Act, 1876.

12. Any Currency Agent to whom currency notes have been supplied under Section 9 may, if he thinks fit, on the demand of any person, issue from his agency any such notes in exchange for the amount thereof in any coin specified in Section 11.

13. The officers in charge of circles of issue shall, on the requisition of the Controller, issue to any Government Treasury currency notes in exchange for gold coin which is not legal tender under the Indian Coinage Act, 1906, or

for gold bullion at the rate of one rupee for 11·30016 grains troy of fine gold.

CURRENCY NOTES WHERE LEGAL TENDER AND WHERE PAYABLE.

14. A universal currency note shall be a legal tender at any place in British India, and any other currency note shall be a legal tender at any place within the circle from which the note was issued,

for the amount expressed in the note in payment or on account of—

(a) any revenue or other claim, to the amount of one rupee and upwards, due to the Government of India, and

(b) any sum of one rupee or upwards, due by the Government of India or by any body corporate or other person in British India ;

Provided that no currency note shall be deemed to be a legal tender by the Government of India at any office of issue.

15. A currency note shall be payable at the following offices of issue, namely:—

(a) a universal currency note at any office of issue;

(b) a currency note other than a universal currency note at any office of issue in the town from which it was issued;

Provided that any such note issued before the 18th day of February, 1910, shall also be payable,

(i) in the case of a note issued from the office at Cawnpore or Lahore, at any office of issue in Calcutta, and

(ii) in the case of a note issued from the office at Karachi, at any office of issue in Bombay.

16. For the purposes of Sections 14 and 15, currency notes issued from any currency agency shall be deemed to have been issued from the town appointed under Section 5

to be the place of issue in the circle of issue in which that agency is established.

17. Where an office of issue is closed, the Governor-General in Council shall, by notification in the *Gazette of India*, direct that, with effect from the date of the closing of such office, all currency notes issued therefrom shall, for the purposes of Sections 14 and 15, be deemed to have been issued from such other office as may be specified in such notification.

Reserve.

18. (1) The provisions contained in this section shall not come into operation until such day (hereinafter referred to as the appointed day) as the Governor-General in Council may direct in this behalf.

(2) A Reserve shall be maintained for the satisfaction and discharge of the currency notes in circulation and all such notes shall be deemed to have been issued on the credit of the revenues of India as well as on that of the Reserve.

(3) The Reserve shall consist of two parts, namely:—

(*a*) the metallic Reserve, and

(*b*) the securities reserve.

(4) the metallic reserve shall consist of the total amount represented by the sovereigns, half-sovereigns, rupees, silver half-rupees, and gold and silver bullion for the time being held on that account by the Secretary of State for India in Council and by the Governor-General in Council;

Provided that no amount of gold coin and bullion held by the Secretary of State in the United Kingdom in excess of fifty millions of rupees in value reckoned at the rate hereinafter provided for shall be included in the metallic reserve.

(5) the securities Reserve shall consist of the securities which are for the time being held on that account by the Secretary of State for India in Council and on behalf of the Governor-General in Council :

Provided that—

(*a*) no securities held by the Secretary of State for India in Council, other than securities of the United Kingdom, the date of maturity of which is not more than one year from the date of their purchase, shall be included in the securities reserve; and,

(*b*) the securities held on behalf of the Governor-General in Council shall be securities of the Government of India and shall not exceed in amount two hundred millions of rupees of which an amount of not more than one hundred and twenty millions of rupees may be securities created by the Government of India and issued to the Controller (such securities being hereinafter referred to as created securities).

(6) For the purposes of this Section the expression "Currency notes in circulation" means the whole amount of currency notes at any time in circulation;

Provided that currency notes which have not been presented for payment, in the case of notes of the denominational value of fifty or one hundred rupees, within forty years and in the case of notes of any denominational value exceeding one hundred rupees, within one hundred years, from the 1st day of April following the date of that issue, shall be deemed to be not in circulation;

Provided further, that all such notes shall be deemed to have been issued on the credit of the revenues of India and shall, if presented for payment, be paid from such revenues.

(7) Save as hereinafter provided in Section 20, the amount of currency notes in circulation at any time shall not exceed the amount of the metallic reserve together with the amount of the securities reserve:

Provided that it shall not be lawful for the Governor-General in Council to direct the issue of currency notes, if or to the extent that such issue would have the effect of raising the amount of notes in circulation to an amount in excess of twice the amount for the time being of the metallic reserve.

(8) For the purpose of determining—

(*a*) the amount of the metallic reserve, gold bullion shall be reckoned at the rate of one rupee for 11·30016 grains troy of fine gold, and silver bullion at the price in rupees at which it was purchased,

Or, in the case of bullion obtained by melting down silver coin issued under the authority of the Governor-General in Council, at the rate of one rupee for 165 grains troy of fine silver;*

(*b*) the amount of the securities reserve, purchased securities shall be reckoned at the price at which they were purchased and created securities at the market price of similar securities on the date of their issue.

(9) The securities of the Government of India in the Reserve shall be held by the Controller and the Master of the Mint at Calcutta or of such other

* This paragraph was added to the Act by the Indian Paper Currency (Amendment) Act of 1923.

Mint as the Governor-General in Council may direct in this behalf, in trust for the Secretary of State for India in Council.

19. (1) As soon as conveniently may be after the relation of the amount of the Currency notes in circulation to the amount of the Reserve has been brought into conformity with sub-sections (2) to (8) of Section 18 and the metallic reserve is not less than half the amount of currency notes in circulation, the Governor-General in Council shall fix the appointed day.

(2) The provisions contained in this Section shall be in force until the appointed day, but shall as from that day be deemed to be repealed.

(3) Save as hereinafter provided in Section 20, the whole amount of currency notes at any time in circulation shall not exceed the total amount represented by the sovereigns, half-sovereigns, rupees, silver half-rupees, and gold bullion and the sum expended in the purchase of the silver bullion and securities, which are for the time being held by the Secretary of State for India in Council and by the Governor-General in Council as a reserve to provide for the satisfaction and discharge of the said notes, and the said notes shall be deemed to have been issued on the credit of the revenues of India as well as on the security of the said coin, bullion and securities;

Provided that for the purposes of this sub-section, currency notes which have not been presented for payment, in the case of notes of the denominational value of fifty or one hundred rupees within forty years, and in the case of notes of any denominational value exceeding one hundred rupees, within one hundred years from the first day of April following the date of their issue, shall be deemed not to be in circulation;

Provided further that all notes which are declared under the first proviso to this sub-section not to be in circulation shall be deemed to have been issued on the credit of the revenues of India and shall, if subsequently presented for payment, be paid from such revenues.

Explanation.—For the purposes of this sub-section, the sum expended in the purchase of silver bullion obtained by melting down silver coin issued under the authority of the Governor-General in Council shall be deemed to be the value of the bullion calculated at the rate of one rupee for 165 gains troy of fine silver.*

(4) The securities mentioned in sub-section (3) shall be securities of the United Kingdom of Great Britain and Ireland or of the Government of India, or securities issued by the Secretary of State for India in Council under the authority of Act of Parliament and charged on the revenues of India, and the value of them at the price at which they are purchased shall not exceed one thousand millions of rupees.†

(5) If the Secretary of State for India in Council consents to hold in gold coin or bullion or in silver bullion or in securities of the kinds mentioned in sub-section (4), the equivalent in value to notes issued in India as a reserve to secure the payment of such notes, the Governor-General in Council may from time to time direct that currency notes shall be issued to an amount

* This explanation was inserted later by the Indian Paper Currency (Amendment) Act, 1923.

† Originally 850 millions. The Indian Paper Currency (Amendment) Act of 1925 substituted 100 for 85 crores.

equal to the value of the coin bullion, and securities so held by the Secretary of State for India in Council.

(6) Notwithstanding anything to the contrary in this Act, any securities created by the Government of India and issued to the Controller shall, for the purposes of this Act, be deemed to be securities purchased by the Governor-General in Council and the market price, on the day such securities were so issued, of similar securities shall be deemed to be the price at which the securities so created were purchased, and all references to securities so purchased, wherever occurring in this Act shall be deemed also to refer to securities so created, and all references to sums expended in such purchases or to prices paid therefor shall be deemed, in the case of securities so created, to refer to such prices, and this Act shall be construed accordingly.

(7) As long as the value of securities created by the Government of India and issued to the Controller and deemed in accordance with the provisions of the foregoing sub-section to be securities purchased by the Governor-General in Council exceeds one hundred and twenty millions of rupees, all interest derived from the securities in the reserve shall, with effect from 1st day of April, 1923, be applied in reduction of such excess holding of securities and the Auditor-General shall in every year grant a certificate of the amount of such interest and shall also certify whether or not it has been so applied. For the purposes of this sub-section securities so created and issued shall be deemed to carry interest at the same rate as other similar securities.

(8) The securities purchased by the Governor-General in Council shall be securities of the

Government of India and shall be held by the Controller and the Master of the Mint at Calcutta or of such other Mint as the Governor-General in Council may direct in this behalf, in trust for the Secretary of State for India in Council.

20. Notwithstanding anything to the contrary in Section 18 or Section 19, the Governor-General in Council may authorise the Controller to issue Currency notes to an amount in all not exceeding fifty millions of rupees* against bills of exchange which will mature within ninety days from the date of such issue and satisfy such other conditions as the Governor-General in Council may, by general or special order, prescribe. Currency notes so issued shall be in addition to those against which the reserve is held and shall be deemed to have been issued on the credit of such bills and of the revenues of India and shall when presented, be paid from such revenues.

21. Subject to the provisions of Sections 18 and 19, the Governor-General in Council may, at any time, if he think it expedient, convert any of the coin or bullion for the time being held by him as a part of the reserve into coin of any of the kinds mentioned in Section 11 or into gold or silver.

22. Notwithstanding anything to the contrary in this Act, any coin or bullion which is held by or on behalf of the Secretary of State for India in Council in the United Kingdom or under the control of the Government of any part of His Majesty's Dominions for the purpose of coinage for, or transmission to, the Governor-General in Council and any coin or bullion which is in course of transmission from the Secretary of State for India in Council or the Government of any part of His Majesty's Dominions to the Governor-General in Council and any coin or bullion which is in course of transmission from the Governor-

* The Indian Paper Currency (Amendment) Act, 1923 substituted 120 millions for 50 millions.

General in Council to the Secretary of State for India in Council or the Government of any part of His Majesty's Dominions shall be deemed, during the period such coin or bullion is so held or is so in course of transmission, to be part of the reserve referred to in Sections 18 and 19.

23. (1) The Controller may at any time, when ordered so to do by the Governor-General in Council, sell and dispose of any of the securities held under Sub-section (9) of Section 18 or Sub-section (8) of Section 19.

(2) For the purpose of effecting such sales, the Master of the Mint at Calcutta or of such other Mint as aforesaid shall, on a request in writing from the Controller at all times, sign and endorse the securities, and the Controller, if so directed by the Governor-General in Council, may purchase securities of the Government of India to replace such sales.

24. An account showing the amount of the interest accruing on the securities held as part of the reserve under this Act and the expenses and charges incidental thereto, shall be rendered annually by the Controller to the Governor-General in Council, and published annually in the *Gazette of India.*

PRIVATE BILLS PAYABLE TO BEARER ON DEMAND.

25. No person in British India shall draw, accept, make or issue any bill of exchange, hundi, Promissory note or engagement for the payment of money payable to bearer on demand or borrow, owe or take up any sum or sums of money on the bills, hundis or notes payable to bearer on demand of any such person:

Provided that cheques or drafts, payable to bearer on demand or otherwise, may be drawn on bankers, shroffs or agents by their customers or constituents, in respect of deposits of money in the hands of those bankers, shroffs or agents and held by them at the credit and disposal of the persons drawing such cheques or drafts.

26. (1) Any person contravening the provisions of Section 25 shall, on conviction by a Presidency Magistrate or a Magistrate of the first class, be punishable with a fine equal to the amount of the bill, hundi note or engagement in respect whereof the offence is committed.

(2) Every prosecution under this Section shall be instituted by the officer in charge of the circle of issue in which the bill, hundi note or engagement is drawn, accepted, made or issued.

SUPPLEMENTARY PROVISIONS.

27. An abstract of the accounts of the Currency Department showing—

(*a*) the whole amount of currency notes in circulation;

(*b*) the amount of coin and bullion reserved, distinguishing gold from silver, and showing separately the amount of coin or bullion held on behalf of the Secretary of State for India in Council or in transit from or to India, or in the custody of the Mint Master during coinage;

(*c*) the nominal value of, and the price paid for, the securities held as part of the reserve, showing separately those held by the Secretary of State for India in Council and those held in India under sub-section (9) of Section 18 or sub-section (8) of Section 19; and

(*d*) the amount of currency notes issued against Bills of Exchange under the provisions of Section 20: shall be made up four times in each month by the Controller and published as soon as may be in the *Gazette of India*.

28. Notwithstanding anything contained in any enactment or rule of law to the contrary, no person shall as of right be entitled to recover from the Government of India the value of any lost mutilated or imperfect currency note;

Provided that the Governor-General in Council may, by rule, prescribe the circumstances, conditions and limitations under which the value of such notes may be refunded as of grace.

29. (1) The Governor-General in Council may make rules to carry out the purposes and objects of this Act.

(2) In particular and without prejudice to the generality of the foregoing power such rules may—

(*a*) fix the denominational values for which currency notes shall be issued;

(*b*) provide for the alteration of the limits of any of the circles of issue;

(*c*) declare the places at which currency notes shall be issued; and

(*d*) prescribe the circumstances in, and the conditions and limitations subject to, which the value of lost, mutilated or imperfect currency notes may be refunded at the office of issue.

(3) Every such rule shall be published in the *Gazette of India* and on such publication shall have effect as if enacted in this Act.

30. The enactments mentioned in the Schedule are hereby repealed to the extent specified in the last column thereof:

Provided that all securities purchased and notes issued under the Indian Paper Currency Act, 1910 and all securities and notes which under Section 30 of that Act, are to be deemed to have been purchased or issued thereunder shall, if undisposed of or in circulation at the commencement of this Act, be deemed to have been respectively purchased and issued under this Act:

Provided further that all currency notes, which, under the said Section 30, are to be deemed to have been issued from the office of issue in the town of Cawnpore, shall still be deemed to have been issued from that office.

THE SCHEDULE.

Enactments Repealed.

(See Section 30.)

Year.	No.	Short Title.	Extent of Repeal.
1910	2	Indian Paper Currency Act, 1910.	So much as has not been repealed.
1911	7	The Indian Paper Currency (Amendment) Act, 1911.	The whole.
1914	10	The Repealing and Amending Act, 1914.	So much of the second schedule as relates to the Indian Paper Currency Act, 1910.
1917	19	The Indian Paper Currency (Amendment) Act, 1917.	So much as has not been repealed.
1920	45	The Indian Paper Currency (Amendment) Act, 1920.	The whole.
1922	12	The Indian Finance Act, 1922.	Section 6.

Note.—In terms of the Currency Act, 1927 (Act I of 1927) the rate of valuation of gold has been altered to one rupee for 8·47512 (instead of 11·30016) grains of gold.

APPENDIX C

PROPOSED NEW PAPER CURRENCY LEGISLATION

Extracts from Bill No. 2 of 1927

A Bill to establish a gold standard currency for British India and constitute a Reserve Bank of India.

WHEREAS it is expedient to provide for the establishment of a gold standard currency for British India, to constitute a Reserve Bank of India to control the working of that standard and regulate the issue of bank notes and the keeping of reserves with a view to securing stability in the monetary system of British India, and generally to make provisions for matters incidental thereto; it is hereby enacted as follows:—

CHAPTER I.

PRELIMINARY.

§ 1 and 2.—These two sections deal with the title extent, commencement and duration and the definitions of terms.

CHAPTER II.

INCORPORATION, SHARE CAPITAL, MANAGEMENT AND BUSINESS.

§ 3.—This provides for the establishment and incorporation of the Reserve Bank of India.

§ 4 and 5.—These lay down the provisions regarding the share capital of the Bank.

§ 6.—This deals with the Head Office, Branches and Agencies.

§ 7 to 12.—These contain provisions regarding the management of the Bank. Qualifications for directorship, composition of the Board of Management and meetings of the Board are dealt with.

§ 13.—Outlines certain temporary provisions for the formation of the first Board.

§ 14.—Deals with the business of the Bank. Among others it may carry on the business of

* * *

(2) (*a*) the purchase, sale and re-discount of bills of exchange and promissory notes, payable in India and arising out of *bonafide* commercial or trade transactions, bearing two or more good signatures, one of which shall be that of a bank, and maturing within ninety days from the date of such purchase or re-discount;

(*b*) the purchase, sale and re-discount of bills of exchange and promissory notes, bearing two or more good signatures, one of which shall be that of a bank, drawn or issued for the purpose of financing seasonal agricultural operations or the marketing of crops, and maturing within six months from the date of such purchase or re-discount;

* * *

(16) the making and issue of bank notes subject to the provisions of this Act.

§ 15.—After such date as the Governor-General in Council may fix in this behalf, the Bank may, notwithstanding any limitations contained in sub-clauses (*a*) and (*b*) of clause (2) of Section 14, purchase, sell or discount any bills of exchange or promissory notes arising out of *bonafide* commercial or trade transactions, bearing two or more good signatures and maturing within ninety days from the date of such purchase or discount.

§ 16.—Describes the business which the Bank may not transact.

CHAPTER III.

Central Banking Functions.

Relations of the Bank with the Secretary of State in Council and the Governor-General in Council.

§ 17 and 18.—Bank to transact Government business.

Note Issue.

§ 19.—(1) The Bank shall have the sole right to issue bank notes in British India, and may, for a period of one year from the date on which this Chapter comes into force, issue currency notes of the Government of India supplied to it by the Governor-General in Council, and the provisions of this Act applicable to bank notes shall, unless a contrary intention appears, apply to all currency notes of the Government of India issued either by the Governor-General in Council or by the Bank in like manner as if such currency notes were bank notes, and references in this Act to bank notes shall be construed accordingly.

(2) On and from the aforesaid date the Governor-General in Council shall not issue any currency notes or any other kind of paper money.

§ 20.—(1) The issue of bank notes shall be conducted by the Bank in an Issue department which shall be separated and kept wholly distinct from the Banking department, and the assets of the Issue department shall not be subject to any liability other than the liabilities of the Issue department as hereinafter defined in Section 29.

(2) The Issue department shall not issue bank notes to the Banking department or to any other person except in exchange for other bank notes or for such coin, bullion or securities as are permitted by this Act to form part of the reserve.

§ 21.—Bank notes shall be of the denominational values of 5, 10, 50, 100, 500, 1,000 and 10,000 rupees, and of such other denominational values, if any, as may be directed by the Governor-General in Council.

§ 22.—The design, form and material of bank notes shall be such as may be approved by the Governor-General in Council.

§ 23.—(1) Subject to the provisions of sub-section (2), every bank note shall be legal tender at any place in British India in payment or on account for the amount expressed therein, and shall be guaranteed by the Governor-General in Council.

(2) The Governor-General in Council may, by notification in the *Gazette of India*, declare that, with effect from such date as may be specified in the notification, any series of bank notes of any denomination shall cease to be legal tender save at an office or agency of the Bank.

§ 24.—The Bank shall not re-issue bank notes which are torn, defaced or excessively soiled, and any bank note re-issued from any office of the Bank shall be sterilized and disinfected before re-issue.

§ 25.—Notwithstanding anything contained in any enactment or rule of law to the contrary, no person shall of right be entitled to recover from the Bank the value of any lost, stolen, mutilated or imperfect bank note:

Provided that the Bank may, with the previous sanction of the Governor-General in Council, prescribe the circumstances in and the conditions and limitations subject to which the value of such bank notes may be refunded as of grace.

Prohibition of Issue of Private Bills or Notes payable to Bearer on Demand.

§ 26.—No person in British India other than the Bank or, as expressly authorized by this Act, the Governor-General in Council shall draw, accept, make or issue any bill of exchange, hundi, promissory note or engagement for the payment of money payable to bearer on demand, or borrow, own or take up any sum or sums of money on the bills, hundis or notes payable to bearer on demand of any such person:

Provided that cheques or drafts payable to bearer on demand or otherwise may be drawn on bankers, shroffs or agents by their customers or constituents in respect of deposits of money in the hands of those bankers, shroffs or agents and held by them at the credit and disposal of the persons drawing such cheques or drafts.

§ 27.—(1) Any person contravening the provisions of Section 26 shall, on conviction by a Presidency Magistrate or a Magistrate of the first class, be punishable with a fine equal to the amount of the bill, hundi, note or engagement in respect whereof the offence is committed.

(2) No prosecution under this section shall be instituted except on complaint made by the Bank.

Assets of the Issue Department.

§ 28.—(1) The Reserve shall consist of gold coin, gold bullion, gold securities, rupee coin and rupee securities to such aggregate amount as is not less than the total of the liabilities of the Issue department as hereinafter defined.

(2) Of the total amount of the Reserve not less than two-fifths shall consist of gold coin, gold bullion or gold securities:

Provided that the amount of gold coin and gold bullion shall not at any time be less than three hundred million rupees in value and shall not be less than one-fifth of the total amount of the Reserve after the end of the fifth year, or than one quarter of the total amount of the Reserve after the end of the tenth year, from the date on which this Chapter comes into force.

(3) The remainder of the Reserve shall be held in rupee coin, Government of India rupee securities of any maturity and such bills of exchange and promissory notes drawn and payable in British India as are eligible for purchase by the Bank under sub-clause (*a*) or sub-clause (*b*) of clause (2) of Section 14 or under Section 15:

Provided that the amount held in rupee coin shall not exceed—

(*a*) during the three years after the date on which this Chapter comes into force, seven hundred million rupees.

(*b*) during the next three years, five hundred million rupees,

(*c*) during the next four years, three hundred and fifty million rupees, and

(*d*) two hundred and fifty million rupees thereafter,

or one-tenth of the total amount of the Reserve whichever amount is greater:

Provided further, that the amount held in Government of India rupee securities shall not at any time exceed one-fourth of the total amount of the Reserve or five hundred million rupees, whichever amount is less.

(4) For the purposes of this section, gold coin and gold bullion shall be valued at 8·47512 grains of fine gold per rupee, rupee coin shall be valued at its face value and gold and rupee securities shall be valued at the market rate for the time being obtaining.

(5) Of the gold coin and gold bullion held in the Reserve not less than one-half shall be held in British India, and all gold coin and gold bullion forming part of the Reserve shall be held in the custody of the Bank or its agencies:

Provided that gold belonging to the Bank which is in any other bank or in mint or in transit may be reckoned as part of the Reserve.

(6) For the purposes of this section, the gold securities which may be held as part of the Reserve shall be securities of any of the following kinds payable in the currency of any gold standard country, namely:—

(*a*) balances at the credit of the Issue department with a bank which is the principal currency authority under the law for the time being in force of such country;

(*b*) bills of exchange bearing two or more good signatures and drawn on and payable at a place in any such country and having a maturity not exceeding ninety days;

(*c*) securities of the Government of any such country maturing within five years;

Provided that, for a period of two years from the date on which this Chapter comes into force, any of such securities may be securities maturing after five years, and the Bank may at any time before the expiry of that period dispose of such securities notwithstanding anything contained in Section 14.

Liabilities of the Issue Department.

§ 29.—(1) The liabilities of the Issue department shall be an amount equal to the total of the amount of the currency notes of the Government of India and bank notes for the time being in circulation and of an initial amount of five hundred million rupees for the purpose of providing for rupee redemption, which last-mentioned amount shall be reduced by one rupee for every five rupees delivered to the Governor-General in Council under the provisions of Section 31, and shall be increased by one rupee for every five rupees received from him under Section 32.

(2) For the purposes of this section, any currency note of the Government of India or bank note which has not been presented for payment within forty years from the 1st day of April following the date of its issue shall be deemed not to be in circulation, and the value thereof shall, notwithstanding anything contained in sub-section (2) of Section 20, be paid by the Issue department to the Governor-General in Council or the Banking department, as the case may be; but any such note, if subsequently presented for payment, shall be paid by the Banking department, and any such payment in the case of a currency note of the Government of India shall be debited to the Governor-General in Council.

Initial Assets and Liabilities.

§ 30.—On the date on which this Chapter comes into force, the Issue department shall take over from the Governor-General in Council the liability for all the currency notes of the Government of India for the time being in circulation, and the Governor-General in Council shall transfer to the Issue department gold coin, gold bullion, gold securities, rupee coin and rupee securities to such aggregate amount as is equal to the total of the amount of the liability so transferred and of a sum of five hundred million rupees. The coin, bullion and securities shall be transferred in such proportion as to comply with the requirements of Section 28:

Provided that the total amount of the gold coin, gold bullion and gold securities so transferred shall not be less than one half of the whole amount transferred.

Supply of Coin, and of Different Forms of Legal Tender Currency.

§ 31.—The Bank may deliver to the Governor-General in Council all rupee coin held by it in excess of the amount which the Issue department is permitted to hold as part of the Reserve under Section 28, against payment of four rupees in bank notes, gold or gold securities for every five rupees so delivered.

§ 32.—When the amount of rupee coin for the time being held in the Reserve does not exceed two hundred and fifty millions or one-tenth of the total amount of the Reserve, whichever is greater, the Bank may demand delivery of rupee coin from the Governor-General in Council, on payment of four rupees in bank notes, gold securities for every five rupees so delivered.

§ 33.—The Governor-General in Council shall undertake not to re-issue any rupee coin delivered under Section 31, nor to put into circulation any new rupees, except through the Bank and on the Bank's demand; and the Bank shall undertake not to dispose of rupee coin otherwise than for the purposes of circulation or by delivery to the Governor-General in Council under that section.

§ 34.—The Bank shall issue rupee coin on demand in exchange for currency notes of the Government of India, and shall issue currency notes or bank notes on demand in exchange for rupee coin, and it shall, in exchange for currency notes or bank notes of five rupees or upwards, supply currency notes or bank notes of lower value or rupees or other coins which are legal tender under the India Coinage Act, 1906, in such quantities as may, in the opinion of the Bank, be required for circulation; and the Governor-General in Council shall, subject to the provisions of Section 32, supply such rupees or other coins to the Bank on demand. If the Governor-General in Council at any time fails to discharge this duty, the Bank shall be released from its obligation to supply such coins to the public.

§ 35 to 37.—Deal with the terms of the purchase and sale of gold by the Bank, also lay down certain interim provisions in this connection.

Suspension of Reserve Requirements and Tax on Note Issue.

§ 38.—(1) The Bank may, with the previous sanction of the Governor-General in Council, for periods not exceeding thirty days in the first instance, which may, with the like sanction, be extended from time to time by periods not exceeding fifteen days, hold in the Reserve gold coin, gold bullion or gold securities of less aggregate amount than that required by sub-section (2) of Section 28 and, whilst the holding is so reduced the proviso to that sub-section shall cease to be operative.

(2) In respect of any period during which the holding of gold coin, gold bullion and gold securities is reduced under sub-section (1), the Bank shall pay to the Governor-General in Council a tax upon the amount by which such holding is reduced below the minimum prescribed by sub-section (2) of Section 28; such tax shall be payable at the bank rate for the time being in force, with an addition of one per cent. per annum when such holding exceeds thirty-two and a half per cent. of the total amount of the Reserve and of a further one and a half per cent. per annum in respect of every further decrease of two and a half per cent. or part of such decrease:

Provided that the tax shall not in any event be payable at a rate less than six per cent. per annum.

§ 39.—Save as provided by Section 38, the Bank shall not be liable to the payment of any stamp duty or other duty or tax in respect of bank notes issued by it.

Duration of the Privilege of Note Issue.

§ 40.—If at any time the Bank fails to comply with any provision of this Chapter or with any other provision of this Act, the Governor-General in Council may, by notification in the *Gazette of India*, declare that the Bank has forfeited the right of note issue, and shall thereupon take over the liabilities of the Issue department together with such portion of the assets of the Bank as is required to meet such liabilities, and thereafter the business of the Issue department shall be carried on in the manner prescribed by this Act by such agency as the Governor-General in Council may determine.

§ 41 and 42.—Provide for the keeping of cash reserves by certain banks with the Reserve Bank and authorise it to enter into agreement with the Imperial Bank of India.

CHAPTER IV.

General Provisions.

Reserve Fund and Allocation of Surplus.

§ 43 and 44.—Deal with the allocation of surplus and the Bank rate respectively.

§ 45 to 47.—Deal with audit and powers and duties of auditors.

§ 48 and 49.—Lay down provisions regarding the publication of returns and liquidation respectively.

§ 50.—Defines the power of the Bank to make regulations regarding certain matters.

§ 51 and 52.—Indicate amendments and repeals of past Acts.

There are three schedules—the third one prescribes the form in which weekly returns of the Issue Department are to be made and published.

Issue Department.

LIABILITIES.	Rs.	ASSETS.	Rs.
Bank notes held in the Banking Department		Rupee coin ...	
Bank notes in circulation		Government of India rupee securities ...	
Total Bank notes ...		Internal bills of exchange and other commercial paper ...	
Government of India notes in circulation ...		Gold securities ...	
Rupee redemption ...		Gold coin or bullion ...	
Total ...		Total ...	

Ratio of gold and gold securities to liabilities per cent.

INDEX

(Reference to Pages.)

Abrahams, Lionel 182, 197, 200
Agency Houses 4, 10

Bank (See also Presidency Banks)
—of Asia 27
—Agra and United Service Ltd. 11,23
—Bengal 4, 12
—of Bengal (Presidency Bank) . . 5, 6, 14-20, 22, 24, 27-28, 57, 64, 71, 197
—of Bombay (Presidency Bank) . . . 20-21, 29, 57
—Calcutta 22
—Commercial 22
—of England 86, 118
—Government Bank of Madras 6, 13, 21
—of Hindustan 4, 6, 10-12
—Imperial Bank of India . . . 68, 70-73, 96, 207
—of India 23
—of India, Australia and China 27
—of Madras 13, 21-22, 29, 71
—of Mirzapore 23
—Nordwest Von Indien 23
—Oriental Bank Corporation 23, 24, 27
—Union 22
—of Western India 23
Bank Charter Act 3, 46, 47, 49
Blackett, Sir Basil 72, 117, 208, 211, 270
Budget, balancing of the 269

Calcutta Review, article on Indian Paper Currency, 1863 . . 52
Cannan, Edwin 166, 195
Cassel, Gustav 164
Central Bank, in connection with the issue . . . 68, 69, 70, 74-75
Chamber of Commerce, Bengal 211
Charters of the Bank of Bengal 5, 24, 27-28
Circle System . . 17, 18, 42, 45, 48, 50, 57, 60, 61, 78, 90-94, 285

Circulation statistics—
of Bank of Bengal 20
" Bombay 21
" Madras 21-22
—by Circles 239
—gross and active 235
—gross, active and net 232
—increase in average circulation 229
—and price level 236
Commission—
—of 1867 . . . . 19, 20, 23, 79, 88
—Chamberlain (1914) . . . 70, 71, 101, 106, 117, 133, 136, 148, 150, 153, 204
—Hilton-Young (1926) . . . 74, 75, 89, 116, 132, 152, 190, 272 *et seq.*
—Indian Fiscal 62
Commissioner, Head of Paper Currency . . 19, 23, 79, 80, 82
Committee—
—Babington-Smith . . . 117, 139, 153, 205, 209, 213
—Fowler 198
—Herschell 89, 144
Comptroller-General of Accounts 79, 80, 81
Controller of the Currency 80
Convertibility—
—difficulties during the War . . . . . 166 *et seq.*
—Plan outlined by Hilton-Young Commission . . 274-75
Currency—
—Agency 84, 94-95
—Chest 84, 95-97
—Department, Profits of 243
—Forgeries 243-44
—Legislation, Progress of . . . . . . 244 *et seq.*
—Office . . . . 82 *et seq.*
—Officer 83
—Report 242
—Return, specimen of 237

Dalal, Sir Dabida 105, 109, 137, 200
Dawkins, Sir Clinton 201
Denominations of notes . . . 8, 20, 42, 45, 48-50, 87, 240, 285
Deputy Controller of the Currency 81
Discount on notes 108
Dunbar 98

East India Company 3, 4
Elasticity of the issue . . . 114 *et seq.*, 192 *et seq.*, 284-285

Encashment—
—facilities for . . . . 104 *et seq.*
—Difficulties about 106-7

Federal Reserve system . . . . . 200, 205, 217 *et seq.*, 272
Forgeries of notes 243-44

Gold—
—issue against 47, 85, 134
—Reserve (see Reserve of gold)
—Valuation of 152

Hailey, Sir Malcolm 109, 127, 176, 182, 185, 269
Hamilton, Sir Daniel 118, 200, 286
Harrington, H. B. 120
Harrison 132
Howard, H. F. 72, 169, 201, 205
Hunter 200

Interest charges on seasonal issue . . . . . 222 *et seq.*
Issue—
—against gold (see Gold and Reserve of gold)
—against silver (see Silver and Reserve of silver)
—against securities (see Securities and Reserve of securities)
—against bills of exchange . . . . . . 205 *et seq.*
Iyer, S. 105, 138

Jevons, Prof. 183

Keynes, J. M. 70, 71, 203
Kinley 200

Laing Samuel 37, 40-41, 45-47, 55-56, 58-66, 256-57, 273
Law, Sir Edward 69, 70, 125, 136
Legal tender . . . . 103 *et seq.*
Legislation, course of paper currency . . . . . 244 *et seq.*
Lushington, C. H. 35-37, 39-41, 251-52

Maine, Sir Henry 52, 120
Massey, W. N. 62
McWatters, A. C. 158
Meston, Lord 100, 104, 132, 201
Mill, J. S. 194
Mints 78, 80
Mint chest 84, 97

Mint Master 79, 80
Mitra, Sir B. N. 105
Morley, John 147

Napier, Sir R. 52
Newmarch 101, 132
Notes—
—design and printing of 85-87
—lost and mutilated 101

Pittman Act 108, 140, 155
Presidency Banks (see also Banks) . . 5, 6, 14, 20, 23, 26, 29, 55-57, 65, 71, 205
Profits of note circulation 243

Reichsbank 198
Reserve Bank of India 272-73
Reserve Gold standard . . . . 117, 124, et seq.
—relation with Paper Currency reserve . 124-33, 283-84
Reserve—
—of gold 47, 50, 116, 143-54
—of silver 50, 154-157
—of ingot silver 155
—of securities . . . . 50, 158 et seq. 213 et seq.
—location of paper currency reserve . . . . 133 et seq.
Reverse bills, sale of . . . . 172 et seq.

Seasonal—
—issue (see Issue against bills of exchange)
—Currency problem . . . . 208 et seq.
—interest on seasonal issue . . . . . . 222 et seq.
Securities—
—depreciation of 214
—reserve (see Reserve of securities)
Sicca Rupee 8, 13
Silver—
—purchase procedure 157
—reserve (see reserve of silver)
—reserve (see Reserve of silver)

Treasury bills 6
Trevelyan, C. E. 51, 61, 64, 66, 120
Tucker, C. S. 4

Udny, G. 17
Universal currency notes 89, 92, 100

War—
—crisis regarding convertibility . . . . 106 *et seq.*
—growth of circulation during 228
—inflation of issue during . . . . . 161, 166 *et seq.*
Webb, Sir Montague 137, 148, 186, 192
Wilson, James 7, 35, 36, 38, 40, 41, 43, 44, 253-54
Wood, Sir Charles 35, 37, 40, 41, 46, 48, 49, 56, 58, 59-66, 255, 273

ERRATA

Page 5.	Omit line 25 and substitute 'development of the Paper Currency of the country'		
Page 20.	Second foot-note. Line 1	Add '5' after 'Three Noten von'	
Page 93.	Line 24.	Read	'Province' for 'Providence'.
Page 98.	Line 25.	Read	'antithesis' for 'anthesis'.
Page 127.	Line 8.	Read	'reverse' for 'reserve'.
Page 132.	Line 3.	Read	'proved' for 'provided'
Page 190.	Line 21.	Read	'this' for 'his'.
Page 210.	Last line.	Read	'more' for 'wore'.